POSTCARD HISTORY SERIES

Joplin

On the Front Cover: The photographer took this image of West Fourth Street from an upper window of the Keystone Hotel on 405 Main Street around 1907. The building on the right, 111 to 119 West Fourth Street, housed Joplin Waterworks, Western Union, Joplin Gas Works, and the *Joplin News Herald*. West Fourth Street, with its banks, churches, and office buildings, was quite a contrast to Main Street, where numerous saloons occupied each block. (Courtesy of the Joplin Public Library.)

On the Back Cover: Beginning in 1935, many souvenir postcards featured three-dimensional letters with colorful backgrounds. The Curt Teich Company of Chicago, the most prolific postcard printer of the time, produced the majority of these cards. In 1942, the company began incorporating color photograph montages inside the large letters and using bright backgrounds embellished with hand-drawn artwork. The large letter style was outdated by the 1950s, when real photo postcards surged in popularity. (Courtesy of the Joplin Public Library.)

POSTCARD HISTORY SERIES

Joplin

Leslie Simpson

ARCADIA PUBLISHING

Featuring postcard images from the digitized collection of the Joplin Public Library.
ISBN 978-0-7385-8322-8

Published by Arcadia Publishing
Charleston, South Carolina

Printed in the United States of America

Library of Congress Control Number: 2011925045

For all general information contact Arcadia Publishing at:
Telephone 843-853-2070
Fax 843-853-0044
E-mail sales@arcadiapublishing.com
For customer service and orders:
Toll-Free 1-888-313-2665

Visit us on the Internet at www.arcadiapublishing.com

Dedicated to the Post Memorial Art Reference Library on its 30th anniversary.

Contents

Acknowledgments

It all began with a postcard! Not long after I moved to Joplin in 1979, I saw a postcard of the brightly lit Electric Park with its Ferris wheel, roller coaster, and daisy loop. I was shocked that my new hometown once had so much to offer. I wanted to know more, which is how I got hooked on Joplin's history and its architecture.

Several years ago, then–Joplin Public Library director Carolyn Trout and I embarked on a huge endeavor to digitize historic materials. The project was made possible by a grant from the Missouri State Library. I researched and wrote the narratives for over 500 postcards. The site, which went online in 2004, is a phenomenal resource. The University of Missouri Digital Library provided the repository for the digitized items. The collection is accessible at http://joplinpubliclibrary.org/ and http://digital.library.umsystem.edu/.

Most of the postcards featured in Postcard History Series: *Joplin* came from the Joplin Public Library's collection and from two large private collections belonging to Rodney Blaukat and Galen Augustus. I am indebted to current Joplin Public Library director Jacque Gage and the Library Board of Directors for allowing me to use the digitized collection as the basis of this book. I am also grateful to Blaukat and Augustus for generously sharing their collections.

Brad Belk, curator of the Joplin Museum Complex, provided helpful information regarding Joplin's mining history. Charles Gibbons's excellent book, *Angling in the Archives*, was an invaluable resource. I would also like to thank my staff at the Post Memorial Art Reference Library; Ali Wilbert, Nancy Erwin, Danya Walker, Stephanie Cope, Paula Gillespey, and Jill Halbach were always willing to help with whatever I needed. I especially appreciate Jill for her thorough proofreading and astute suggestions.

I would like to express my appreciation to the Winfred L. and Elizabeth C. Post Foundation for sponsoring this project. The foundation, which is dedicated to promoting the arts, administers the Post Memorial Art Reference Library. All proceeds from the sale of this book go to support the library. To learn more about the Post Library, visit www.postlibrary.org.

INTRODUCTION

Historic postcards provide a delightful way to travel back in time and stroll down the streets of a bygone era. Although postcards are ephemeral in nature, they are also plentiful; many have survived to tell their stories. They are also very personal. People updated loved ones on the weather, their health, and their activities—an early day text message with attached photograph, so to speak! People kept them as souvenirs of places they visited or sent them to show off the charms of their hometown. On one of the mining postcards, for instance, the sender penciled, "This is where we get our money!"

The images in this collection depict all aspects of Joplin's history, beginning with the exhilarating days of two rival towns—Joplin and Murphysburg. It is interesting to read what an unbiased observer had to say. An article in the *St. Louis Globe-Democrat* published on February 14, 1873, described "two thriving hamlets situated in the southwestern part of Jasper County. A narrow gulch, the valley of a mineral washing stream, divides them and for all practical purposes is one town. Jealousies over the name, and a struggle for priority of location, have, however, divided them, and to some extent injured their prosperity." After the towns settled their differences, merged, and incorporated as Joplin on March 23, 1873, prosperity ensued. Mining was king; huge fortunes were blasted from the ground daily. Joplin's slogan "The City that Jack Built" referenced the zinc, also known as blackjack, that brought wealth to the district. The postcards illustrate everything from the grimy existence of the lowly miners deep in the bowels of the earth to the glitzy lives of the mine operators who became millionaires overnight.

The photographs also demonstrate what people did for amusement. Whether rich or poor—there was something for everyone to enjoy. In the early days, Joplin was infamous for its saloons and gambling houses. The House of Lords, visible in many of the street scene postcards, was one of the most notorious gambling houses in the Midwest. Joplin saloons aroused the wrath of those bent on ridding the town of alcohol, which was viewed as the source of all poverty, crime, and violence. The local branch of the Women's Christian Temperance Union led the charge on social issues, determined to stamp out vice. The group also established Joplin Children's Home to care for orphans. In 1901, the crusaders brought in axe-wielding activist Carrie Nation, who spoke at the Club Theatre about the evils of alcohol. She toured several drinking establishments in downtown Joplin. Expressing shock at the risqué paintings hanging in the saloons, she demanded that they be removed. In 1909, evangelist Billy Sunday pitched a huge tent in the 500 block of Virginia Avenue and held a revival that went on every night for six weeks. Over 6,000 attended the rally, the aim of which was to shut down the saloons and remedy societal ills. Local church people convinced county officials to hold local option elections in 1910. In all precincts except Joplin, Jasper County residents voted to prohibit the sale of liquor. Nine years later, temperance activists accomplished their goal with the ratification of the 18th Amendment, establishing national prohibition of alcohol.

Many of the postcards feature Joplin's architecture. Brash characters, many from Ireland and Germany who came to the area with nothing but the clothes on their backs, constructed Joplin. Patrick Murphy, a hot-tempered Irishman, founded the town of Murphysburg. Thomas Connor, also from Ireland, built a luxurious high-rise hotel that was renowned all over the world. Many of Joplin's prominent business owners and leaders were German emigrants—a situation that created tensions during World War I. German brewers Charles Schifferdecker and Edward Zelleken made fortunes in mining, then used their wealth and influence to replace the wood structures downtown with brick edifices worthy of the fastest growing city in Missouri.

In 1888, Zelleken made a remarkable challenge. Disturbed at the lack of decent housing in Joplin, he chastised mine operators and investors who were content to dwell in hired houses.

Most miners lived in shacks, while many of the capitalists resided in hotels. Zelleken promised that if well-to-do citizens would join him in building houses costing at least $3,500 to $4,000, he would be the first to start. Whether this challenge was the catalyst or not, the 1890s ushered in an unprecedented housing boom. New residential areas were continually being opened for development. All one has to do today is drive around the old neighborhoods to observe the patterns of Joplin's architectural evolution. There are the Victorian houses constructed from the 1880s through 1900. Next came the Arts and Crafts period from 1900 to 1930, with bungalows and American Foursquares predominant. The 1930s ushered in modest designs, such as Cape Cod and Colonial Revival. The demand for ranch houses in the late 1940s and 1950s rendered the previous decades' designs hopelessly old-fashioned.

Another theme that surfaced in many of Joplin's postcards was transportation. After installation of trolley and rail lines, Joplin became the hub of southwest Missouri and the center of the Tri-State District. Later on, the city was known as "The Crossroads of America" due to its location at the intersection of several important highways. US Route 71 connected Joplin with Kansas City to the north and Fort Smith, Arkansas, to the south. Missouri Route 43, which coincides with Main Street in Joplin, extends north and south as well. Joplin gained additional renown as one of the stops on historic US Route 66, even being cited in the song "Get Your Kicks on Route 66," made popular by Nat King Cole.

Historic postcards presented the best that Joplin had to offer, from its businesses, churches, and schools to its scenery. The city boasted an exceptional park system that benefited both residents and visitors. Many of the images depicted the natural wonders to be found in the Ozark region of southwest Missouri. These included Grand Falls, Crystal Cave, clear-water springs, and the world's largest chert glade. The tourism industry began in earnest in 1919, when delegates representing 60 towns in southwest Missouri and northwest Arkansas convened at the Connor Hotel. They established the Ozark Playgrounds Association, headquartered in Joplin, to promote the region as a recreation area and destination spot.

During World War II, Joplin was a hot spot thanks to the proximity of a major training facility, Camp Crowder, 20 miles south of town. The United Service Organizations (USO) and other civic groups rose to the occasion, providing plenty of diversions for the soldiers, who arrived en masse whenever they had time to spare. The demand for services escalated as Camp Crowder's population swelled to 17,000 soldiers. By the way, cartoonist Mort Walker used Camp Crowder as his inspiration for Camp Swampy in the *Beetle Bailey* comic strip. Joplin was also the hub for six defense centers that eventually employed 30,000 to 40,000 defense workers.

The post–World War II years introduced suburbanization and new commercial development on Range Line Road. Meanwhile, many homes built by Joplin's early leaders were demolished, divided into apartments, or abandoned to become decaying eyesores. The demise of passenger train service and the construction of Interstate 44 funneled traffic away from US Route 66 and from downtown. The grand buildings, formerly the heart and soul of Joplin, quickly deteriorated. Some ultimately became victims of urban renewal, when block after block of buildings were razed to the ground. Urban renewal ended in 1972, after destroying 35 acres of Joplin's older structures.

Historic preservation became an important element in Joplin's economic development at the beginning of the 21st century. Unfortunately, this is a lesson that was learned too late. The postcard images document what was lost and provide invaluable clues in the restoration of structures that survived.

This Joplin postcard album should be of interest to longtime residents of Joplin, as well as to newcomers. The former will enjoy the nostalgia trip while also learning the history behind places they may have taken for granted. Newcomers will be intrigued to find out what a significant city Joplin was in its infancy. Perhaps it will inspire everyone to learn more about the community and work to preserve its treasures for future generations.

One

From the Ground Up

The mining boomtown of Joplin grew by leaps and bounds after its incorporation in 1873. The biggest impetus for growth and development came with the arrival of the railroads a few years later. An assortment of towns and camps in Missouri, Kansas, and Oklahoma comprised the 2,500-square-mile region called the Tri-State Mining District; Joplin served as its center. Joplin claimed to have more wealth per capita than any other city its size in the state. In 1897, the "Klondike of Missouri" produced more capital than the gold mines of Alaska. Contemporary historian Thomas Millard poetically described the mining operations around Joplin as a "wilderness of smoking funnels standing against the sky like a limbless forest," and he went on to say, "pervading it all, the indelible impression of restless, untamable energy." As poor miners became wealthy overnight, Joplin bristled with excitement. Every Saturday night, miners, operators, landowners, and ore buyers gathered at the hotels and banks to settle accounts. The already-crowded sidewalks became impassable as thousands more poured into town from outside camps. Banks remained open until 11:00 p.m., and most businesses closed at midnight. Men liberally patronized the gambling halls, saloons, and other facilities that offered amusement. According to Millard, although an occasional street brawl broke out, the crowds were surprisingly well behaved. He claimed that the superior character of the miners in the district was due to the fact that most were from nearby farms and villages. Cash was not the only legal tender in those days. Miners routinely paid theater admission or purchased supplies by depositing chunks of lead in collection boxes. Even children gathered minerals from waste dumps; these shiners could be traded at the grocery store for 5¢ worth of candy.

In 125 years of Tri-State mining history, an estimated half-billion rock tons were mined in the region. Two world wars helped the local economy with increased demand for lead bullets and zinc for brass shell casings. Peacetime use of these minerals included lead for batteries, plumbing supplies, paints, high-octane gasoline, cable sheathing, and bearings. Zinc was needed for galvanized iron and steel goods and zinc oxide for tires and pharmaceuticals. Other valuable mine output included cadmium, germanium, and sulfuric acid.

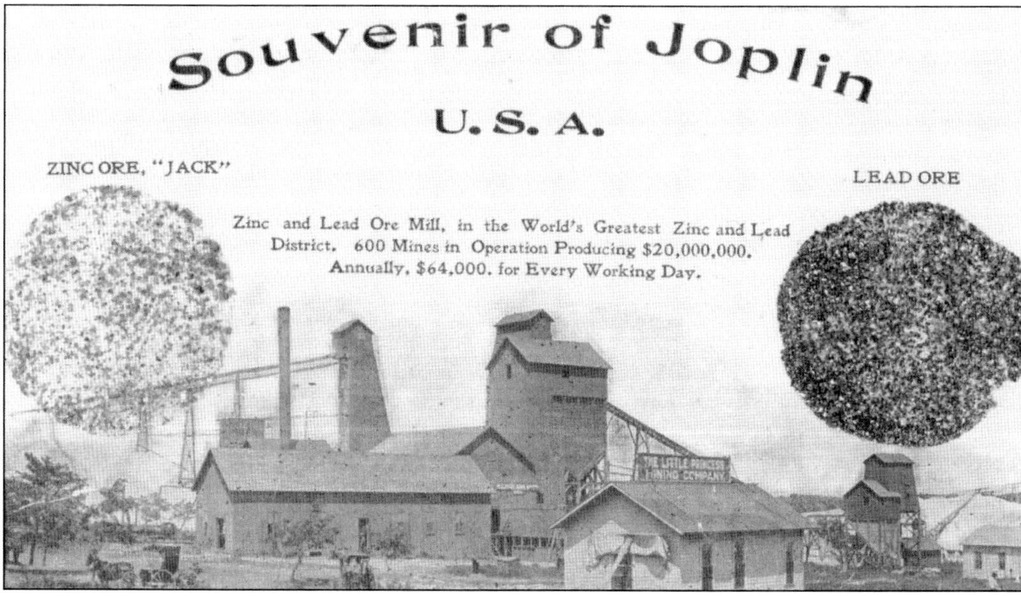

Miners Elliot R. Moffet and John B. Sergeant sparked a mining boom that put Joplin on the map. In 1870, they struck a rich vein that produced more than $60,000 worth of lead ore in the first 90 days. They erected 14 smelters in the Joplin Creek valley. Wagons hauled the lead pigs from the smelters to Kansas City for distribution to manufacturers of bullets, pottery, paint, glass, and pipes. (Courtesy of Rodney Blaukat.)

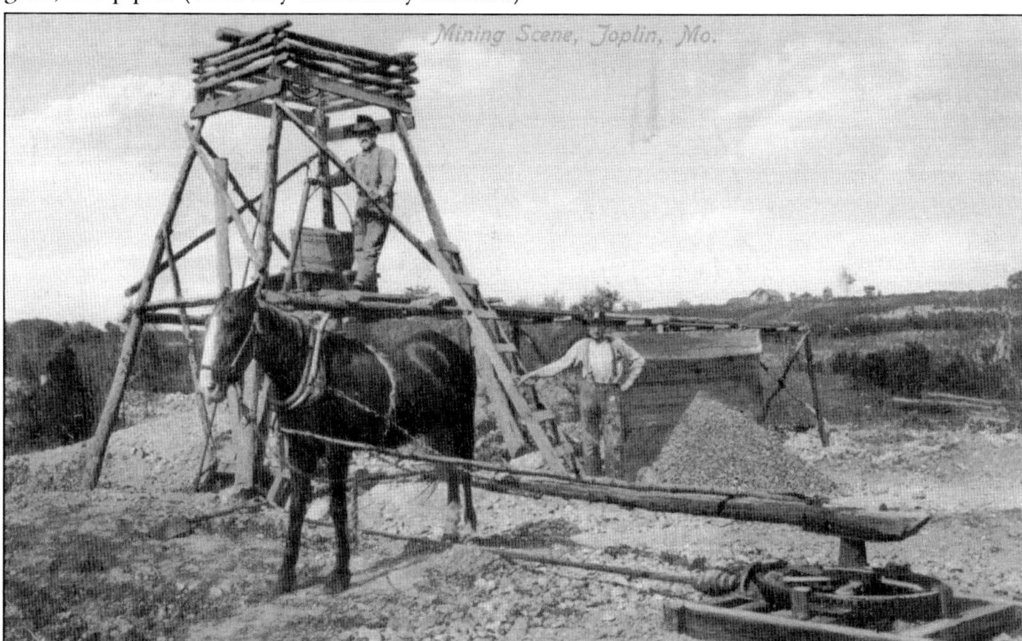

Prospectors streamed into the area. There were no roads, so they came by horse, mule, covered wagon, or on foot. There were no places to live. John Cox platted the town of Joplin on the east side of Joplin Creek in 1871, and Patrick Murphy and W.P. Davis platted Murphysburg on the west side. The rival settlements merged and incorporated as the town of Joplin on March 23, 1873. (Courtesy of the Joplin Public Library.)

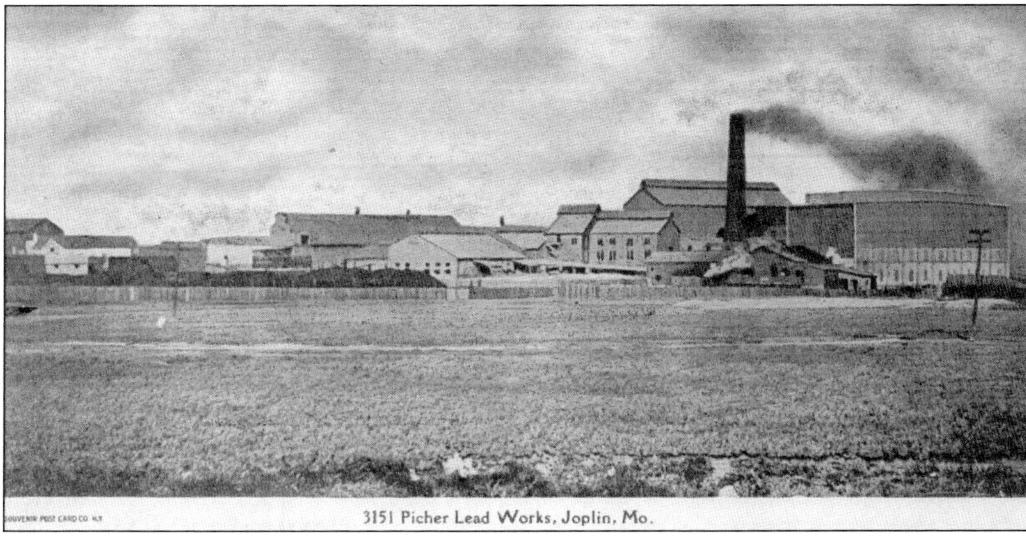

Pennsylvania metallurgist Eayre O. Bartlett came to Joplin to work with Moffet and Sergeant. He sought financial backing for his sublimed white lead process, which produced highly durable lead-based paint. The US government purchased the paint to protect its battleships. Oliver and William Picher organized Picher Lead and Zinc around 1875. Later, they purchased the Moffet/Sergeant operation and reorganized it as Picher Lead Company, which dominated the area's smelting industry. (Courtesy of the Joplin Public Library.)

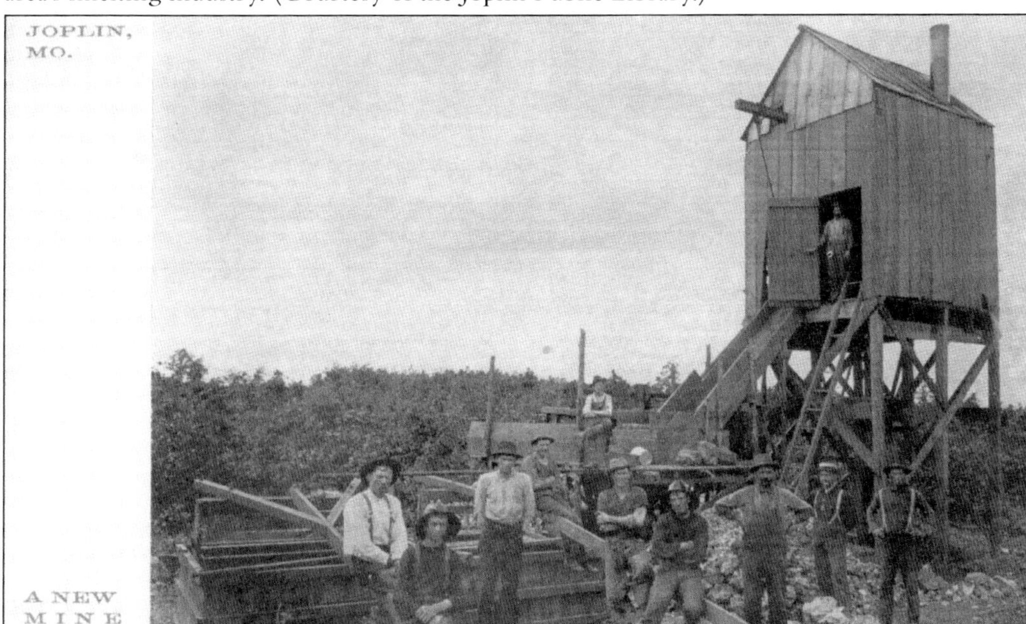

During those grubstake days, landowners leased plots to prospectors and advanced them money and equipment. The miners hand drilled holes and blasted them with dynamite. After mining out the holes, they moved to another spot. Abandoned shafts dotted the landscape, earning Joplin the epithet "city of holes" and creating hazards for those who stumbled into them at night. Joplin grew by leaps and bounds; poor miners became wealthy overnight. (Courtesy of Galen Augustus.)

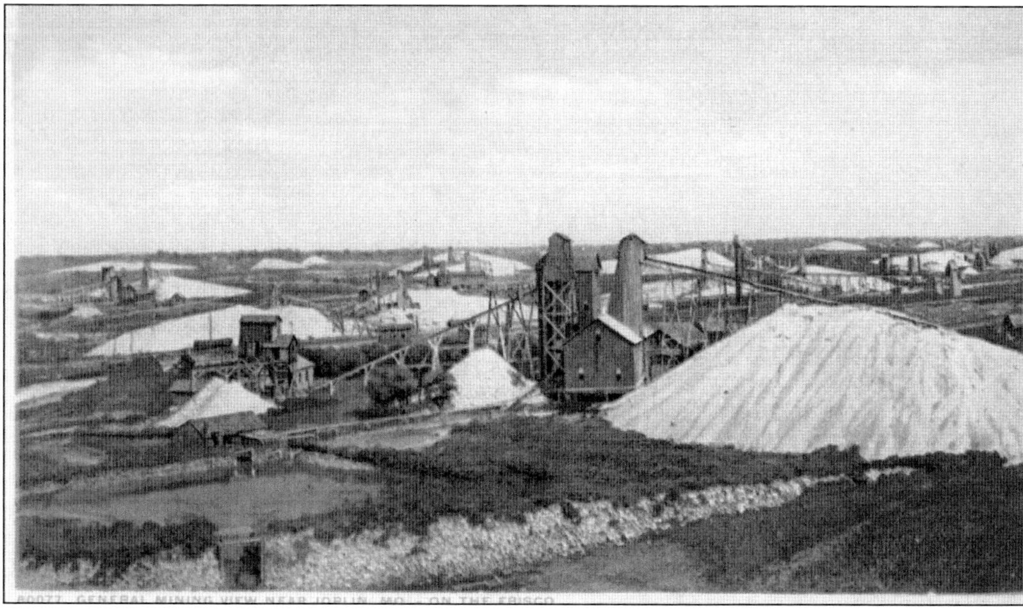

An assortment of towns and camps in Missouri, Kansas, and Oklahoma comprised the 2,500-square-mile region called the Tri-State Mining District; Joplin served as the hub. In its first 20 years, Joplin's population grew to 18,000, with more wealth per capita than any other city its size in the state. In 1897, the Klondike of Missouri produced $1 million more in capital than the gold mines in Alaska. (Courtesy of the Joplin Public Library.)

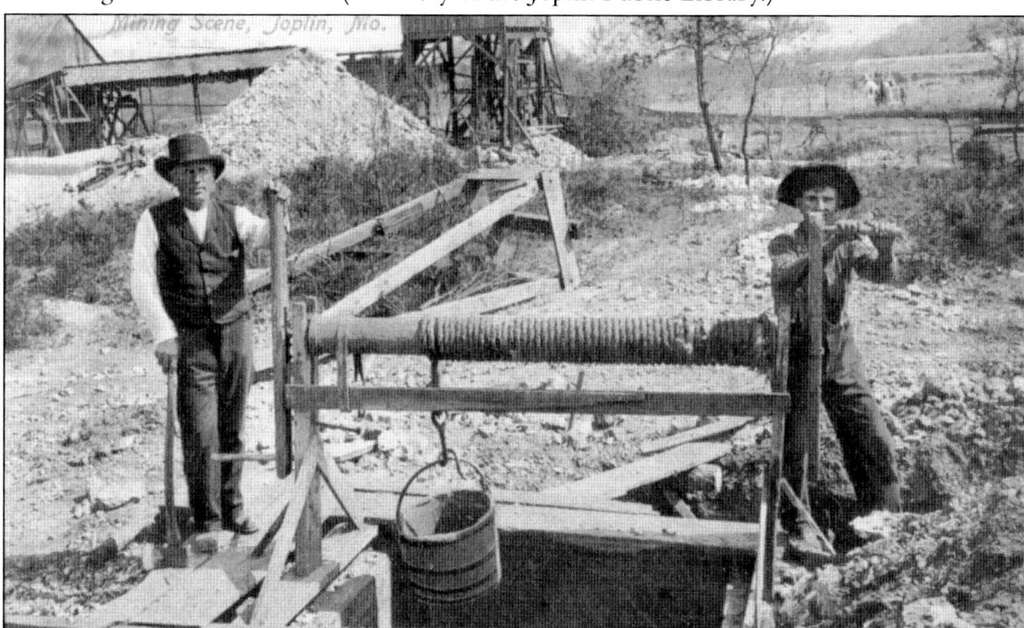

In the primitive days of mining, a prospector paid $5 for a pick, a shovel, a windlass, a rope, and an ore can. With a little luck, he could dig up a fortune. The windlass, which retrieved ore buckets from below ground, depended solely on the strength of the man who operated it. Eventually horsepower, then steam, natural gas, and electricity powered the machinery. (Courtesy of the Joplin Public Library.)

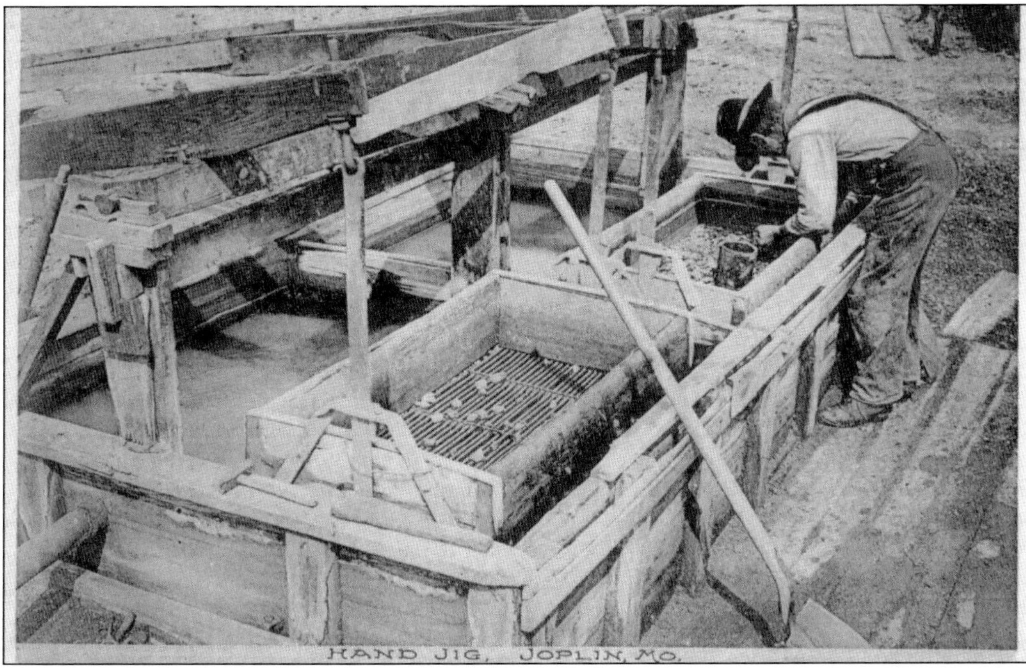

Once the ore arrived at the surface, the valuable minerals were separated from the waste rock. One person operated a hand jig, filling a sluice box with crushed material and water. The heavier ore particles in the mixture sank to the bottom; the zinc and lead were then separated by hand. A good jig operator could process six to 10 tons of ore each workday. (Courtesy of Galen Augustus.)

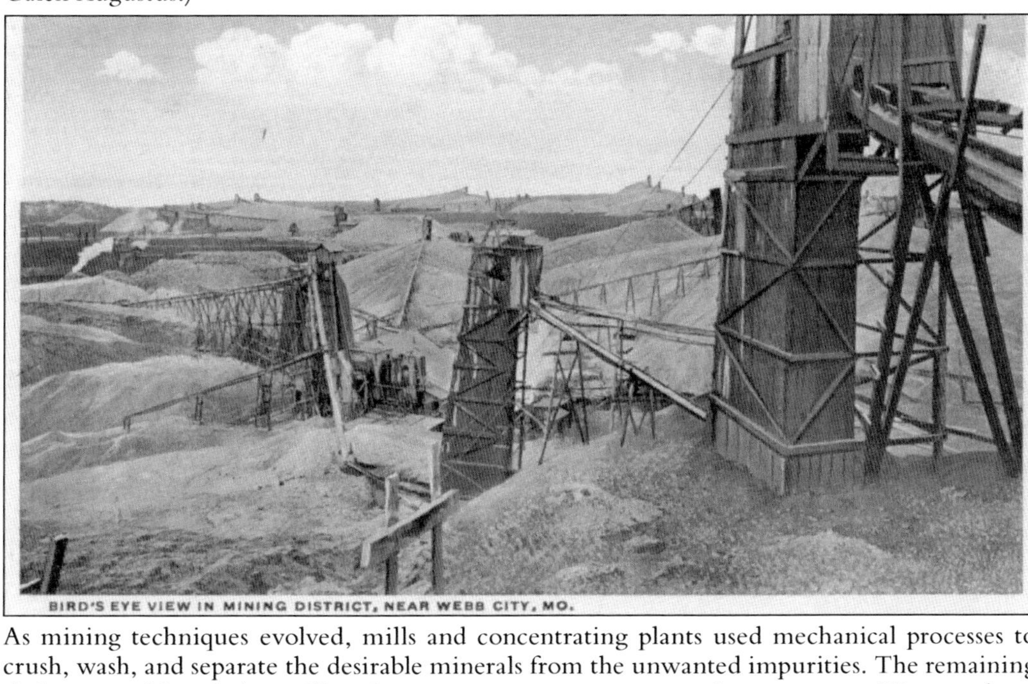

As mining techniques evolved, mills and concentrating plants used mechanical processes to crush, wash, and separate the desirable minerals from the unwanted impurities. The remaining sludge was sold to sludge mills, where water was spun out to retrieve more ore. Waste rock, or "chat," was used for road construction and railroad ballast. (Courtesy of Galen Augustus.)

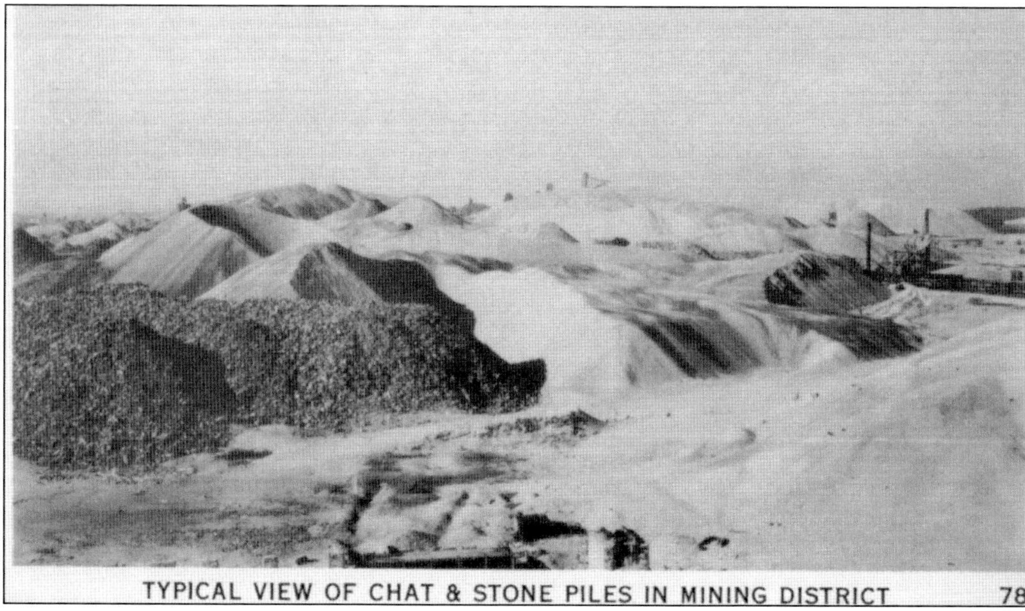

Construction workers also used the gravel-like chat in mixing concrete. Mountains of chat continued to dominate the Tri-State landscape in spite of efforts to dispose of it. Children of yesteryear loved to play on the mountains of chat. They clambered all over them, jumping and sliding, never thinking of the hazards, such as falling into mine shafts or ingesting toxic particles of lead and zinc. (Courtesy of Galen Augustus.)

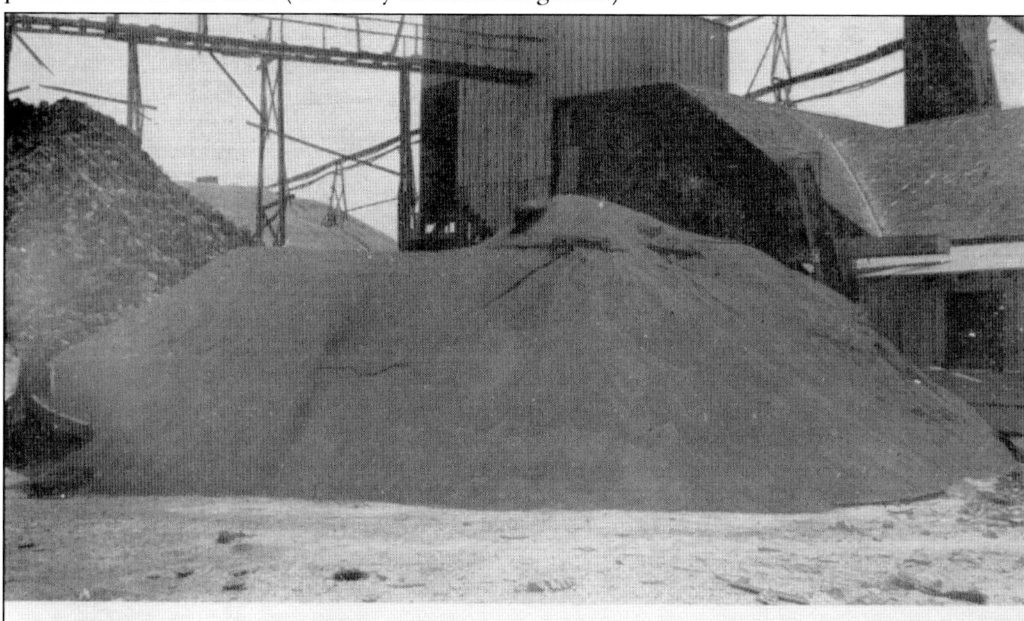

When miners first started digging in southwest Missouri, they only wanted lead. They kept coming across an unknown substance known as blackjack, which they tossed aside as worthless. Later, they found out that it was zinc, a mineral more valuable than lead. Zinc production increased significantly in the early 1900s. It accounted for the majority of the region's wealth and for Joplin's slogan, "The City that Jack Built." (Courtesy of the Joplin Public Library.)

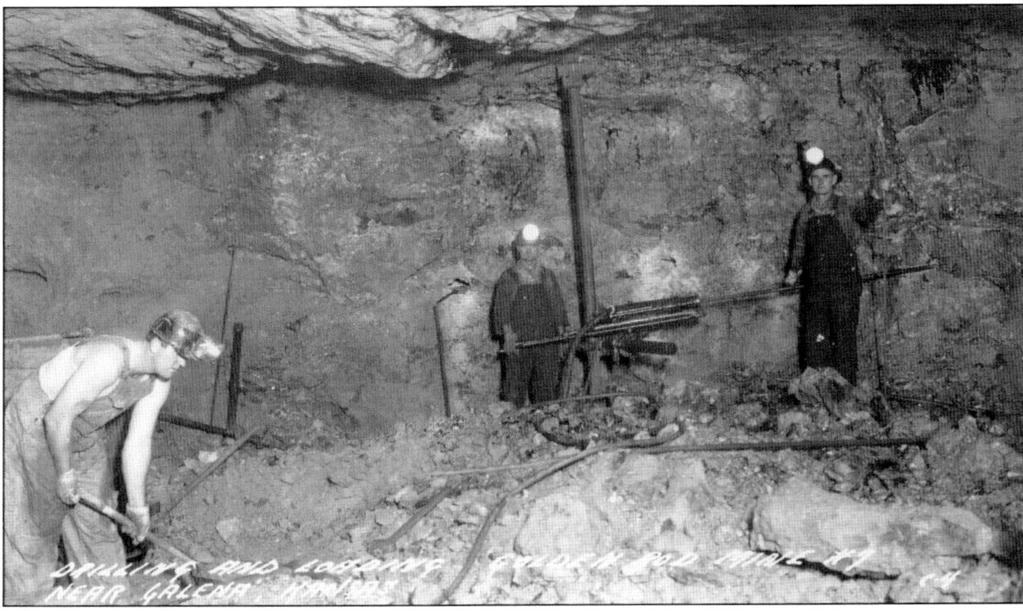

The most grueling and hazardous work involved removing the ore that ran horizontally between layers of hard rock. To blast through the rock, a driller bored a series of holes with hand machinery, inserted sticks of dynamite, lit the charges, and then ran for cover. By the turn of the century, steam power had greatly improved the efficiency of drilling holes. (Courtesy of Galen Augustus.)

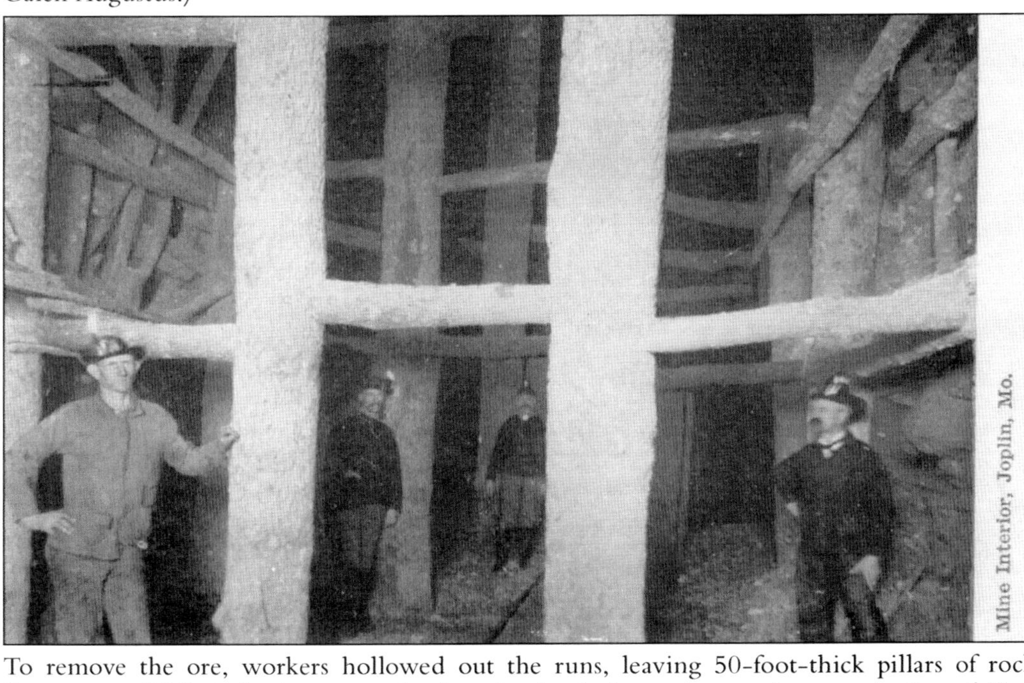

To remove the ore, workers hollowed out the runs, leaving 50-foot-thick pillars of rock for support. Wall timbering was only done in the shafts, to prevent loose rocks from falling and to keep out as much water as possible. Pumps were necessary in shafts over 100 feet deep, since the shafts constantly filled with ground water and runoff during spring rains. (Courtesy of Galen Augustus.)

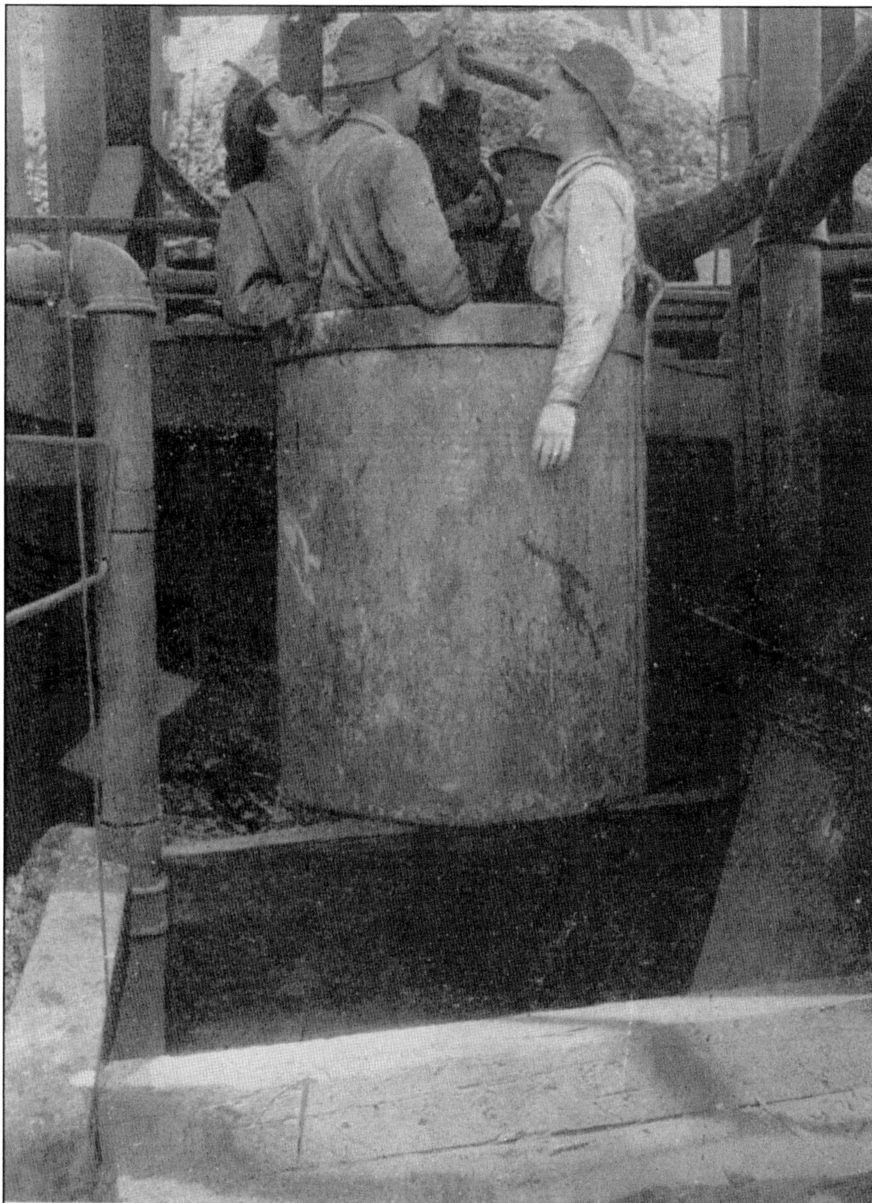

Entering Mine, Joplin, Mo.

After the ore was dislodged, shovelers filled cans, which were taken by track to the shaft and hoisted to the mill above for processing. The standard can held up to 1,200 pounds of ore. Shovelers were paid by the number of cans filled; if they filled more than 100 cans in a day, they earned a bonus. The shoveler's helpers worked to keep the track free of rocks, provide a steady supply of empty cans, and get the filled cans out of the way and headed to the surface. After the cans were emptied, they were returned to the mine for refilling. Miners often hopped inside to use the cans as elevators. Careless men who did not keep their arms and legs inside could easily be mangled when the heavy can bumped against the walls of the shaft. (Courtesy of the Joplin Public Library.)

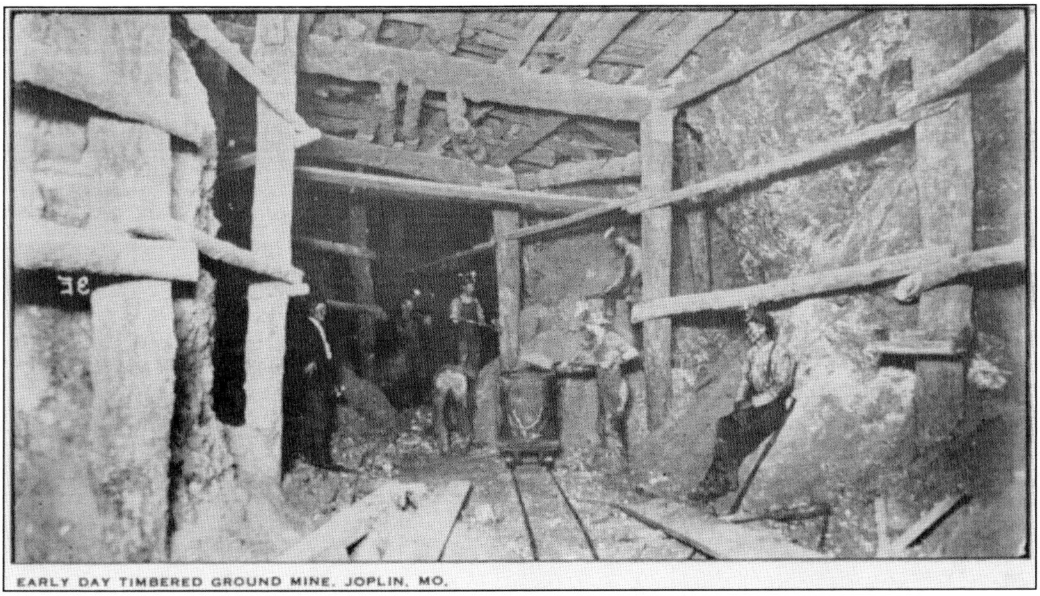

One class of underground laborers worked only for room and board. The attributes of the good old Missouri mule—intelligence, willingness, and strength—ideally suited them for mine work. A law mandated that mules must be brought up every two weeks for fresh air; otherwise, some would have spent their entire lives underground. Mule handlers brought the animals out at night, since they would be spooked by bright sunlight. (Courtesy of Galen Augustus.)

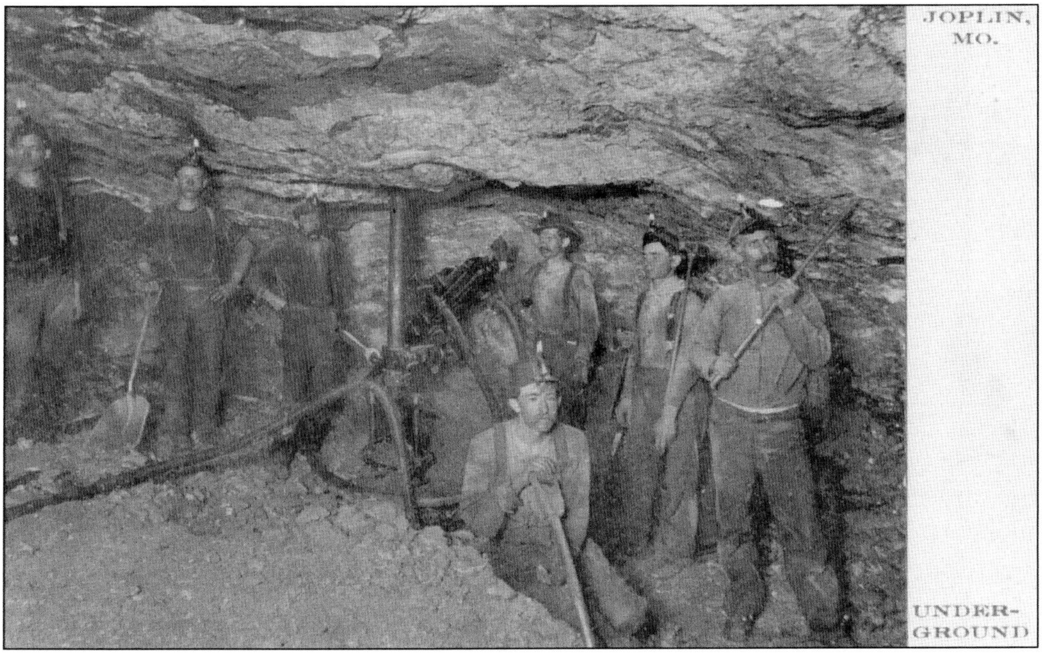

It was a hard life for the workers, whether down in the mines or above ground in the mills and smelters. Area children often worked as well. One 13-year-old smelter's helper made 15¢ per hour working 10-hour days, six days each week. Smelter workers labored in shifts, 15 minutes in front of the furnace followed by a 15-minute cooldown from the fiery blasts that permanently reddened their faces. (Courtesy of Galen Augustus.)

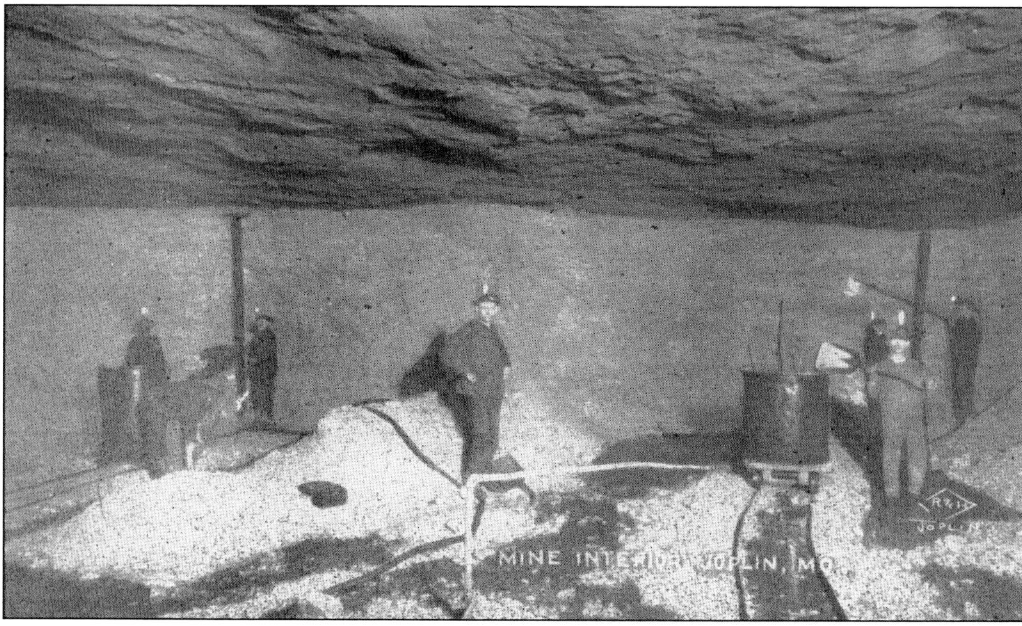

In 1899, mine workers typically worked six nine-hour shifts each week. After 1900, the workday was lowered to eight hours for underground workers and 10 hours for those in the mills above ground. In 1916, typical wages ranged from $2.75 to $4 per day, based upon the degree of difficulty or expertise needed for the job. (Courtesy of Galen Augustus.)

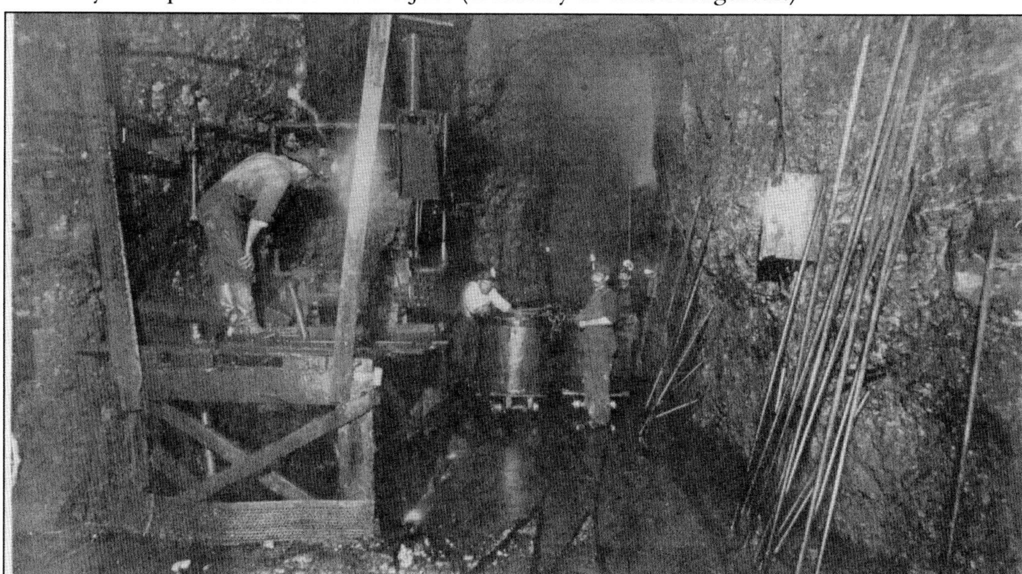

No. 4. Underground Scene, Lead and Zinc Mine, Joplin, Mo.

The workers who benefited the most financially were the mill foremen, ground bosses, mine superintendents, metallurgists, chemists, assayers, ore buyers, lease men, bookkeepers, statisticians, and supply and explosives salesmen. The gulf between miners and management expanded during the teens, with unionization of workers and frequent strikes. In 1915, the American Institute of Mining Engineers met to discuss ways to improve communication, while state inspectors investigated health issues. (Courtesy of Galen Augustus.)

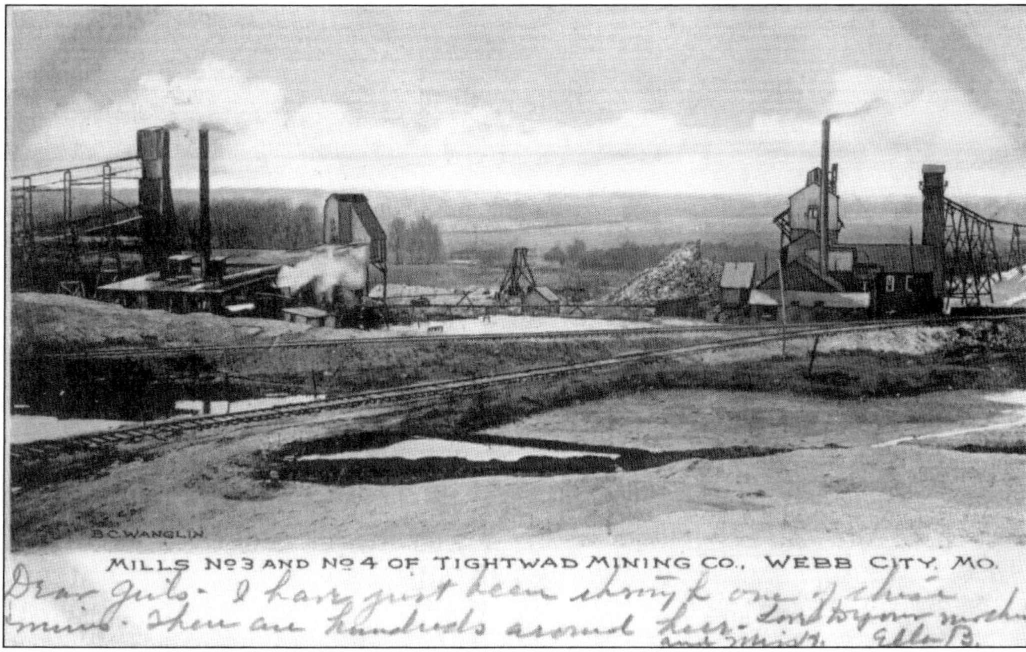

Mine owners assigned a unique name to each of the thousands of Tri-State-area mines. Some chose humorous names such as I Know, You Know, and Damfino. Others selected colors and animals for a theme. For example, there were the Bird Dog, Bull Dog, Yellow Dog, and Green Dog, as well as the Red Bird, Red Rooster, Blue Goose, and the Black Seven, an enterprise owned by seven blacks. (Courtesy of Galen Augustus.)

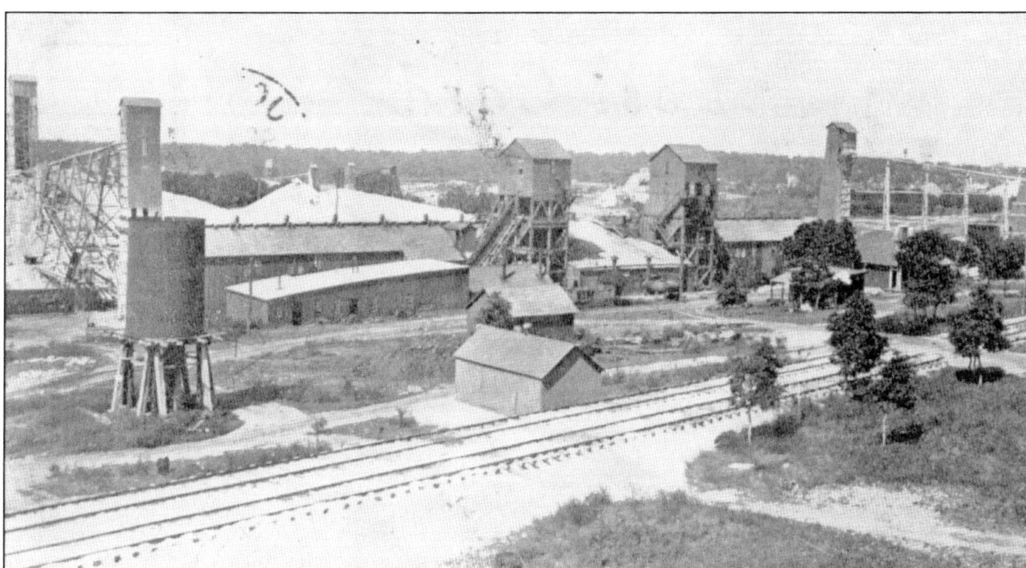

The prolific Yellow Dog Mine, which boasted the most modern steam-driven equipment of the day, earned a reputation for its innovations. The Yellow Dog even provided an unusual setting for an elegant society soiree. In 1906, the Knights Templar held its ball in the mine. Guests danced and strolled amidst the whirl and rumble of the mill in full operation. (Courtesy of Galen Augustus.)

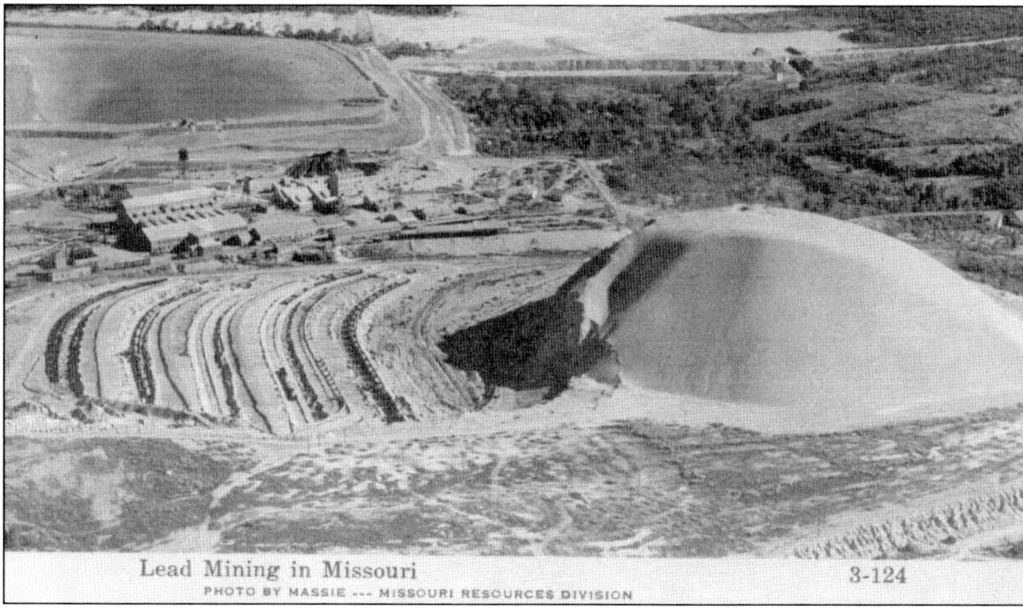

The richest lead and zinc strike in southwest Missouri occurred at the Oronogo Circle Mine, one of the few open-pit mines in the district. The largest chunk of pure lead ever found came from the mine; it was displayed at the Chicago World's Fair in 1893. After World War I, the strip-mining ended. The huge water-filled pit became popular with scuba divers, who liked to explore its depths. (Courtesy of the Joplin Public Library.)

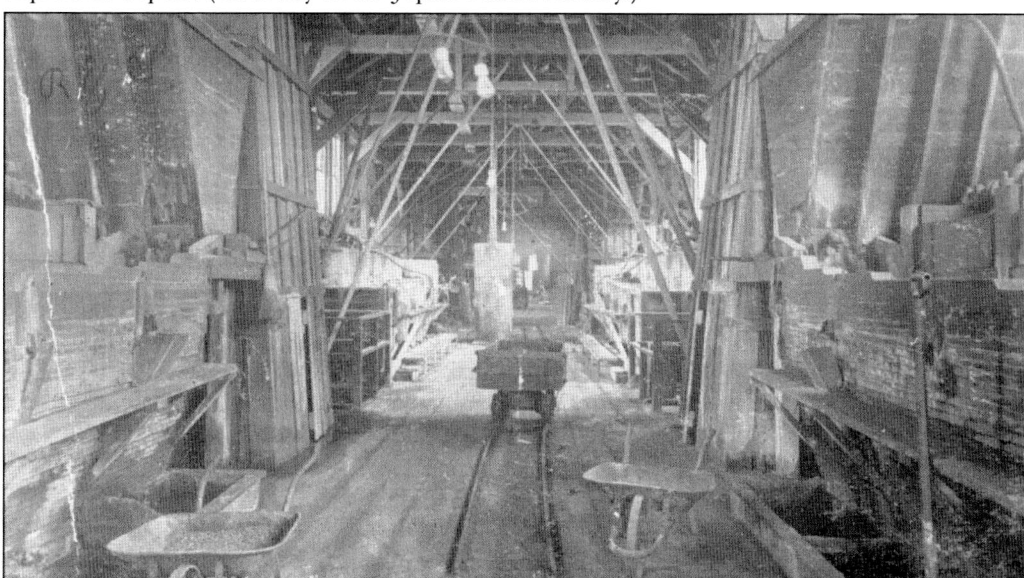

The mining industry came of age in the early 20th century, after electrical power superseded steam-powered machinery. About the same time electricity came into common usage, natural gas was discovered in southeastern Kansas. Both electricity and gas, which yielded a cheap alternative to coal, revolutionized the mining industry. New mines and mills were fitted completely with electricity, while older installations had to be retrofitted with gas burners. (Courtesy of Galen Augustus.)

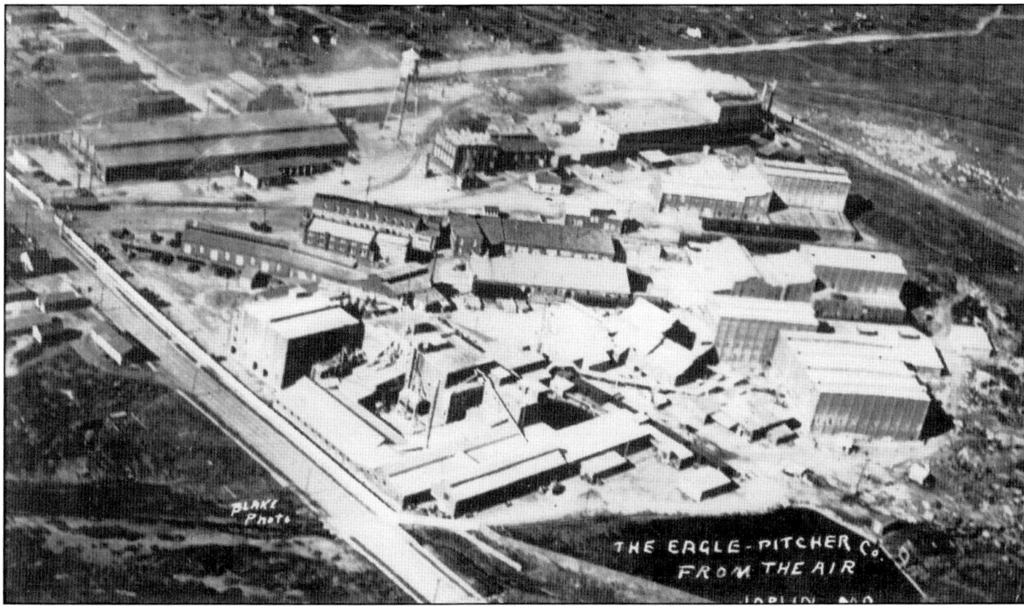

In 1916, Picher Lead Company merged with Eagle White Lead Company of Cincinnati, Ohio. For decades, Eagle Picher was the largest employer in the district. As mining began to phase out, the company branched into other industries. Its laboratories for metallurgy research and development produced the country's most important innovations in battery technology. Eagle Picher batteries played a vital role in NASA space programs. (Courtesy of Galen Augustus.)

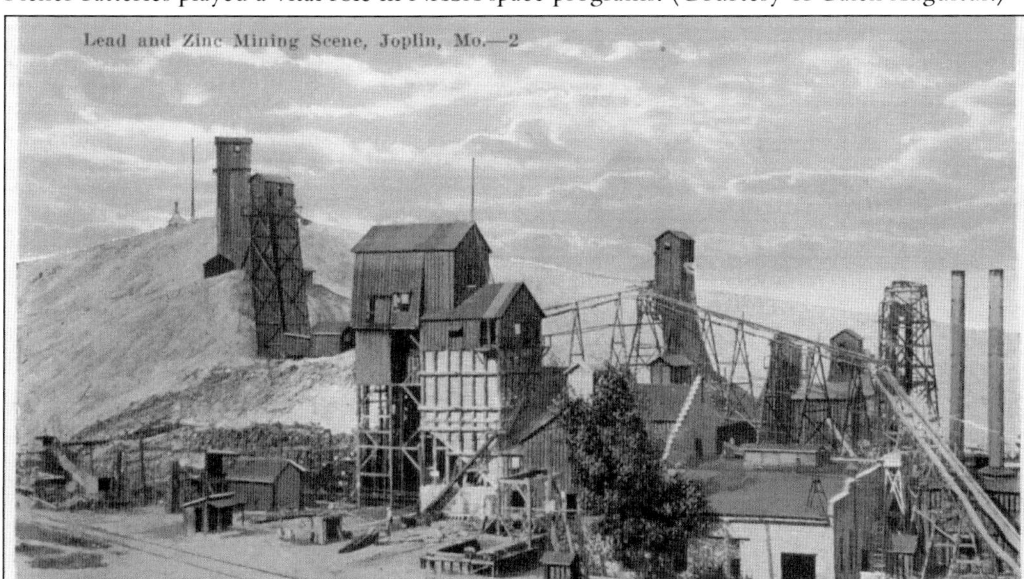

Large companies with expensive machinery and buildings began replacing the small operations. In 1907 and 1908, an economic panic tanked ore prices, forcing many mine closures. World War I brought soaring prices and a scramble for mining land, leases, and machinery. During the Great Depression, demand for ore dropped again, with employment hitting an all-time low. World War II temporarily boosted zinc and lead production in the Tri-State District. (Courtesy of the Joplin Public Library.)

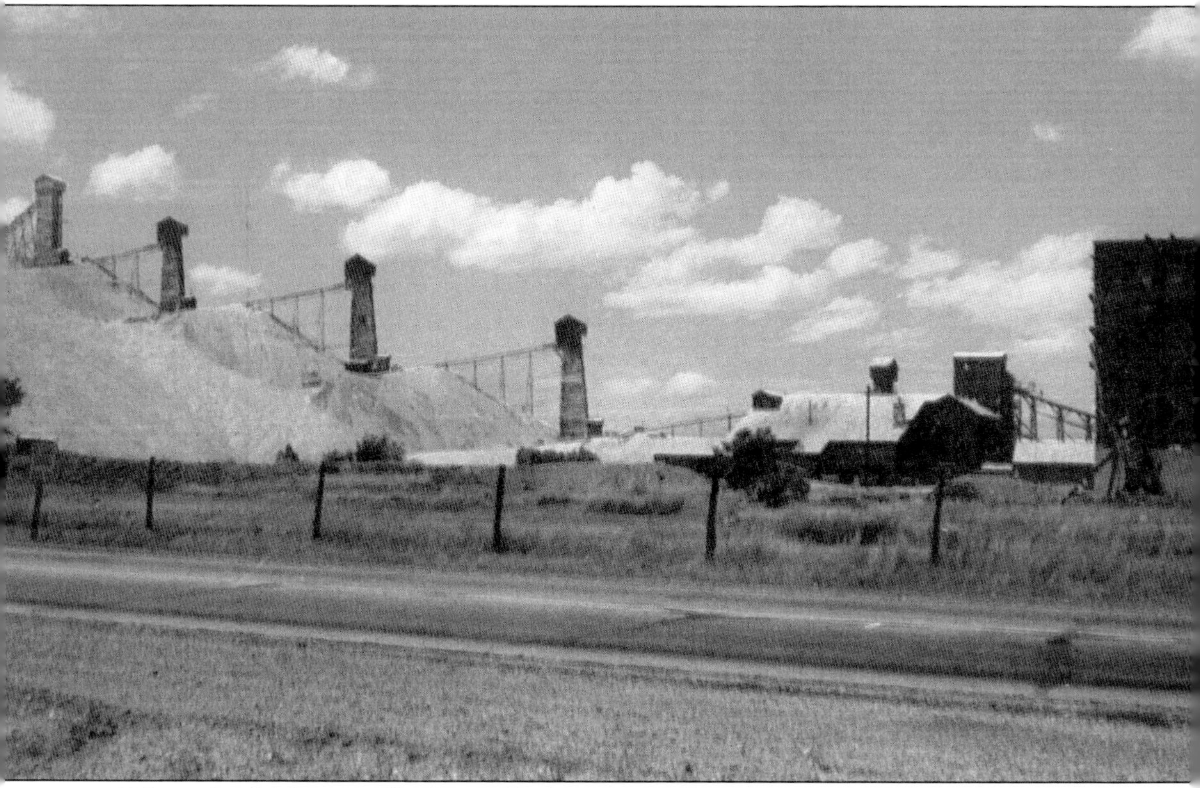

This card, which reputedly shows the last mine still operating in the Joplin area, may well represent the last hurrah of the industry to which Joplin owed its very existence. Mining activity slowed down after World War II, when government subsidies ceased. Thousands of workers found themselves unemployed. Mines filled up with water after the pumping stopped. By the 1960s, Tri-State District mining had ended due to increased operating costs and diminished profits; lead and zinc could be imported from foreign countries at a substantially lower cost. There were also growing environmental concerns, such as surface cave-ins from collapsed mine shafts, contaminated soil in residential areas, contamination of wells and streams, metal-bearing dust, and radon gas. Costly cleanup efforts in the region have been funded by the US Environmental Protection Agency's Superfund. (Courtesy of Joplin Public Library.)

Two

Building Blocks

One of the best ways to learn about the history of a community is to study its buildings. Joplin evolved from a ramshackle mining camp into a thriving city. The influx of people from Europe, as well as from the eastern and southern United States, influenced the way it grew. Meanwhile, the Industrial Revolution radically changed building technology. In 1877, the arrival of the railroad meant that builders were no longer limited to locally available materials. However, local resources continued to play a major role in Joplin's building construction; Carthage limestone, handmade brick, zinc shingles, and an abundance of wood literally provided the building blocks used to create Joplin's finest architecture. Talented architects, such as August and Alfred Michaelis, Thomas Bellas, and Austin Allen, practiced their craft and left indelible marks on Joplin's appearance. They designed imposing buildings in styles that were popular all over the United States. These included Italianate and neoclassical designs and the revival styles of Gothic, Romanesque, Colonial, and Greek. This chapter presents some of Joplin's best structures; many remain vibrant today, but, alas, many have been destroyed through neglect or demolition.

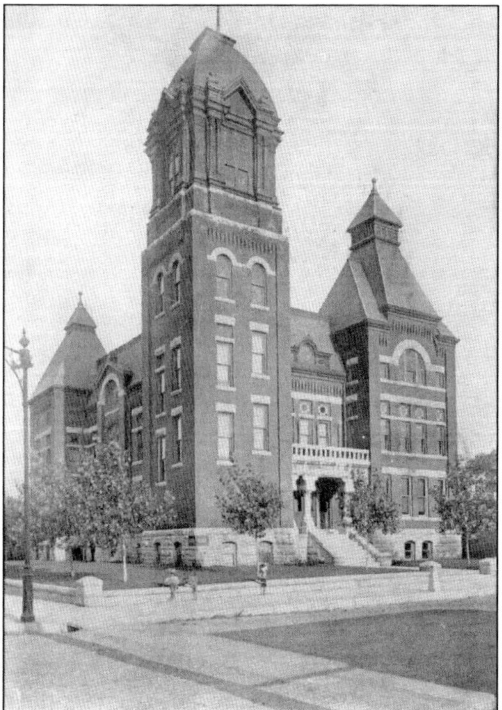

Jasper County Court House, Joplin, Mo.

Jasper County experienced its own civil war in the 1880s, when leaders from both Joplin and Carthage fought bitterly to have the county courthouse built in their cities. A compromise was reached—two grand halls of justice were erected in 1894. The limestone courthouse in Carthage cost $100,000; Joplin's brick and stone courthouse cost a comparatively paltry $20,000. Architect Thomas Bellas designed the towered structure at 701 Virginia Avenue. (Courtesy of the Joplin Public Library.)

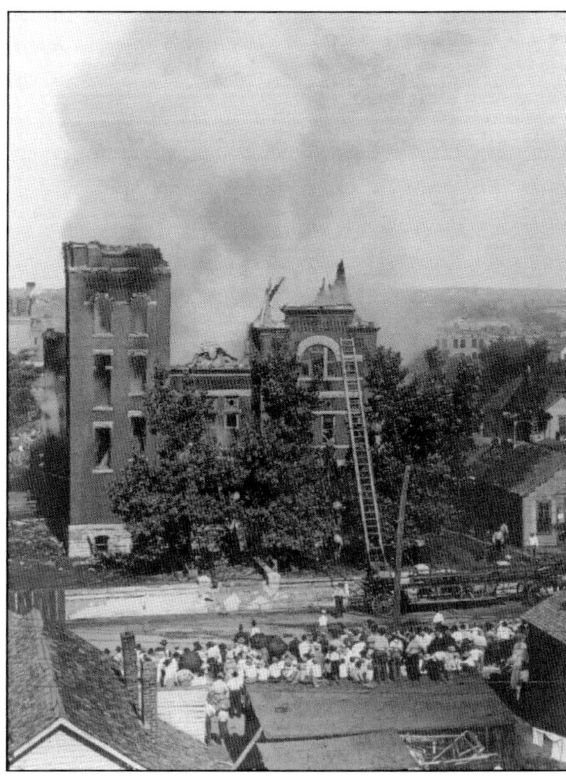

On June 13, 1911, a fire broke out in the courthouse basement when a 10-gallon can of disinfectant exploded. Only three people were in the building, and they escaped unharmed. Four fire departments and 100 volunteers battled the blaze; however, burst hoses and low water pressure hampered their efforts. Large crowds gathered to watch the disaster unfold. Although the county had planned to rebuild on the site, it never did. (Courtesy of Galen Augustus.)

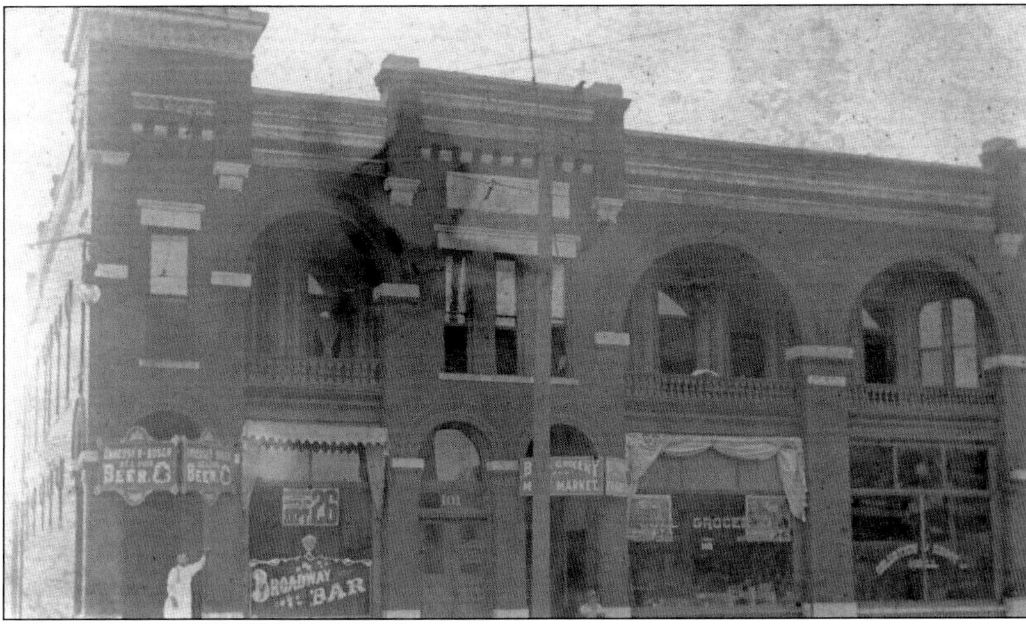

The Broadway Building at 101 Main Street, constructed around 1900, housed Bell Grocery and the Salvation Army Hall, which operated a relief store and labor bureau to help find work for the indigent. Perhaps their efforts were undermined by the presence of the Broadway Bar in the same building! Incidentally, the 1909 Joplin city directory listed 52 saloons and only 16 dry goods stores. Evidently folks preferred wet goods! (Courtesy of Galen Augustus.)

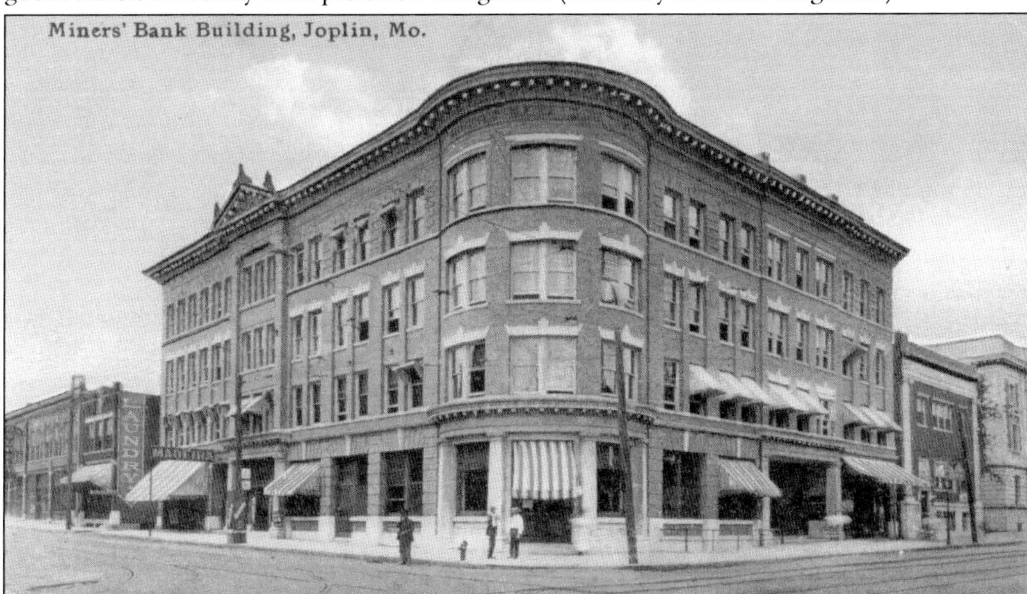

Joplin's first financial institution, the banking house of Patrick Murphy, was established in 1875. On July 1, 1905, the enterprise moved to a new location at 207 West Fourth Street and changed its name to Miners Bank. Architect August Michaelis designed the structure, which the newspaper described as "the finest and most modern between St. Louis and Denver." The building fell into disrepair and was destroyed by fire in 1982. (Courtesy of Rodney Blaukat.)

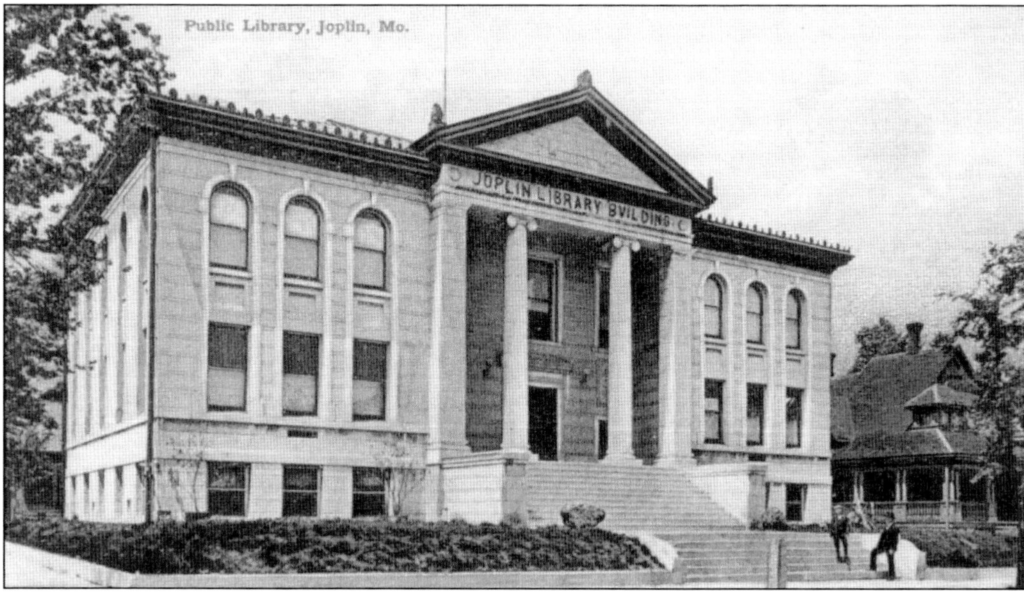

In 1901, philanthropist Andrew Carnegie granted Joplin petitioners $40,000 to build a library. On October 8, 1902, a cornerstone-laying ceremony was held at the northwest corner of Ninth Street and Wall Avenue. Designed by August Michaelis, the building was completed in November 1903. The *Joplin Globe* proclaimed it "the most beautiful in the city." In 1915, Carnegie gave another $20,000 for a two-story addition. (Courtesy of Galen Augustus.)

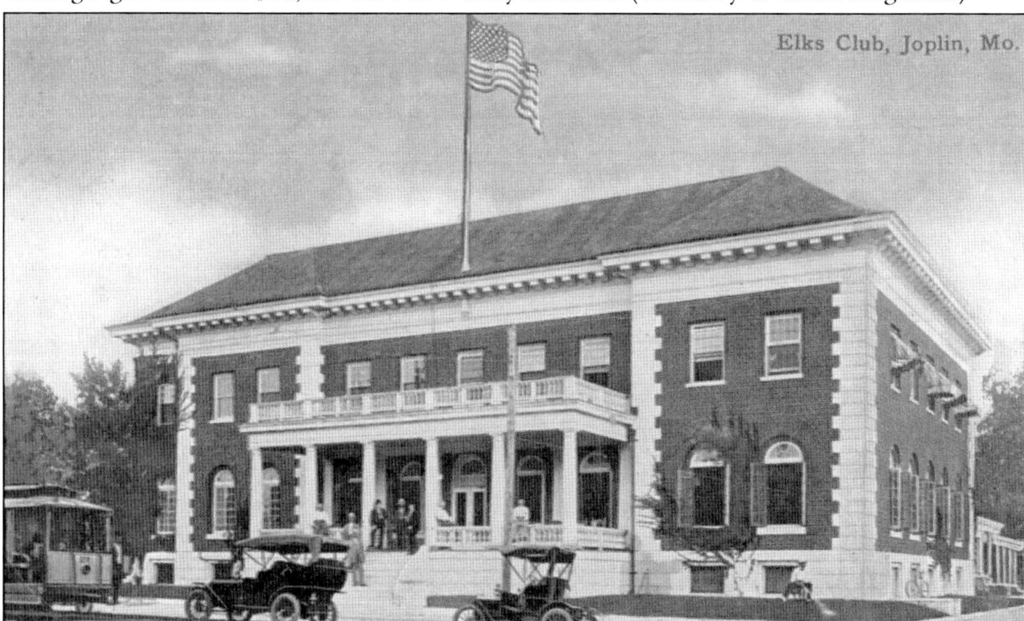

In 1904, Joplin Elks commissioned architect Austin Allen to construct a lodge at 320 West Fourth Street. The first floor featured the lobby, billiard room, reading room, card rooms, dining room, social room, kitchen, and serving rooms. Sleeping quarters, lodge hall, and bathrooms occupied the second floor. The basement housed a four-lane bowling alley, gymnasium, Turkish bath, lockers, and storage rooms. (Courtesy of Rodney Blaukat.)

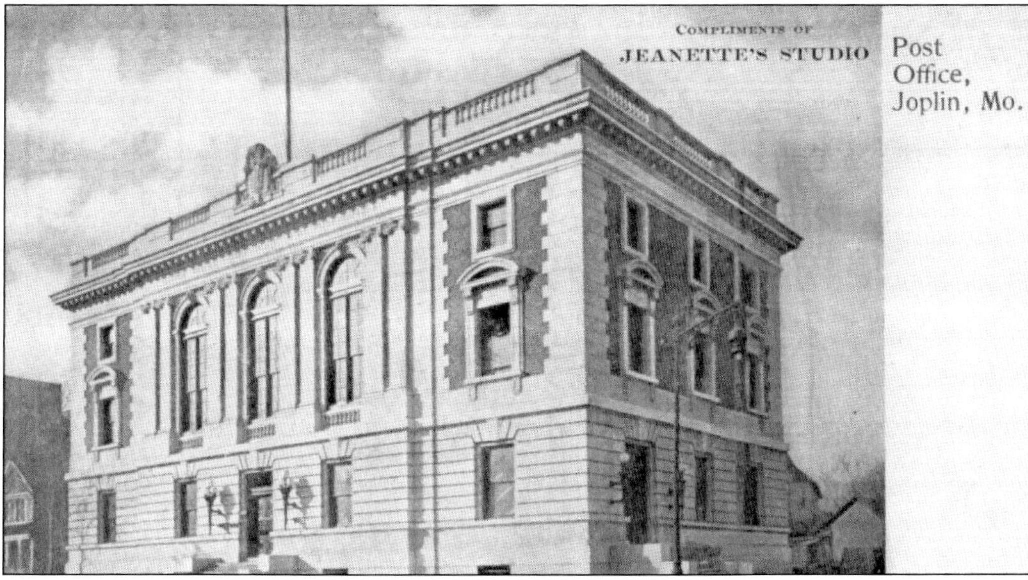

Designed by nationally prominent architect John Knox Taylor, the federal building and post office at 302 Joplin Avenue was completed in 1905. The upper floors of the building housed federal offices and the US Federal Court. The basement and first floor comprised the post office, equipped with the latest in sorting equipment. The main office employed 10 clerks, a postmaster and his assistant, two dispatching clerks, 11 regular mail carriers, and two substitute carriers. (Courtesy of the Joplin Public Library.)

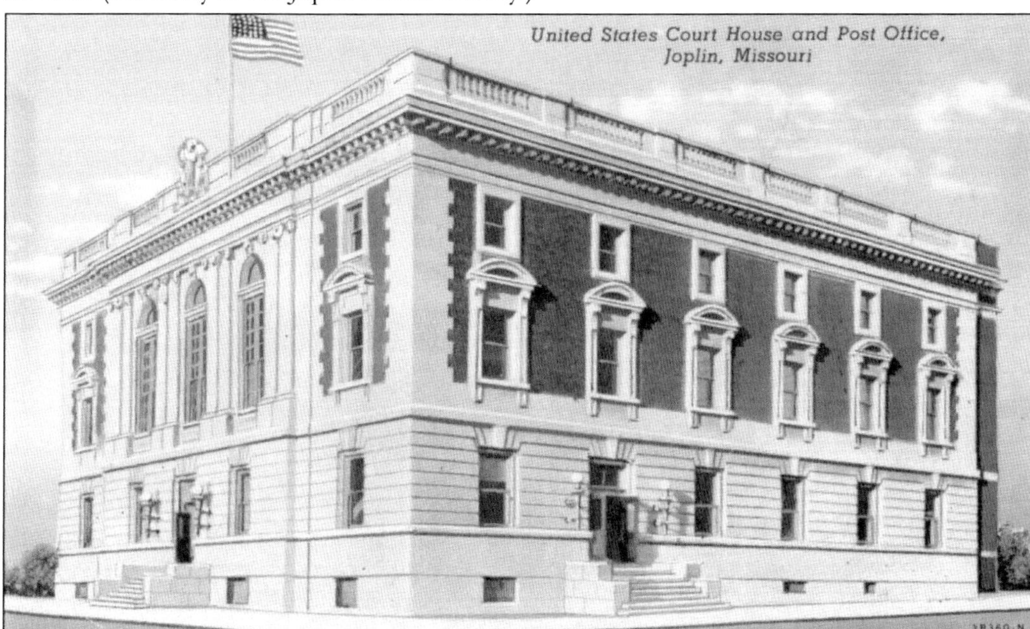

Completed in 1936, a new addition using $150,000 in Works Progress Administration funding doubled the square footage. In 1962, the Joplin Post Office moved into new quarters at First and Main Streets, leaving the federal building for offices and courtroom use. The venerable old building gradually lost all of its tenants. In 1999, the US government declared it a surplus building to be sold. (Courtesy of the Joplin Public Library.)

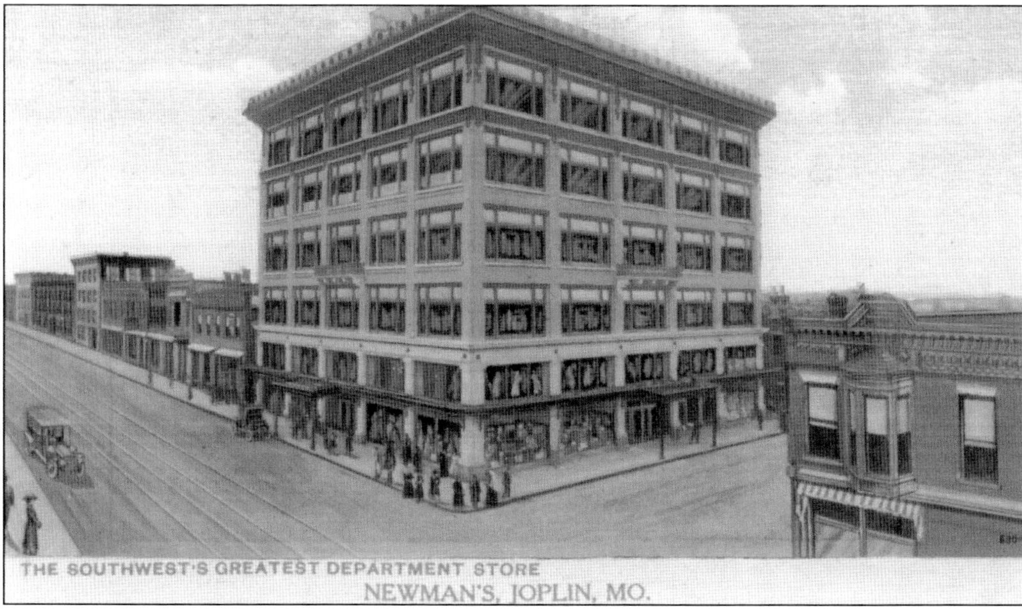

Successful men's clothiers Albert Newman and Gabe Newberger hired Austin Allen to build a palatial home of merchandising at 602 Main Street. Stocking the modern, luxurious store was a major event, as 29 railroad boxcars unloaded the fixtures and merchandise in advance of the grand opening held on November 16, 1910. An illuminated roof sign spelled out Newman's and served as a beacon in the nighttime sky. (Courtesy of Galen Augustus.)

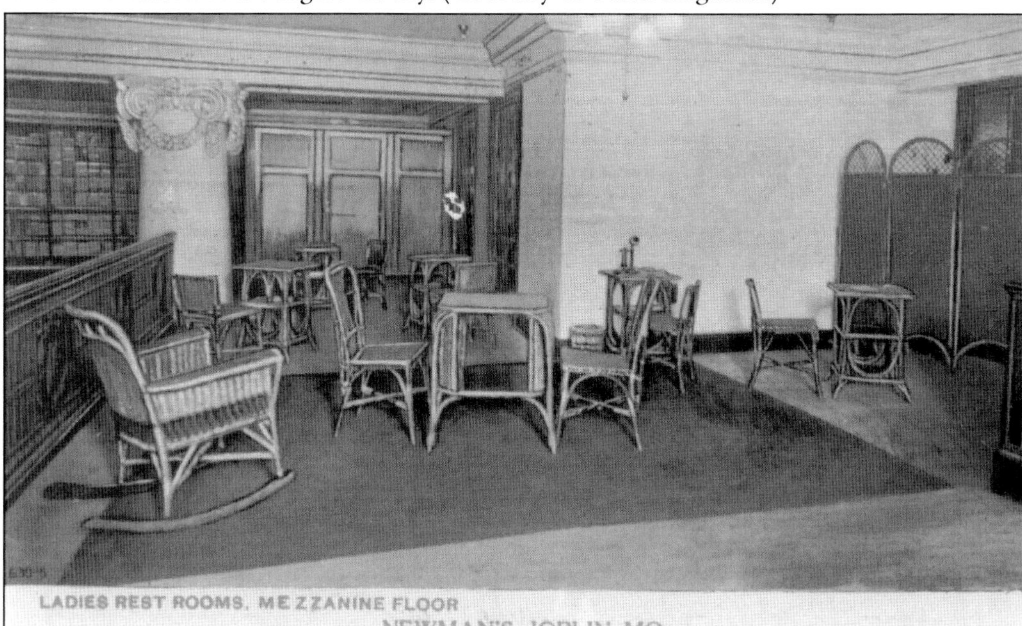

Newman's offered everything from clothing, shoes, hats, toys, books, and trunks to drug sundries. The basement sold miscellaneous dry goods, and the main floor offered a vast array of retail merchandise and a post office substation. Customers dropped off their hats, coats, and packages in the checking rooms. A grand marble staircase led to the mezzanine level with its wicker-furnished ladies' rest area. (Courtesy of Galen Augustus.)

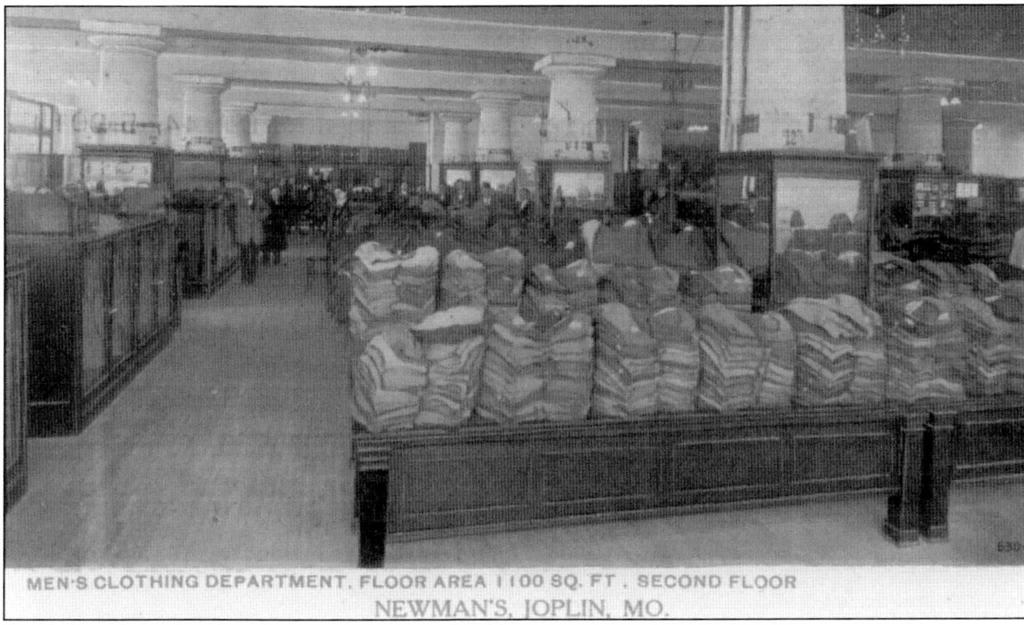

Men's and boys merchandise and luggage were sold on the second floor. Rich woods gleamed everywhere, from the polished floors to the mahogany cabinets and tables. On the third floor, the ladies' department showcased ready-to-wear, millinery, coats, suits, corsets, French muslin undergarments, furs, and infant-wear. Discriminating shoppers came from all over the four-state area to check out the latest fashions displayed at Newman's. (Courtesy of Galen Augustus.)

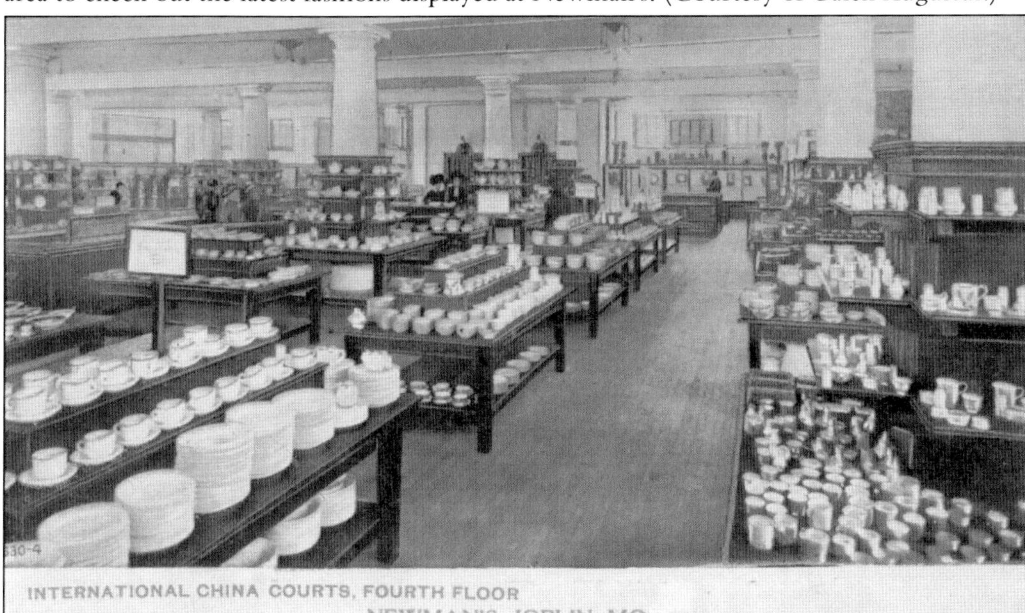

The fourth floor offered domestic and imported porcelain, china, and glass. It also sold toys, sporting goods, books, stationery, house furnishings, and draperies. In addition to the astonishing displays of merchandise, customers also enjoyed an exhilarating view of downtown Joplin. General offices, credit rooms, stock rooms, an alteration department, and a decorator's office were located on the fifth floor. (Courtesy of Rodney Blaukat.)

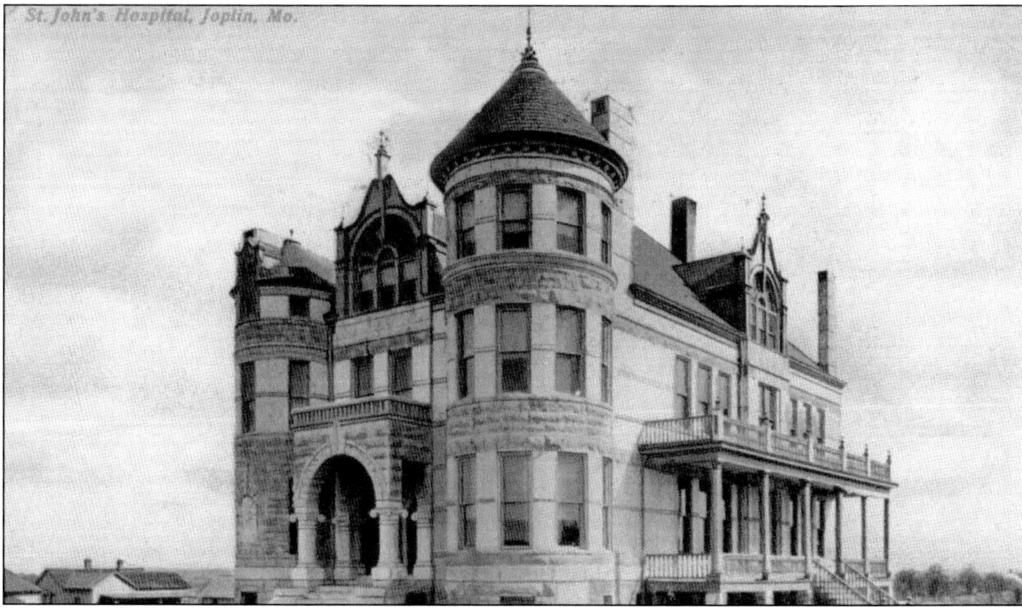

In 1885, Rev. William McCormack and 13 Sisters of Mercy came to minister to the rough mining town of Joplin. At that time, seriously injured miners were transported by buggy to the hospital in Fort Scott, Kansas. Mortality rates ran high, and the Sisters began a massive fundraising campaign to build a hospital. This Romanesque-style limestone edifice, designed by August Michaelis, opened in 1900. (Courtesy of Galen Augustus.)

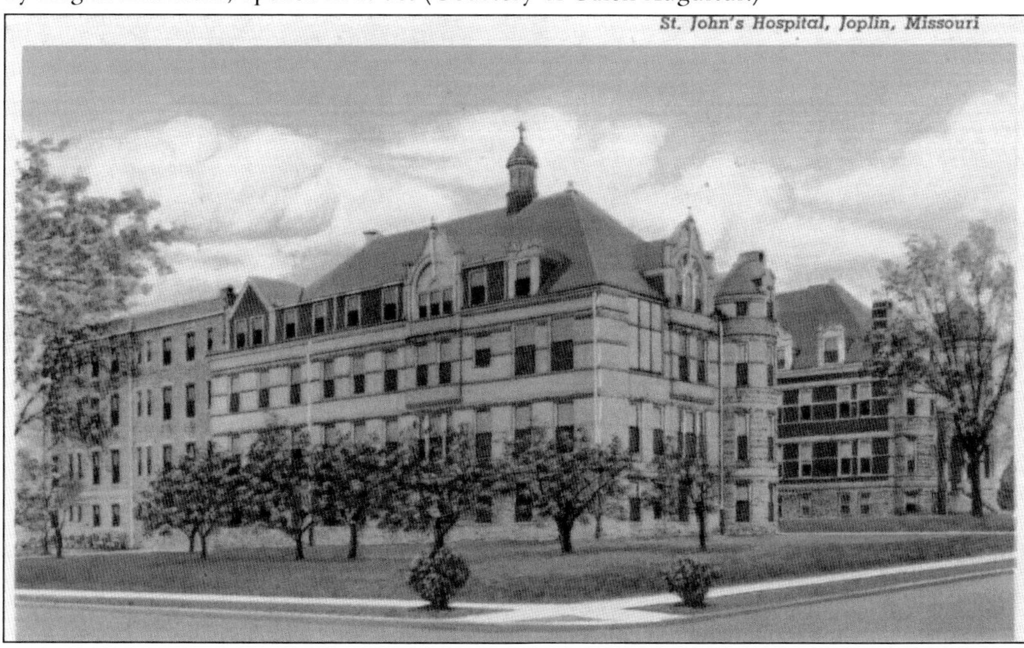

The new St. John's Hospital at 822 West Twenty-second Street opened a nursing school in 1903. It did not take long to outgrow its original 50-bed capacity. In 1926, a four-story, 40-room addition made it the largest hospital in the region. The nursing school was expanded to provide additional classrooms, laboratories, and lodging for 27 nurses. The hospital was enlarged again in 1942, bringing the bed capacity to 210. (Courtesy of Rodney Blaukat.)

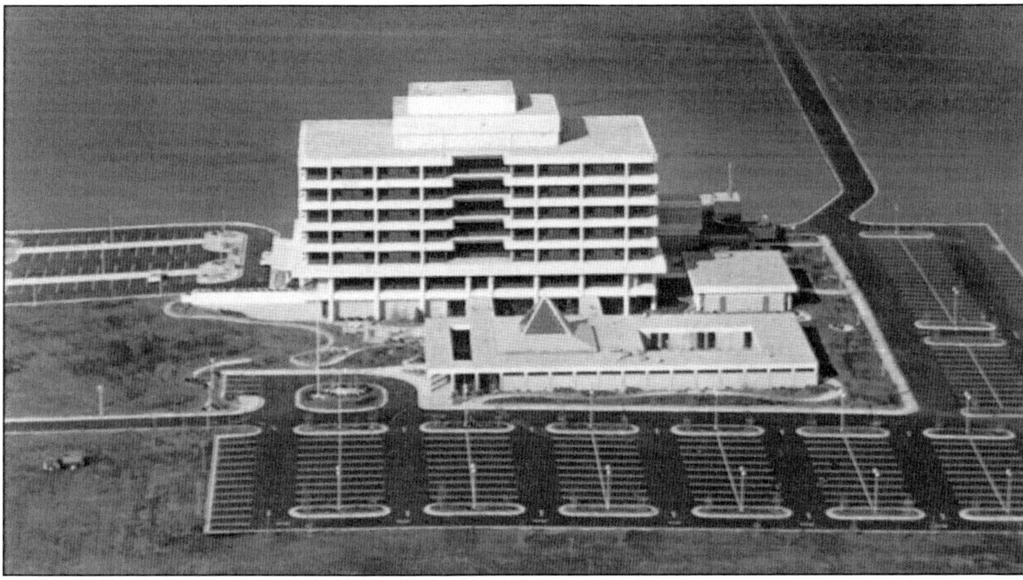

Despite additions and improvements, St. John's Hospital struggled to keep up with the times. Administrators selected 52 acres of abandoned mine land on McClelland Boulevard between Twenty-Sixth and Thirty-Second Streets for the site of a $10-million hospital. On February 25, 1968, St. John's Medical Center opened a seven-story, 267-bed patient tower. Its state-of-the-art computer system made it the first completely computerized hospital in the United States. (Courtesy of the Joplin Public Library.)

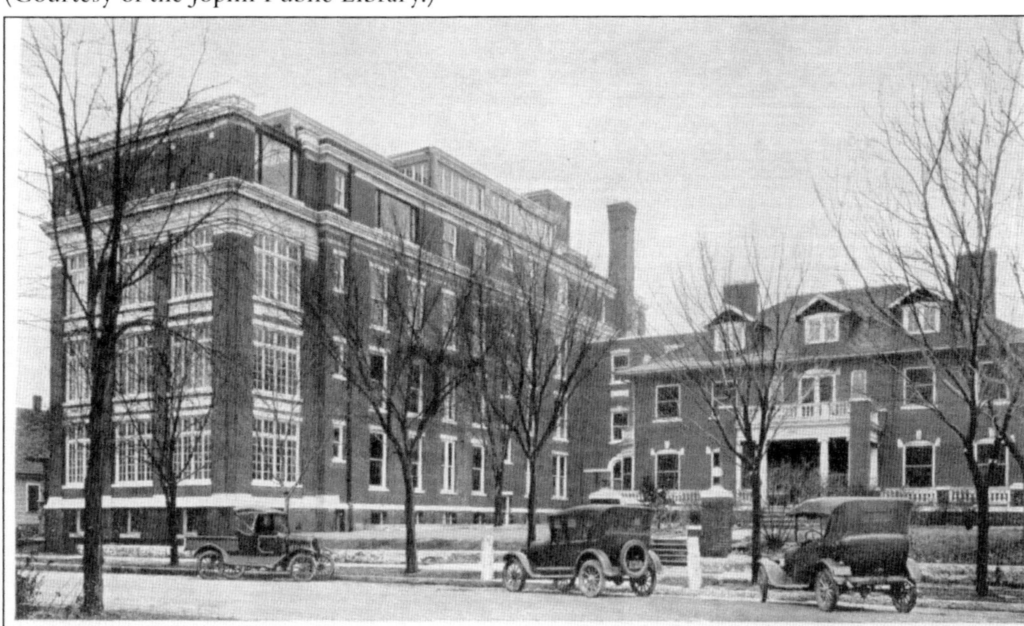

Inventor and entrepreneur John W. Freeman built this house at 2008 Sergeant Avenue. In 1922, the Freemans donated it in memory of their son Orley for use as a hospital. A five-story brick annex opened in May 1925; another large wing opened in 1954. The original home was demolished to make way for a parking lot. The old facility closed in 1975, after construction of a new hospital on West Thirty-Second Street. (Courtesy of the Joplin Public Library.)

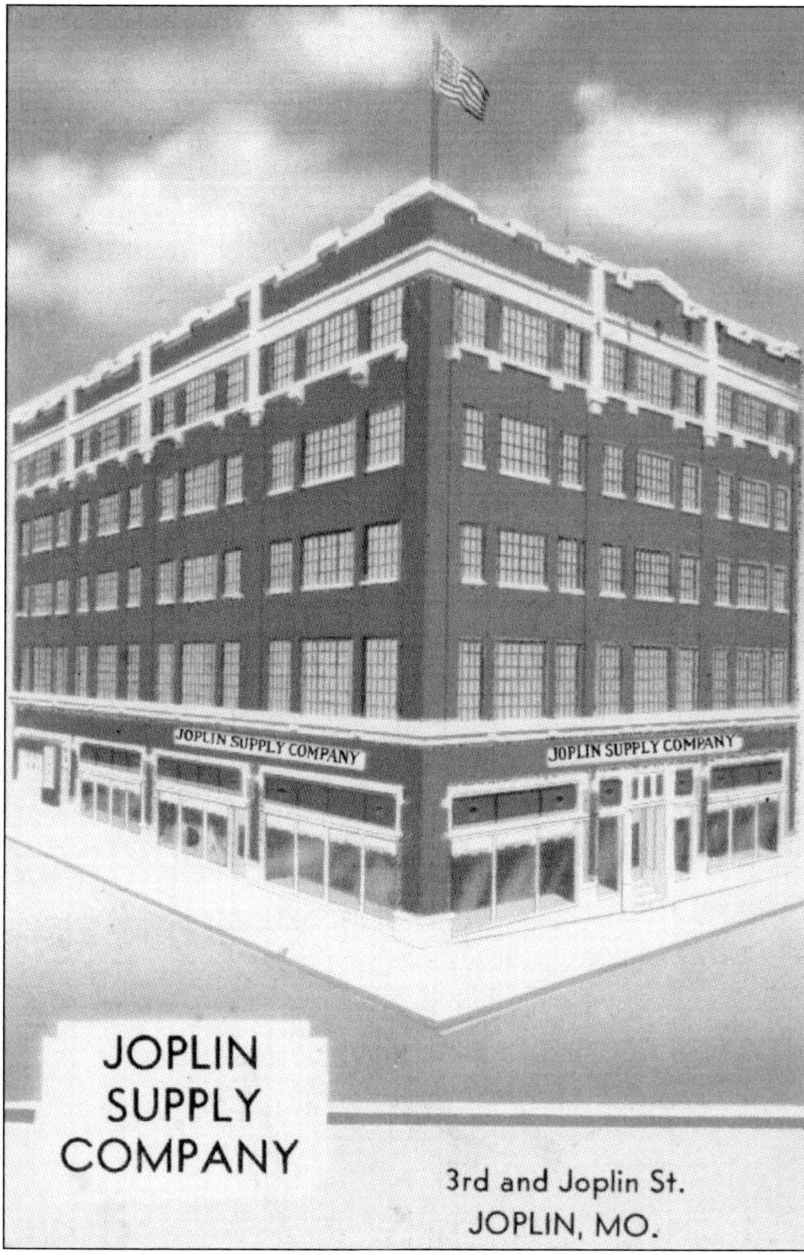

Joplin Supply Company started in 1899 as a mining equipment dealer. In 1903, the company began distributing Ford Model A's. Four years later, the *Joplin Globe* boasted that Joplin, with 125 autos on its streets, had more motorcars for a city its size than anywhere else in the United States. In 1911, Joplin Supply began selling Model T's for $375 each. Joplin Supply's success selling vehicles prompted the Ford Motor Company to select the firm to manufacture them. In 1923, Joplin Supply constructed a five-story brick factory at 220 Joplin Avenue. Parts were freighted in by train and assembled into Model T's, Lincolns, and Ferguson tractors at the plant. In 1930, the company ended its association with Ford Motor and returned to manufacturing mining machinery. It shifted over to plumbing, heating, and refrigeration supplies after the mining industry fizzled out. (Courtesy of Rodney Blaukat.)

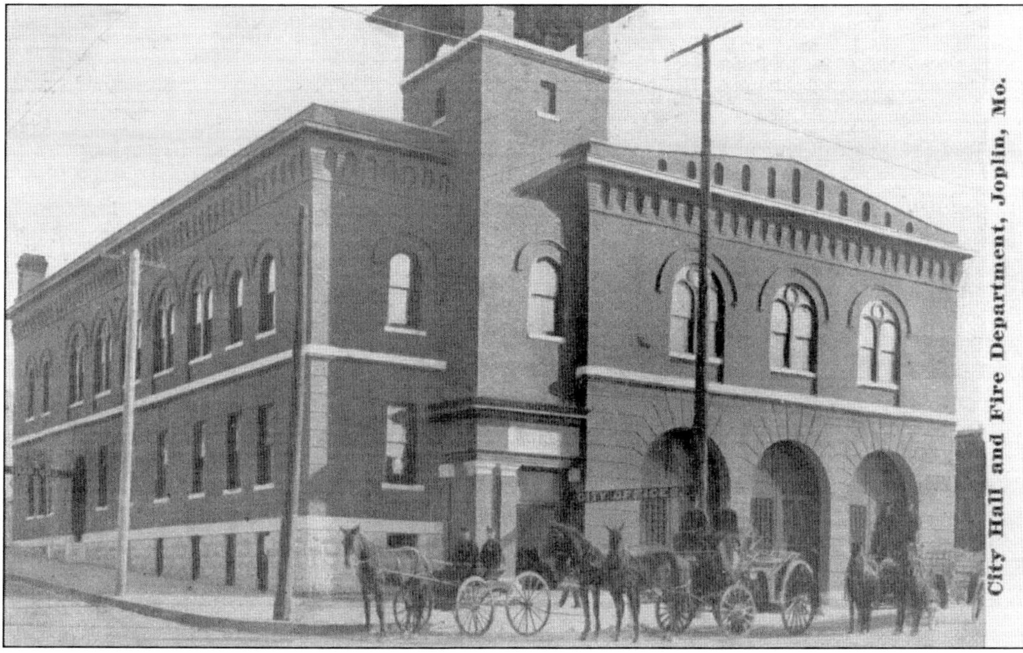

In October 1906, Joplin City Hall opened at 201 Joplin Avenue. The police department, fire department, boys' cells, offices, vault, and city courtroom shared the ground floor. Men's cells, girl's cells, a surgeon's room, a matron's room, and separate cells for white and Negro females filled the second floor. In 1918, a two-story extension was added. It was demolished after the city offices moved to 303 East Third Street in 1967. (Courtesy of Rodney Blaukat.)

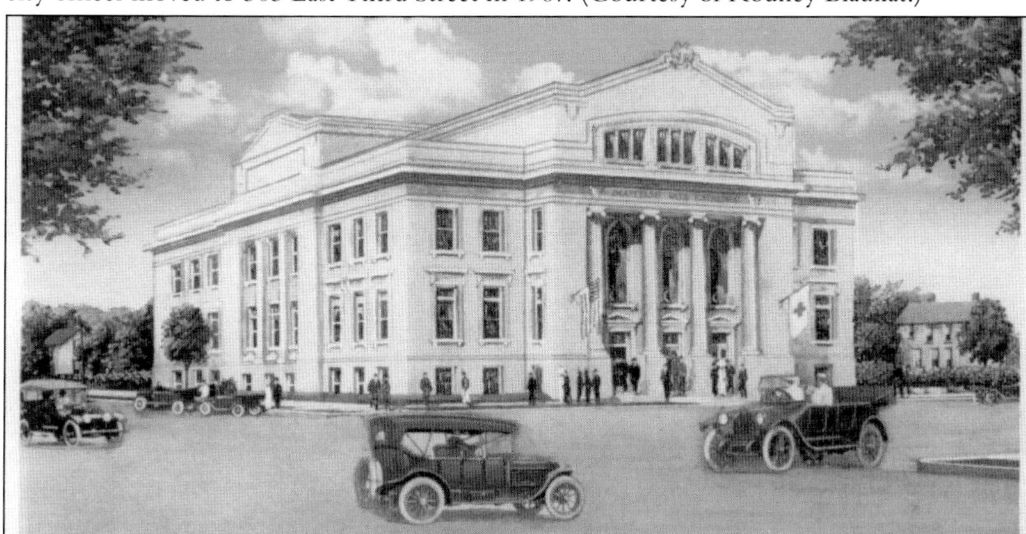

Completed in 1924 at 501 Byers Avenue, the Scottish Rite Cathedral was an architectural masterpiece. Each chamber was decorated extravagantly with marble, plaster reliefs, chandeliers, mosaics, stained glass, rich wood moldings, and decorative painting. Soaring 30 feet above the second floor auditorium was a ceiling crafted entirely of art glass illumined from above. A massive pipe organ, elaborate stage, and 106 hand-painted backdrop curtains completed the room. (Courtesy of Galen Augustus.)

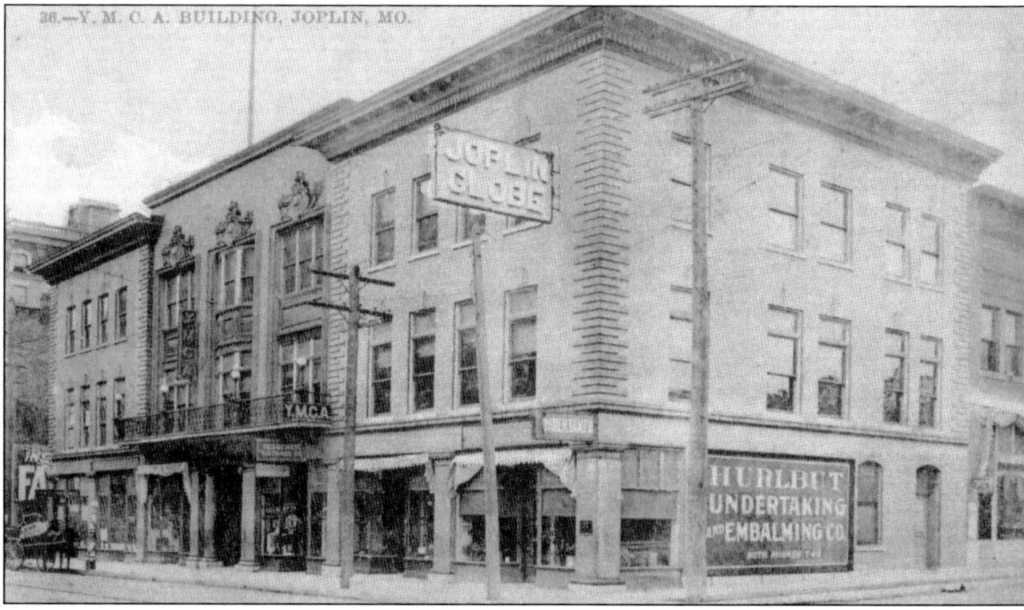

The architectural firm Garstang and Rea designed the YMCA at 117 East Fourth Street. The building formally opened on March 24, 1901. A 1910 advertisement listed membership rates as $3, $5, and $8 for men and $4 and $5 for boys. "Any man or boy of good moral character" was urged to join. The YMCA also encouraged travelers to take advantage of the lodging, bathing, and dining facilities. (Courtesy of Rodney Blaukat.)

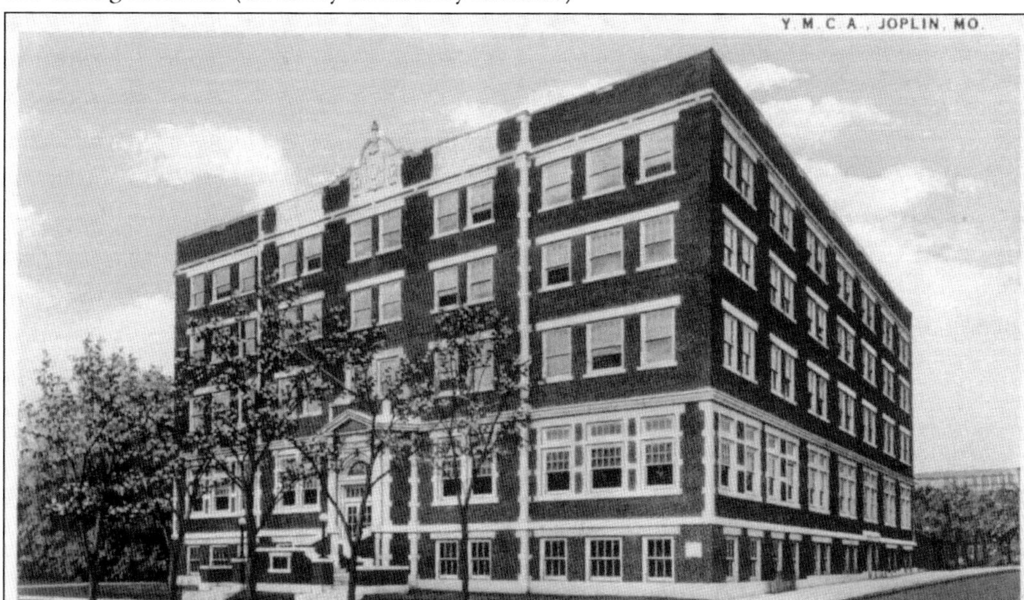

In 1917, the YMCA paid $35,000 for a lot at 510 Wall Avenue then raised $250,000 by popular subscription. The cornerstone was ceremonially laid in October 1919, and the YMCA finally opened on June 16, 1921. The latest in fireproof construction techniques insured that the building would be around for a long time. Twelve-inch-thick brick curtain walls encased the structure, which was partitioned with tile interior walls and concrete floors. (Courtesy of the Joplin Public Library.)

Three

Getting Around

Early settlers to the future Joplin area had few transportation options available. Some arrived on foot; the more fortunate ones came by horseback, horse-and-buggy, or covered wagon. In 1877, a railroad was completed that connected Joplin with Girard, Kansas. Appropriately, the last spike to be driven was made of lead. Other railroad companies laid tracks to connect Joplin with the outside world. They also built freight and passenger depots to service them. The interurban railway system, built in the 1890s, made it possible for people to live outside of the urban center yet still have access to work, shopping, and leisure activities. Local commerce, however, was still dependent on the horse, the ox, and the mule. Horse-drawn delivery wagons conveyed provisions; horse-drawn fire engines responded to fires and other emergencies. People also began riding bicycles for transportation in the 1890s. By 1910, many residents owned automobiles. The Joplin Fire Department made history in 1907, claiming that it was the first fire department in the world to have a motorized fire truck. Nicknamed "The Goat," it was purchased from a local inventor. In the postcard views of downtown Joplin at the beginning of the 20th century, one sees pedestrians, bicyclists, horse-and-buggy rigs, streetcars, and automobiles. Joplin's location at the intersections of several major highways, including US Route 66, earned it the moniker "Crossroads of America." New construction catered to the automobile, as garages, service stations, and car dealerships sprang up all over town. This chapter discusses all of those modes of transportation as well as airplanes, buses, and structural accoutrements, such as viaducts and highways.

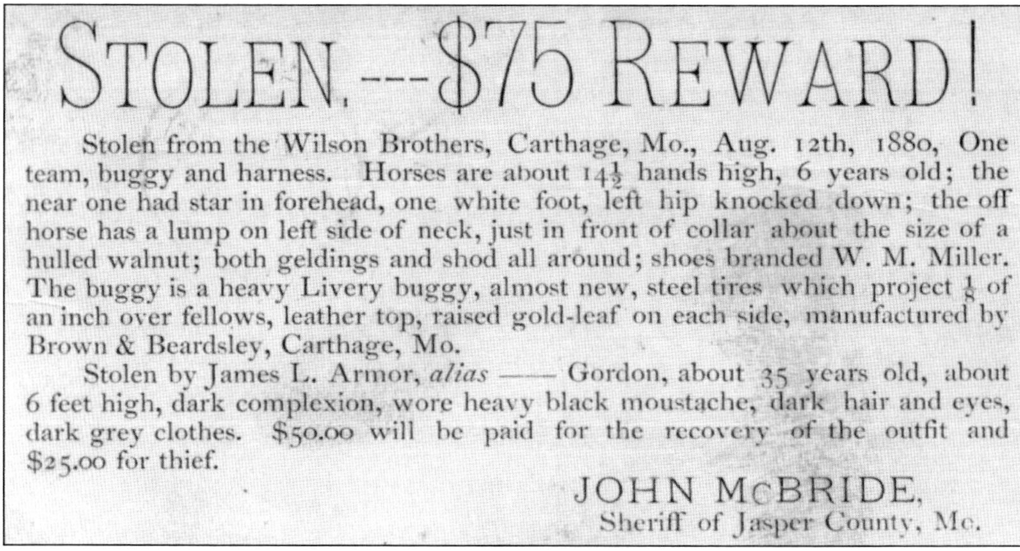

STOLEN.---$75 REWARD!

Stolen from the Wilson Brothers, Carthage, Mo., Aug. 12th, 1880, One team, buggy and harness. Horses are about 14½ hands high, 6 years old; the near one had star in forehead, one white foot, left hip knocked down; the off horse has a lump on left side of neck, just in front of collar about the size of a hulled walnut; both geldings and shod all around; shoes branded W. M. Miller. The buggy is a heavy Livery buggy, almost new, steel tires which project ⅛ of an inch over fellows, leather top, raised gold-leaf on each side, manufactured by Brown & Beardsley, Carthage, Mo.

Stolen by James L. Armor, *alias* —— Gordon, about 35 years old, about 6 feet high, dark complexion, wore heavy black moustache, dark hair and eyes, dark grey clothes. $50.00 will be paid for the recovery of the outfit and $25.00 for thief.

JOHN McBRIDE,
Sheriff of Jasper County, Mo.

In pioneer times, horses provided the easiest source for ill-gotten gains. This postcard alerted area residents to the shocking thievery of James L. Armor. Although Joplin had a police force, citizens formed a local chapter of the Anti–Horse Thief Association (AHTA). For a $1 fee, members were guaranteed protection. When someone reported stolen livestock, police rounded up a posse of the AHTA, which proved amazingly successful at apprehending scoundrels. (Courtesy of Galen Augustus.)

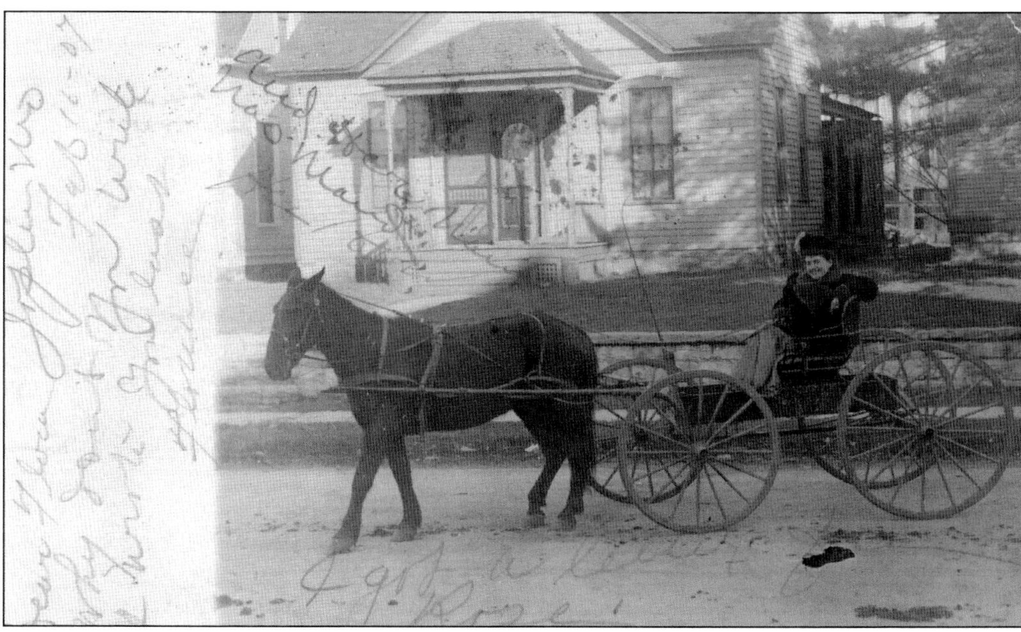

In Joplin's early days, four-legged creatures carried people and goods wherever they needed to go. Horse-drawn vehicles delivered laundry, manufactured goods, and food; they put out fires, functioned as ambulances and hearses, and transported people to work, church, and play. Every dwelling and every public building sported the ubiquitous hitching post out front. (Courtesy of the Joplin Public Library.)

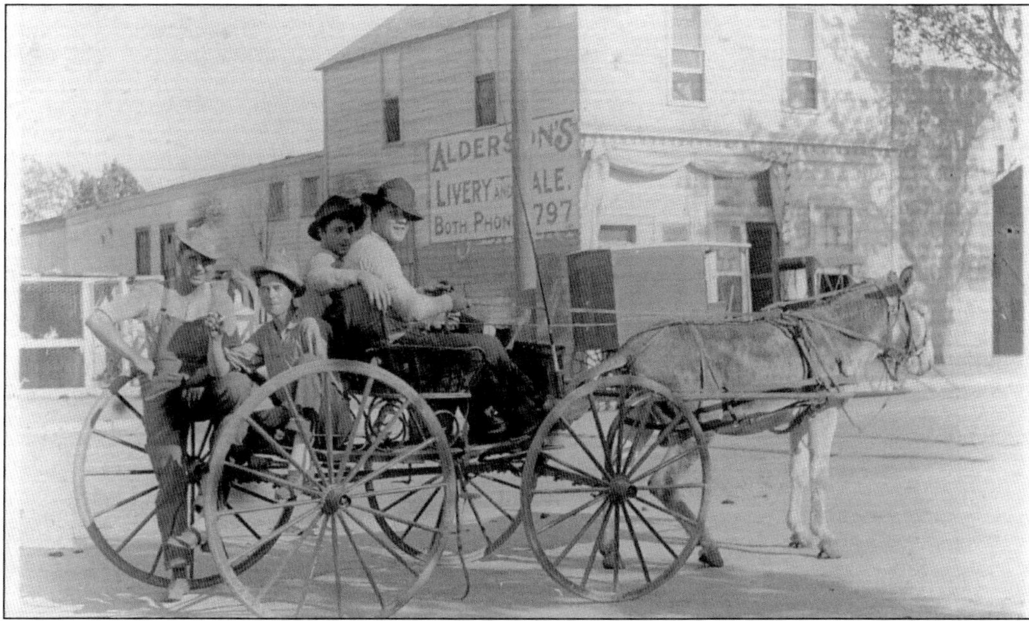

One of the most profitable enterprises in town, the livery stable, provided a place to board horses while owners conducted business or stayed overnight in hotels. Visitors who arrived by train and needed transportation during their stay could hire a horse and carriage. Alderson's Livery and Stable was one of 18 livery stables listed in the 1909 Joplin city directory. The horseless carriage, however, would soon render livery stables obsolete. (Courtesy of Galen Augustus.)

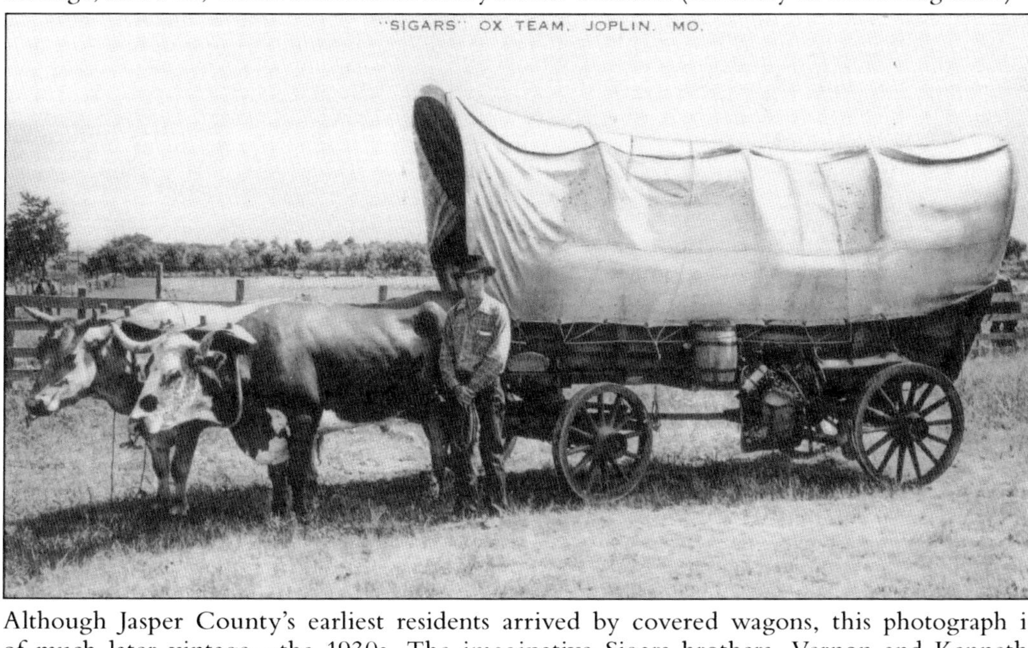

Although Jasper County's earliest residents arrived by covered wagons, this photograph is of much later vintage—the 1930s. The imaginative Sigars brothers, Vernon and Kenneth, invented novel ways to promote and advertise Joplin. They established the Ingenuity Company, whose motto was "The unusual is usual with us." Their homemade Conestoga wagon, pulled by a team of oxen named Jop and Lin, appeared at fairs and parades throughout the region. (Courtesy of the Joplin Public Library.)

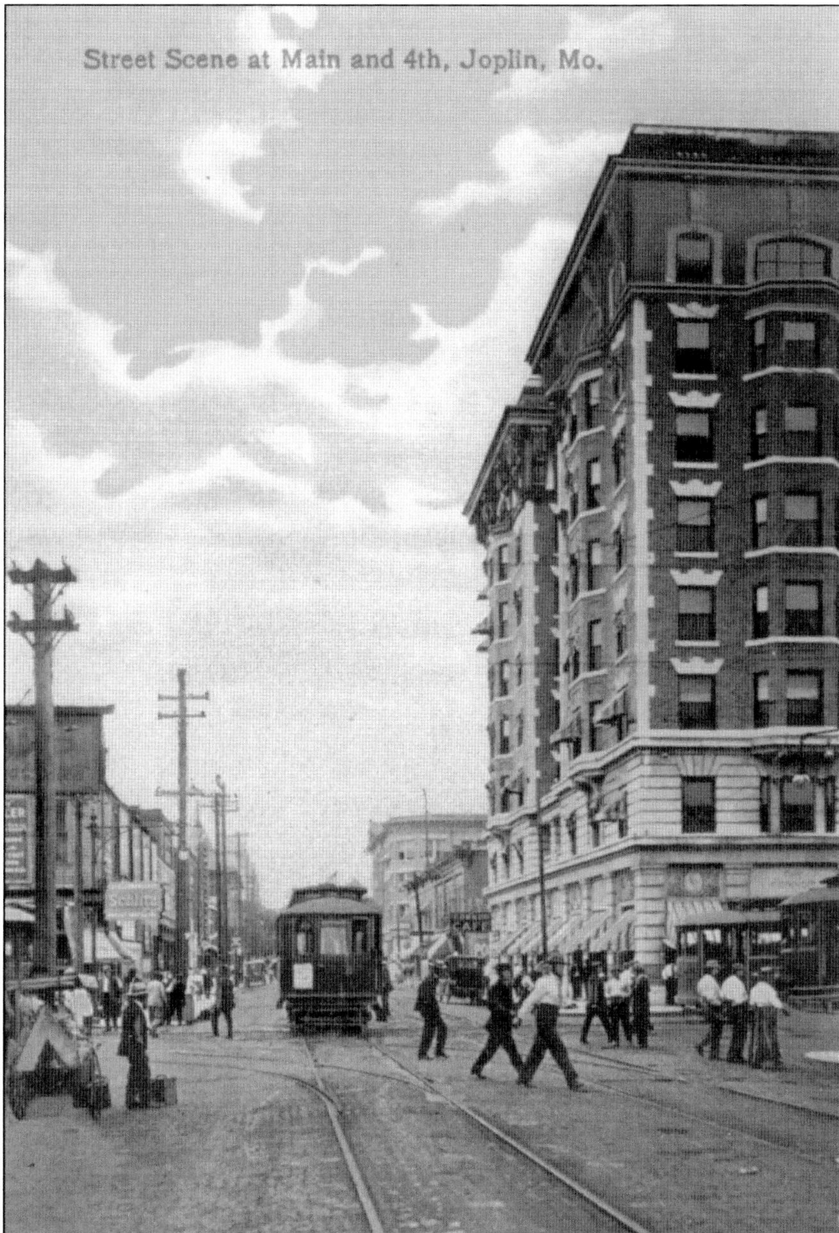

Joplin's first public transportation was a two-mile mule car line started by Alfred H. Rogers in the 1880s. Rogers, along with his financial backers, electrified the system in 1893, and established the Southwest Missouri Electric Railway Company. By 1897, it employed 90 men and operated 12 cars, running over 2,000 miles daily. The electric interurban system, which made fortunes for its investors, was proclaimed the finest in the Midwest. The railway provided interurban service, with runs every 30 minutes between Carthage, Carterville, Webb City, Joplin, and Galena, Kansas, as well as routes to all sections of Joplin. Area residents used the streetcars to get to work, to go shopping, and to get away to Lakeside Park, Midway Park, Castle Rock, Schifferdecker Park, and Miners Baseball Park. At its peak, the company encompassed 94 miles of tracks in three states. (Courtesy of Galen Augustus.)

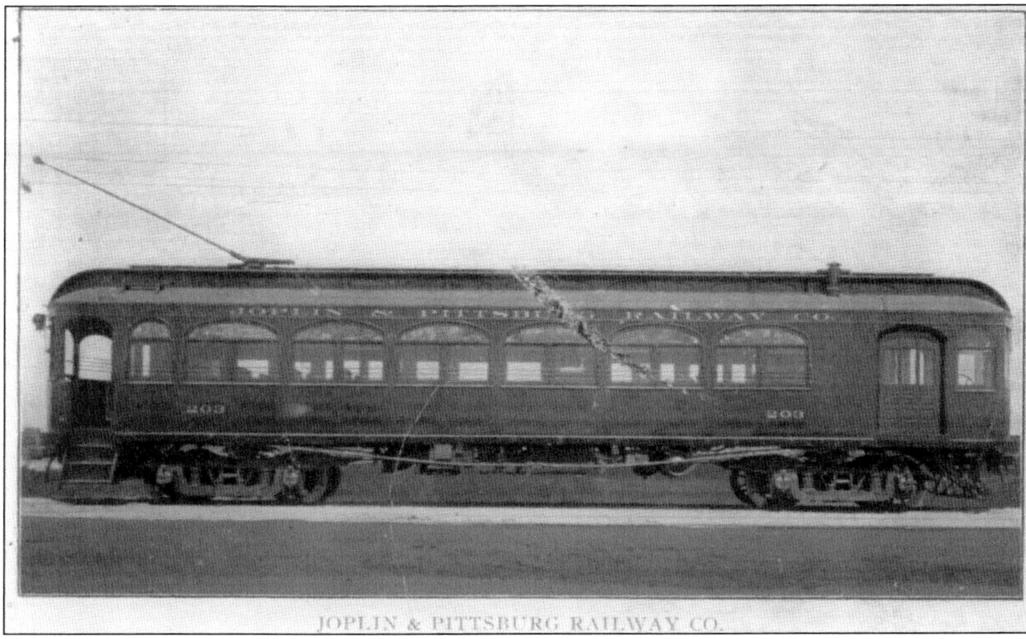

The wood-sided trolleys, painted pea-green and trimmed in yellow, did not provide much in the way of amenities. They had no toilets, fans or heat, at least not until 1906, when electric heaters were installed. Although the cars were built to hold 40 people, many more than that crammed inside on holidays, when folks headed en masse to area parks. (Courtesy of Galen Augustus.)

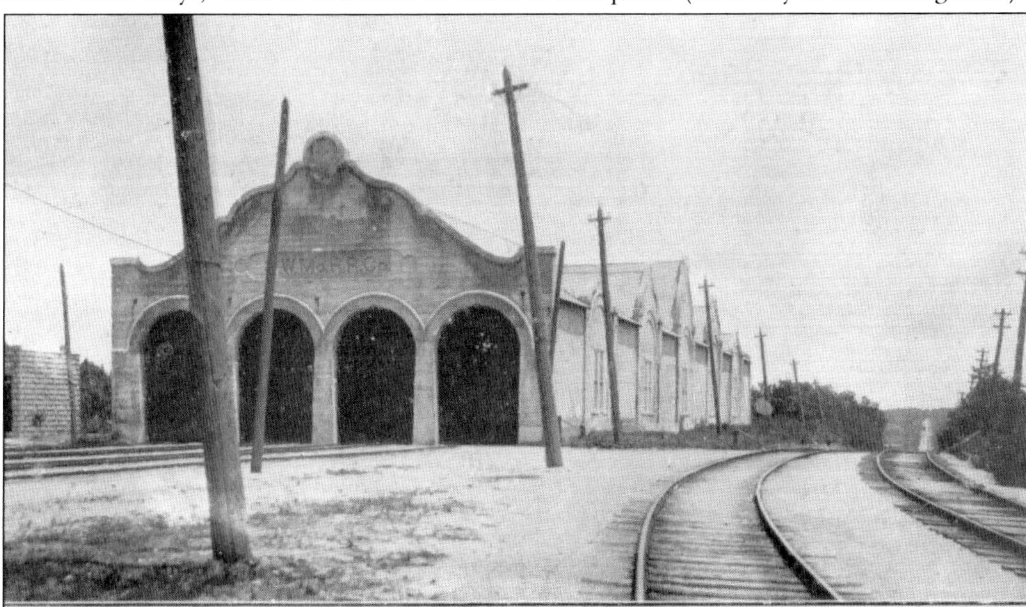

The Southwest Missouri Electric Railway Company played a significant role in Joplin's development. However, as ownership of automobiles increased, streetcar patronage dwindled. The company ended service in 1936 and removed the last of its tracks in 1939. This postcard shows the trolley barn at 601 North High Street, which is now part of the Tamko Roofing complex. (Courtesy of the Joplin Public Library.)

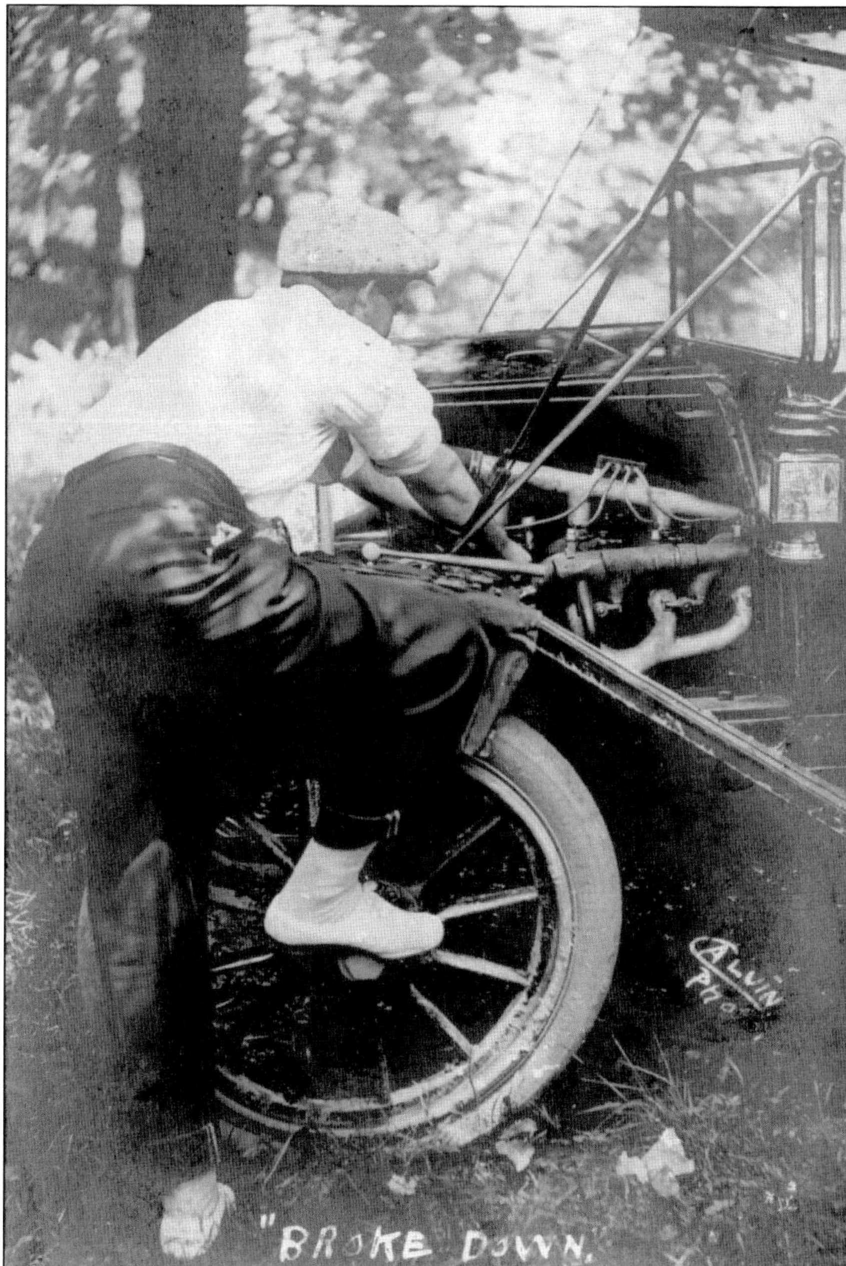

In 1903, George Graves opened the Joplin Automobile Company, the first automobile agency in Joplin. By 1909, 520 automobiles had been registered in the city. The popularity of automobile ownership brought many changes to downtown Joplin. People needed places to park their cars and to get them serviced. Parking lots, parking and service garages, and car dealerships sprang up on Joplin and Wall Avenues. In 1921, the city began installing modern traffic lights at the major corners. Before that, motorists frequently crashed into traffic posts, which stood in the middle of the intersections. Around the city and across the country, road systems were built to handle the increasing traffic. By 1930, one out of every 1.3 American households owned a car. (Courtesy of Galen Augustus.)

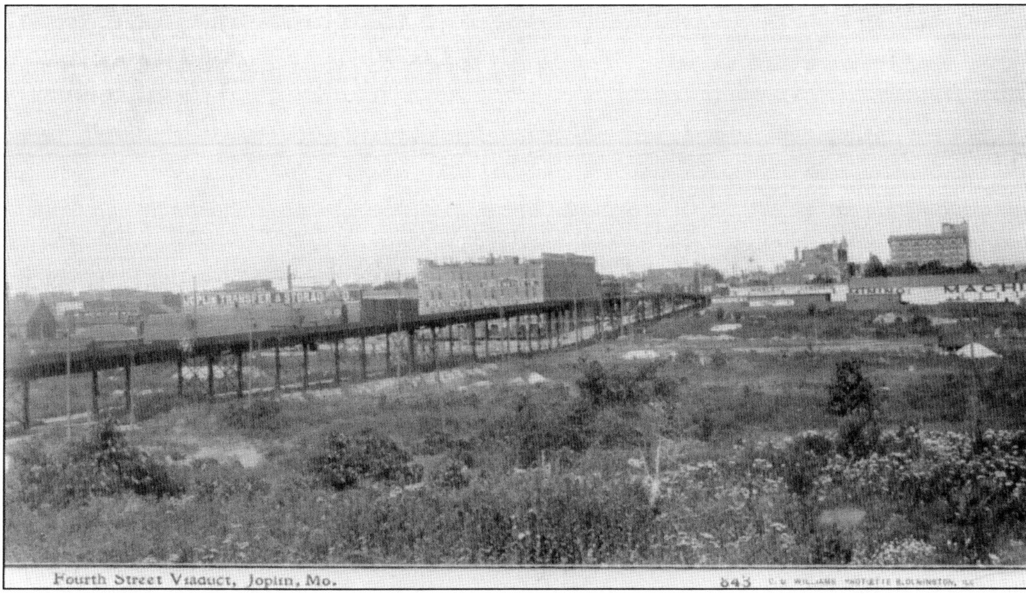

At the turn of the century, Fourth Street east of Grand Avenue cut through undeveloped land. The steel Fourth Street Viaduct, completed in 1907, was one-fourth of a mile in length, spanning the Kansas City Bottoms, the lowlands surrounding the railroad tracks. Built for the streetcars, the bridge's double-tracks ran passenger routes to and from Carthage and Webb City. Notice the Keystone and Connor hotels in the distance. (Courtesy of Rodney Blaukat.)

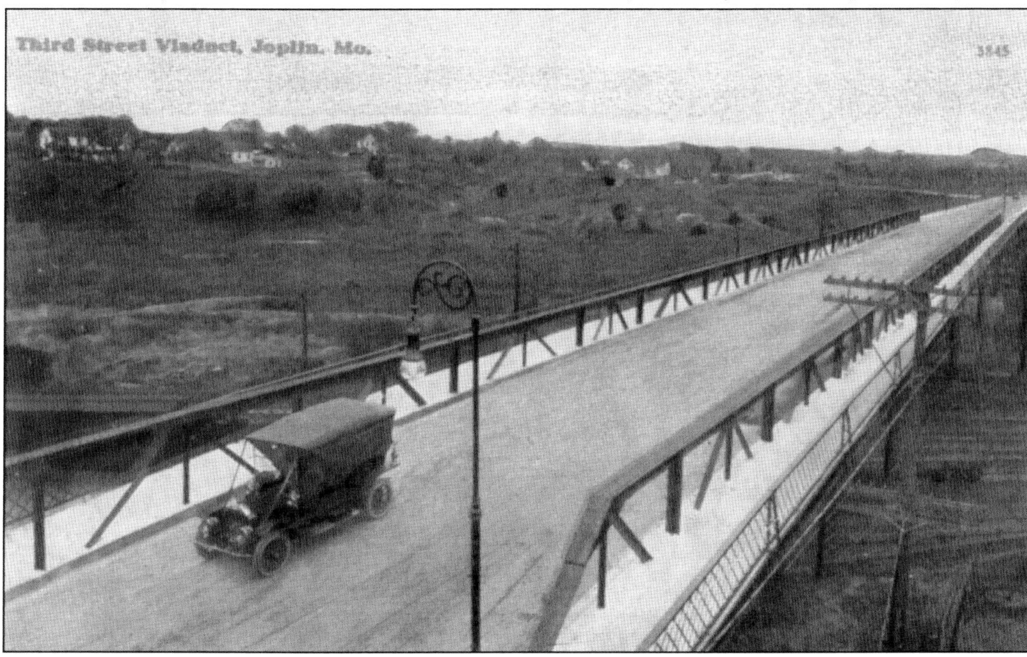

Completed in 1909, the Third Street Viaduct spanned the Kansas City Bottoms, providing a sorely needed connector between east and west Joplin. Previously, the only route was on Broadway, through a dangerous, squalid area that respectable citizens avoided. The immediate effect of the new bridge was much higher real estate values in east Joplin. The viaduct was closed to vehicular traffic in 1945 and torn down in 1955. (Courtesy of Rodney Blaukat.)

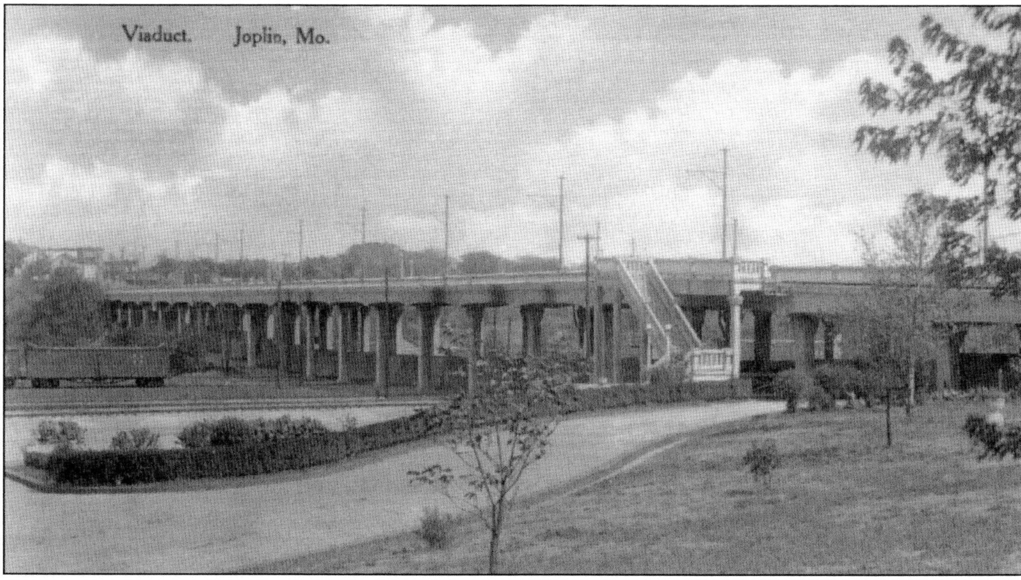

Built in 1914, the First Street Viaduct originally accommodated pedestrian, motor vehicle, and streetcar traffic. Twenty-nine streetlights illuminated the expanse, creating an impressive sight at night. An elegant stairway led down to a curving brick path that meandered through a landscaped area to the Union Depot. The bridge, which was demolished in 1981, provided a safe walkway for pedestrians from east Joplin to go downtown or to the Union Depot. (Courtesy of Galen Augustus.)

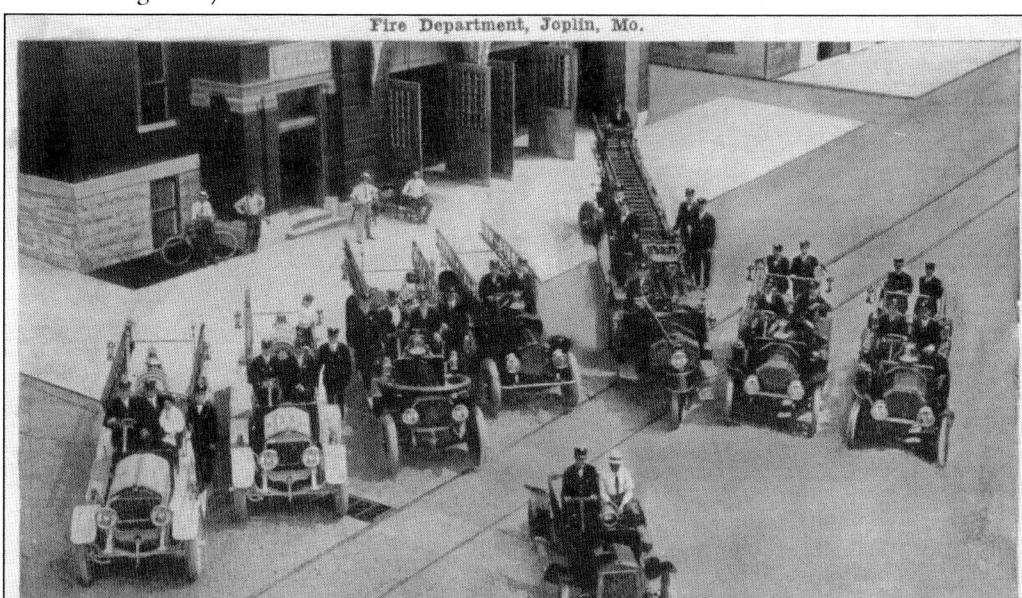

Joplin's fire department was established 1882. Although its first firefighters were volunteers, the department offered monetary incentives to bring out their best effort. Joplin made history by being the first fire department to use motorized vehicles. Firefighting provided entertainment as well as an indispensable service. In 1908, Joplin hosted a tournament at Barbee Park; firemen came from all over the district to compete and demonstrate their firefighting skills. (Courtesy of Rodney Blaukat.)

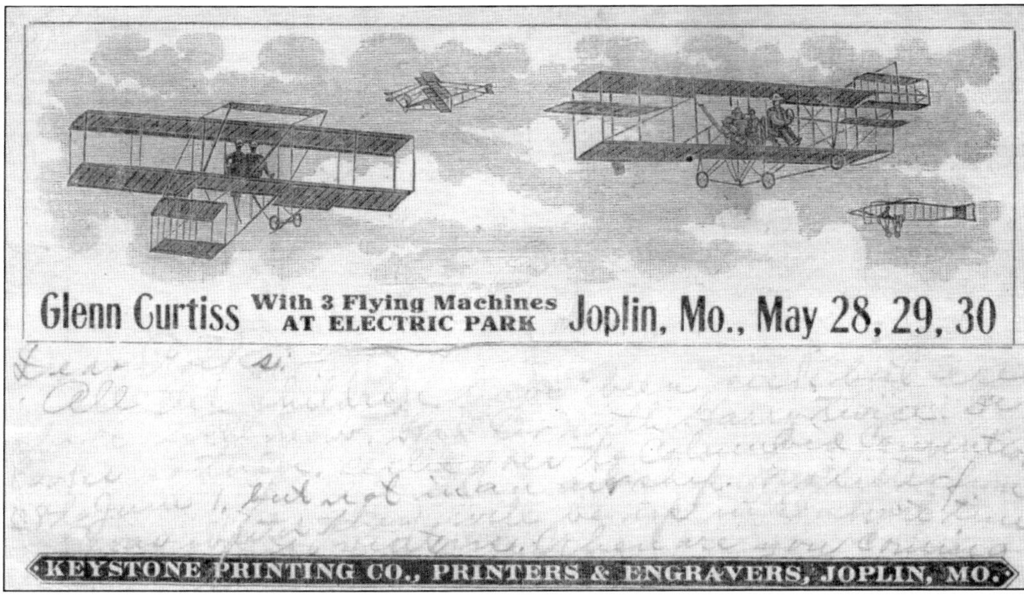

In the early teens, Joplin had a grass landing field at Schifferdecker Park, where people came to watch aerial shows. Thomas Webber, a former World War I pilot, established Joplin Aviation School at the park in 1919. In 1927, Joplin Aviation opened an airport near Seventh Street and Schifferdecker Avenue. The 160-acre site included two runways, a steel hangar, an office, a waiting room, and storage buildings. (Courtesy of Galen Augustus.)

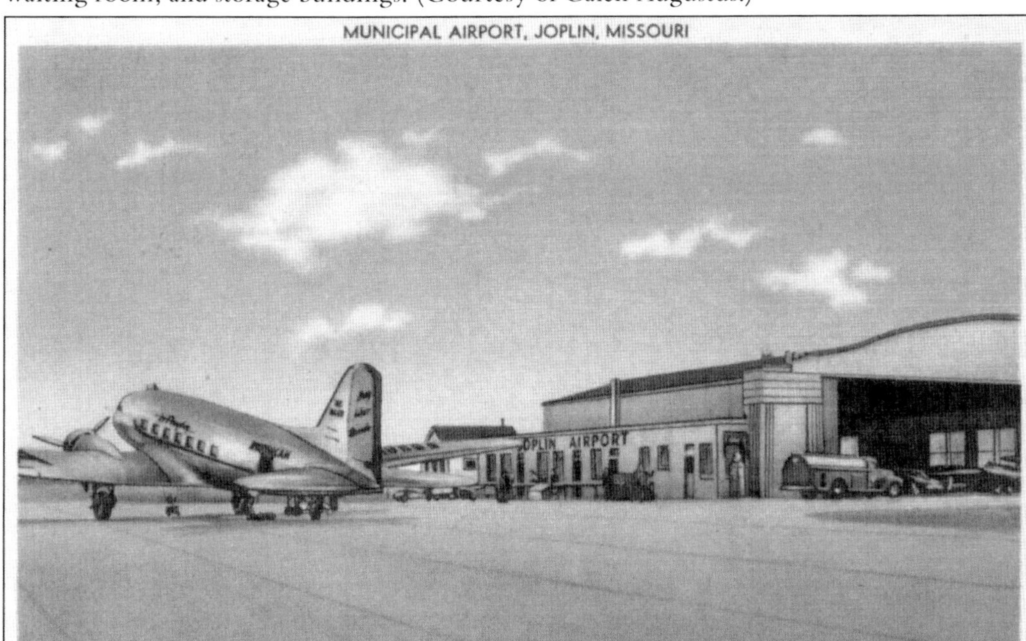

In 1932, the hangars and office building of the airport at Seventh Street and Schifferdecker Avenue were moved to a 400-acre site north of Joplin. The city leased the privately owned airport and eventually bought it in 1935. Federal funding financed paved runways, hangars, an administration building, lights on the field, and a huge 750-pound beacon atop a 50-foot steel tower. The new terminal shown here was completed in 1937. (Courtesy of Rodney Blaukat.)

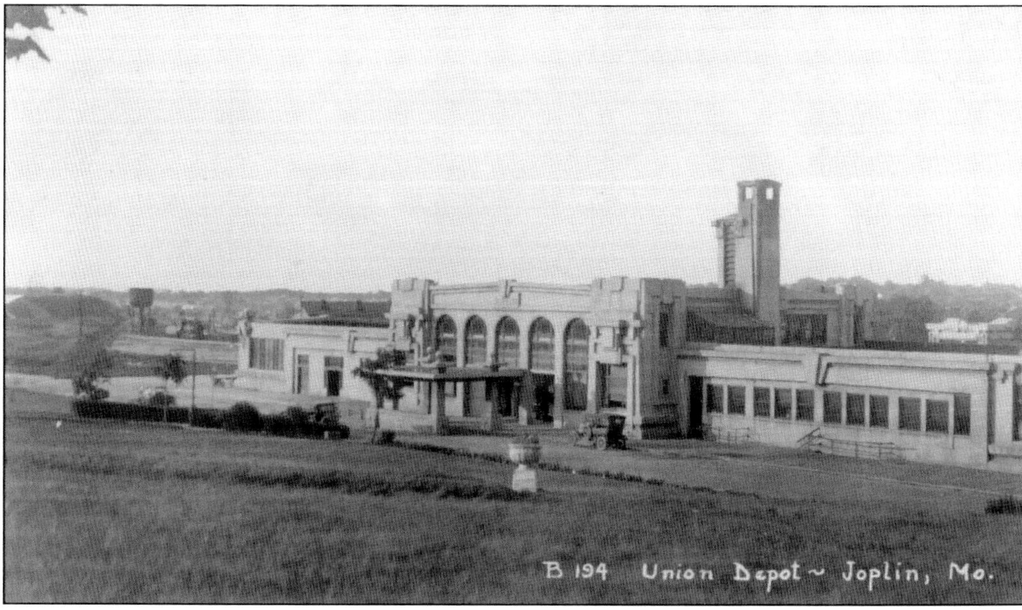

In 1909, the Joplin Union Depot Company commissioned Louis Curtiss, an unconventional Kansas City architect, to design a depot. The Joplin project, completed in 1911, helped establish the architect's reputation as a pioneer in fireproof concrete construction. He attracted considerable attention by utilizing local chat in the concrete mixture for the depot. *Popular Mechanics* magazine published an article about this creative use of mine waste in its January 1912 issue. (Courtesy of Galen Augustus.)

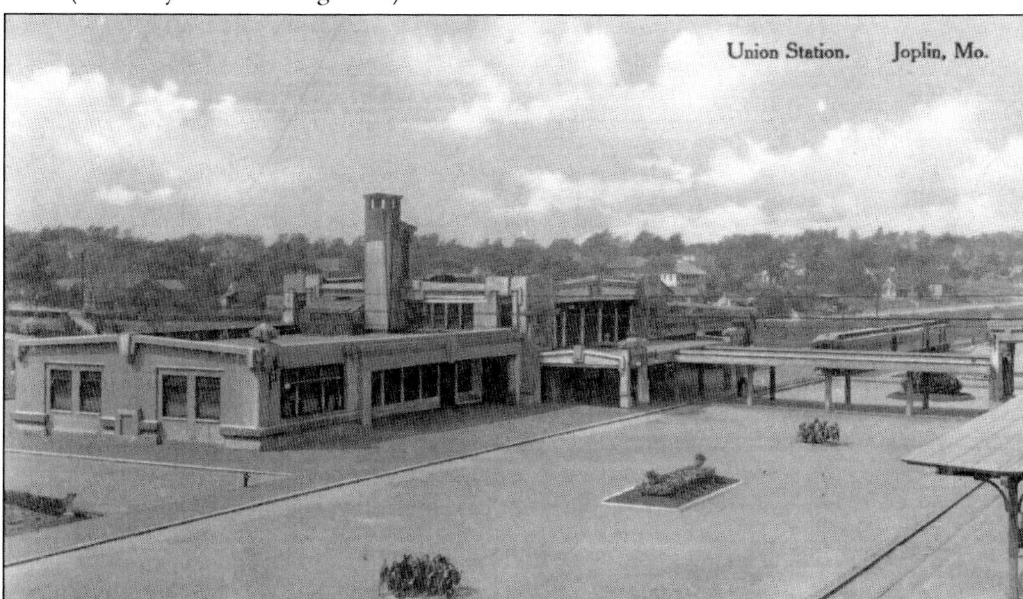

The depot's central area contained waiting rooms, restrooms, a ticket booth, a telegraph office, a newsstand, a men's smoking room, and a retiring room for ladies only. The south wing housed the Rose Room restaurant, a coffee shop, and a kitchen. Eight terminal tracks led into the station, and 800-foot long train sheds provided shelter to boarding passengers. The last train left the station on November 3, 1969. (Courtesy of Rodney Blaukat.)

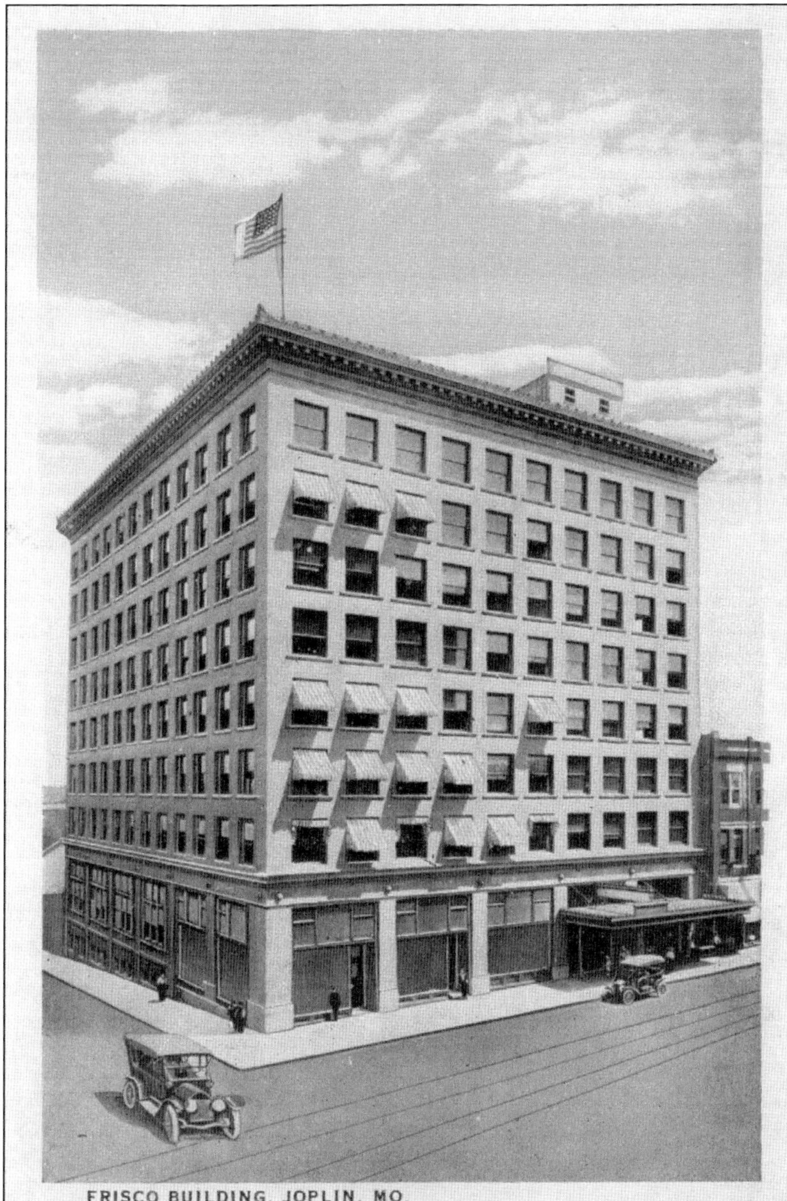

FRISCO BUILDING, JOPLIN, MO.

In 1913, the Odd Fellows lodge constructed a high-rise building that also served as the Frisco Depot. The first floor held ticket booths, waiting rooms, telegraph offices, and a lunch counter. Upper floors housed offices for railroad officials, dentists, doctors, insurance agents, barbers, and beauticians. The basement contained rooms for telegraph operators, conductors, freight handlers, and baggage. The huge furnace required 10 to 12 tons of coal nightly to warm the lobby and the Pullman sleeping cars sheltered there. East of the building were train sheds, a concourse, tracks, and a paved area where passengers embarked and disembarked. The lofty marble lobby featured a brass elevator tended by a uniformed operator. The Frisco's decline began in 1955, with the end of passenger train service and the exodus of its tenants to new offices. Occupancy dwindled until the last occupants moved out in 1987. (Courtesy of the Joplin Public Library.)

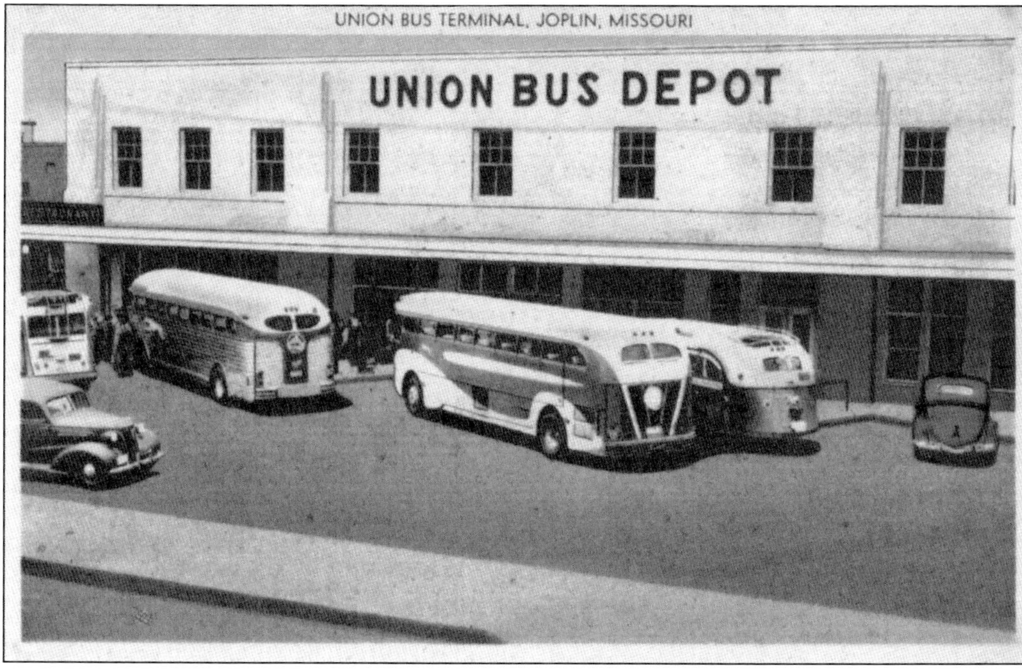

A bus station opened in the Connor Hotel Annex around 1930. Recognizing Joplin as a key traffic center, Crown Coach selected it as a regional headquarters. Transcontinental service mushroomed with other lines adding routes. Union Bus Depot, at 301 Joplin Avenue, introduced its new Art Deco–style terminal in 1936. The 1940s and 1950s represented the heyday of the depot; in 1948, 156 buses arrived and departed daily. (Courtesy of the Joplin Public Library.)

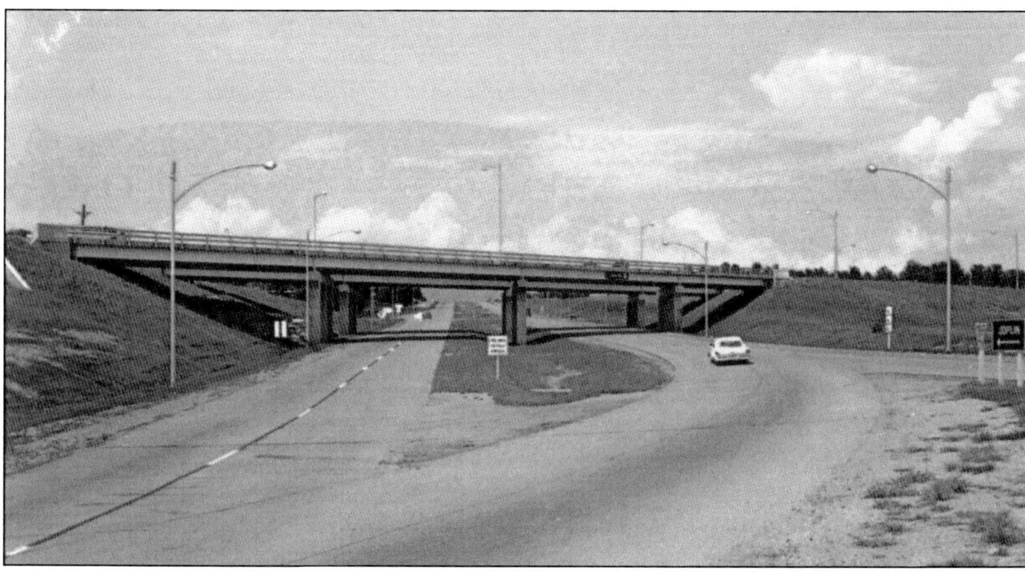

This 1961 postcard shows the newly opened Interstate 44 at the Missouri Highway 43 exit. Interstate 44 follows the general path of US Route 66, the historic highway that it replaced. It extends 290 miles across Missouri, beginning in St. Louis, continuing across Oklahoma as the Will Rogers Turnpike, turning south at Oklahoma City, and ending at Wichita Falls, Texas. (Courtesy of the Joplin Public Library.)

Four

Making a Living

The 1870s mining boom caught the quiet Joplin settlement totally unprepared for the sudden onslaught of people hoping to strike it rich. The next people to arrive on the scene were those offering products, services, and other necessities. These entrepreneurs conducted business in tents or in whatever wood structures they could assemble in a few hours. In January 1872, Joplin had a general store, a hardware store, a pawnshop, a clothing store, a newsstand, a meat market, a shoe store, a drugstore, a dry goods store, a restaurant, a bakery, four saloons, and two liveries. It also had one doctor, one barber, and a hack line. Murphysburg had similar offerings plus four general stores, four hotels, a billiard hall, and a blacksmith. Lumberyards and brick factories soon appeared, making it possible to construct more substantial buildings. Among the earliest industrial enterprises were flour mills, factories, and foundries. A key factor in Joplin's progress was the development of public services such as the water works, gas works, and fire department. Telephone companies and electric plants came a little later. As families moved in and prospered, there was more demand for these services as well as for fashionable clothing shops, furniture stores, and music stores. After mining panned out in the post World War I period, other industries rose to take its place—agriculture, trucking, medical, retail, transportation, and manufacturing. This chapter introduces some of Joplin's earliest businesses and shows how they evolved with the times.

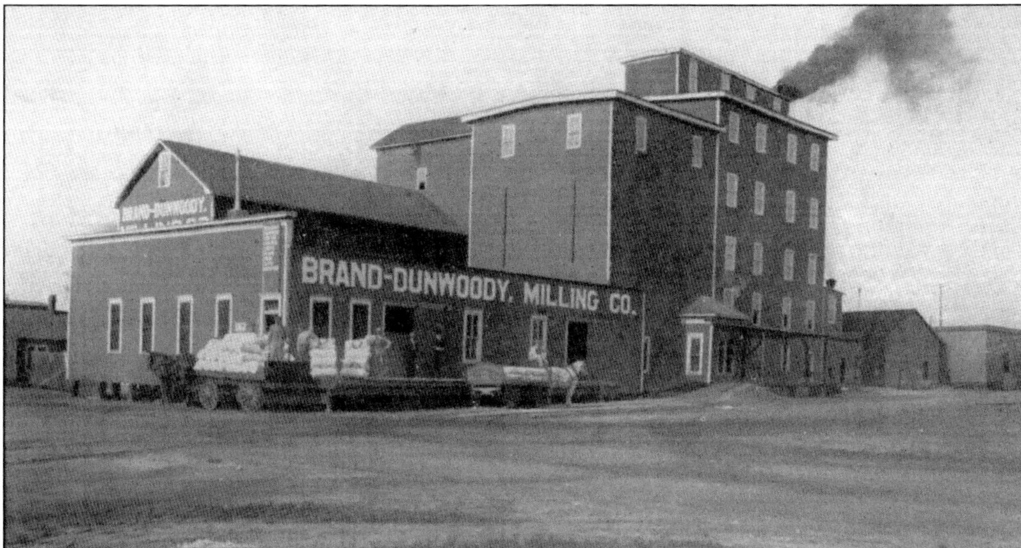

Flour Mill, Joplin, Mo.

Pioneer citizen John B. Sergeant built Joplin's first flour mill in 1882. Flour produced in Joplin shipped to markets in Louisiana, Arkansas, and Mississippi. In 1895, Brand-Dunwoody purchased Sergeant's plant, expanded it, and installed state-of-the-art equipment. The impressive operation included a brick pump house and engine room, a four-story grain elevator, a mill room, a warehouse, and a cooperage to manufacture wooden barrels for shipping the processed flour. (Courtesy of Rodney Blaukat.)

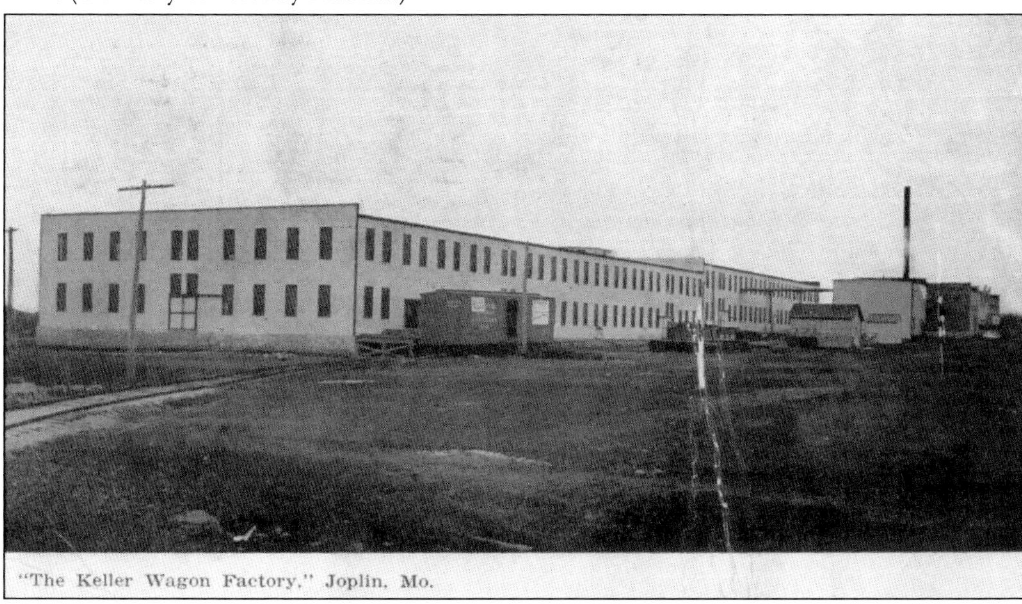

"The Keller Wagon Factory," Joplin, Mo.

Built in 1908 on Oliver Avenue between Fourth and Fifth Streets, the Keller Wagon Factory encompassed two acres of floor space. Perhaps investors Peter Christman and William Houk regretted their involvement, as wagons would soon become obsolete. In fact, Bentonville Cooperage Company purchased the plant in 1913. With railroad connections already in place, the nine-acre site provided an ideal location to manufacture and distribute its products—whiskey barrels. (Courtesy of the Joplin Public Library.)

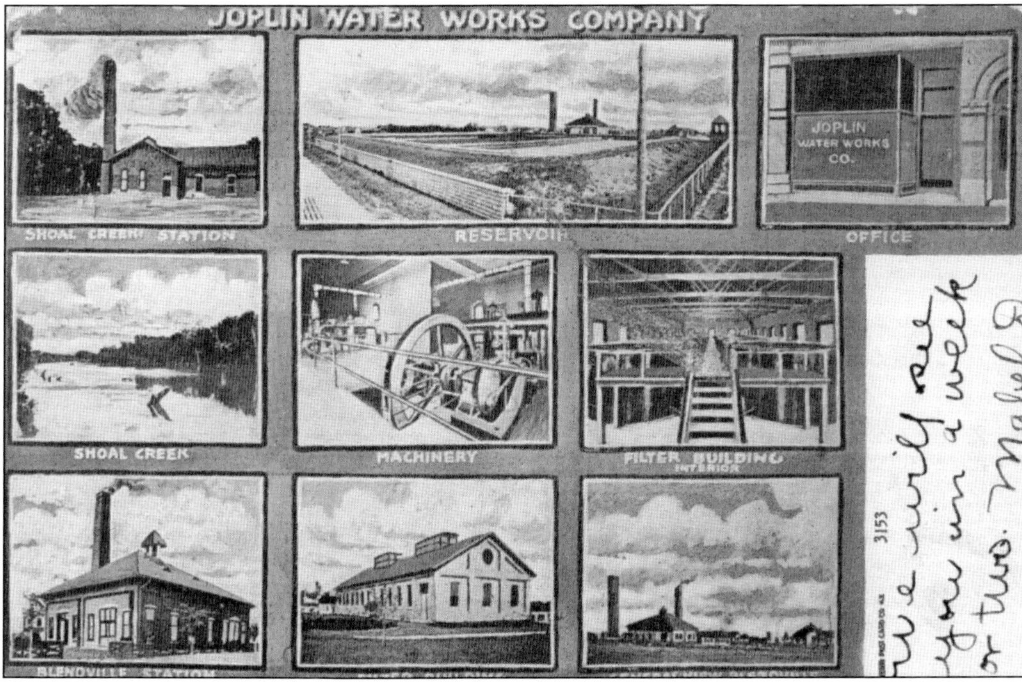

Water service in early Joplin was simply mine water, delivered by wagons and stored in open whiskey barrels without any concern for sanitation. The Joplin Water Company, established in 1880, pumped clean water from spring-fed Shoal Creek. Joplin Water Works Company purchased the company in 1893. The complex, bounded by Picher and Murphy Avenues from Twenty-First to Twenty-Second Streets, included a pump station, filter house, and coagulant house. (Courtesy of Rodney Blaukat.)

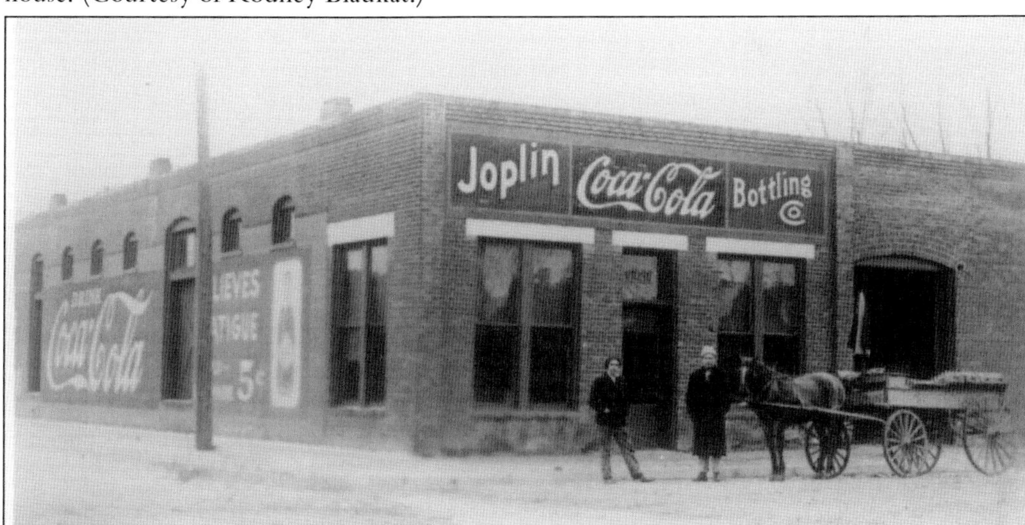

In 1907, after the Coca-Cola Company tested Joplin's water and determined that the unexcelled water supply required no further treatment, a local bottling plant was established. Joplin Coca-Cola Bottling Company moved to new quarters at 1301 Virginia Avenue in 1912. In the early days, workers bottled the soda by hand and delivered it using horse-drawn wagons. (Courtesy of Galen Augustus.)

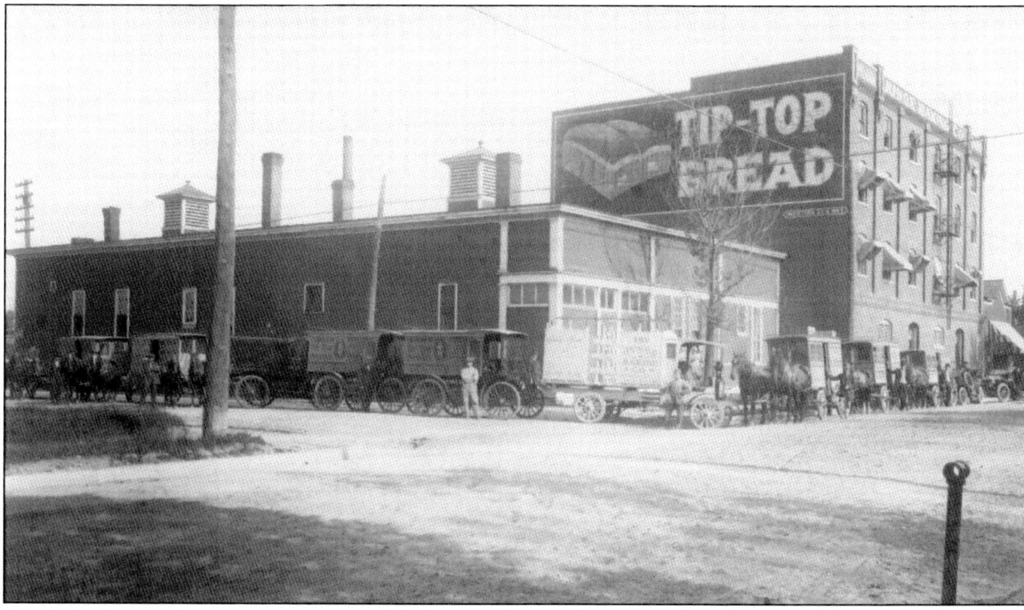

In 1900, German native August C. Junge, with sons Albert and August Jr., established a bakery at the southeast corner of Eighteenth Street and Joplin Avenue. In 1904, the brothers expanded into a large four-story brick building south of the original frame one. Junge Bakery produced wholesale goods and delivered them to area grocery stores. Junge claimed to be the first company in Joplin to use motorized trucks. (Courtesy of Galen Augustus.)

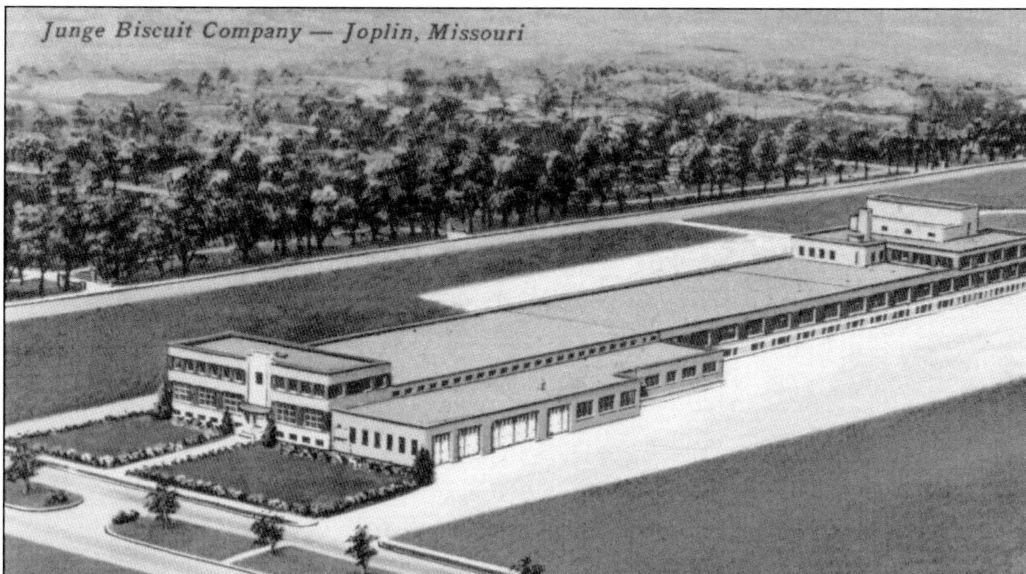

In 1946, Junge Bakery expanded its operation and built a streamlined factory at 1501 Junge Boulevard. The million-dollar cracker and cookie plant doubled the company's production and increased its distribution to a national scale. The plant, which employed over 400 people plus 55 salesmen, manufactured more than 260 varieties of cookies, crackers, and bread. In 1952, the Junges sold the cracker and cookie plant to the Safeway Corporation. (Courtesy of Rodney Blaukat.)

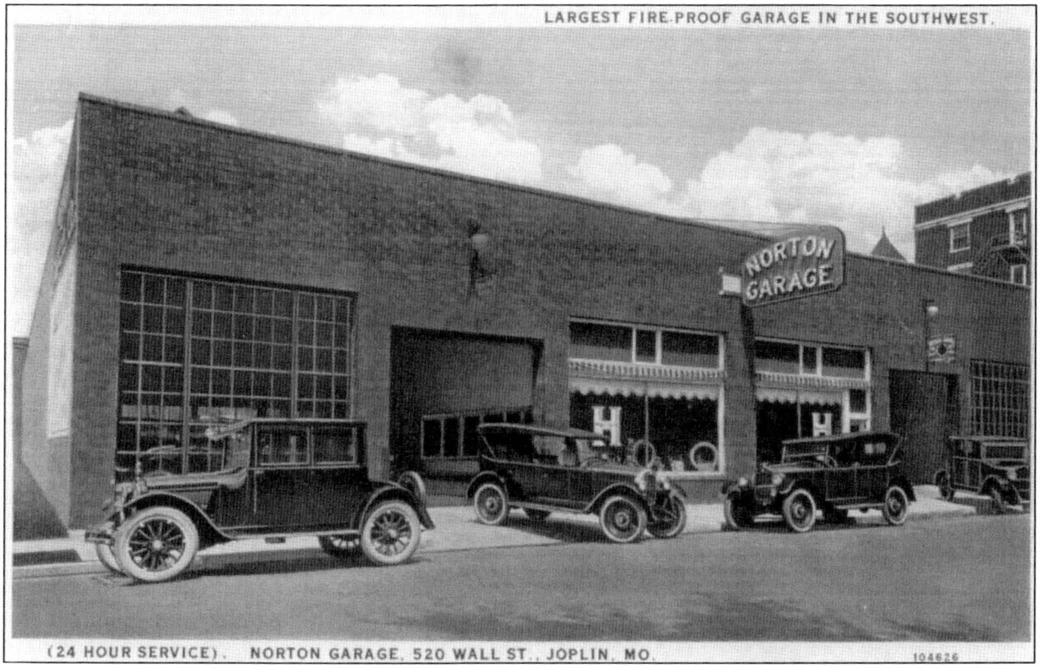

Verne Norton started the Norton Taxicab Company some time around 1912. As more and more people started driving their own cars, he decided it would be profitable to sell and service automobiles. He built this brick garage at 520 Wall Avenue in 1922. Norton offered 24-hour service, continued to run a taxi fleet, and also operated a Hupmobile dealership. The garage closed in the mid-1930s. (Courtesy of Galen Augustus.)

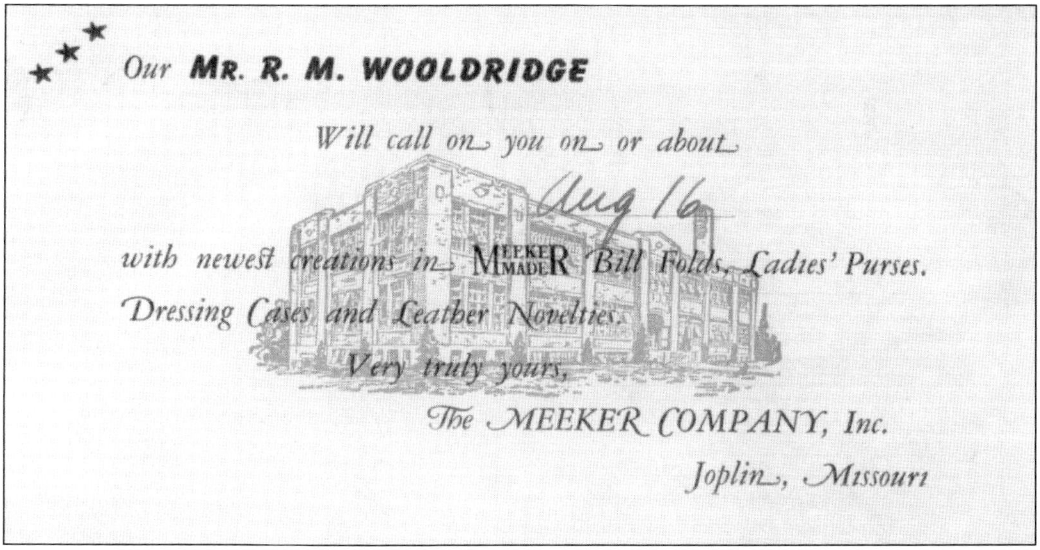
Our MR. R. M. WOOLDRIDGE

Will call on you on or about

Aug 16

with newest creations in MEEKER MADE Bill Folds, Ladies' Purses, Dressing Cases and Leather Novelties.

Very truly yours,

The MEEKER COMPANY, Inc.

Joplin, Missouri

Corry Meeker established a small advertising specialties company in 1907. By 1912, the company had shifted to manufacturing quality leather goods. In 1927, Meeker purchased the entire block between Sixth and Seventh Streets from Michigan to School Avenues to build a state-of-the-art factory. During its heyday, the company employed as many as 400 workers. Cheaper imports and higher production costs eventually terminated Meeker's 80-year run in 1987. (Courtesy of Galen Augustus.)

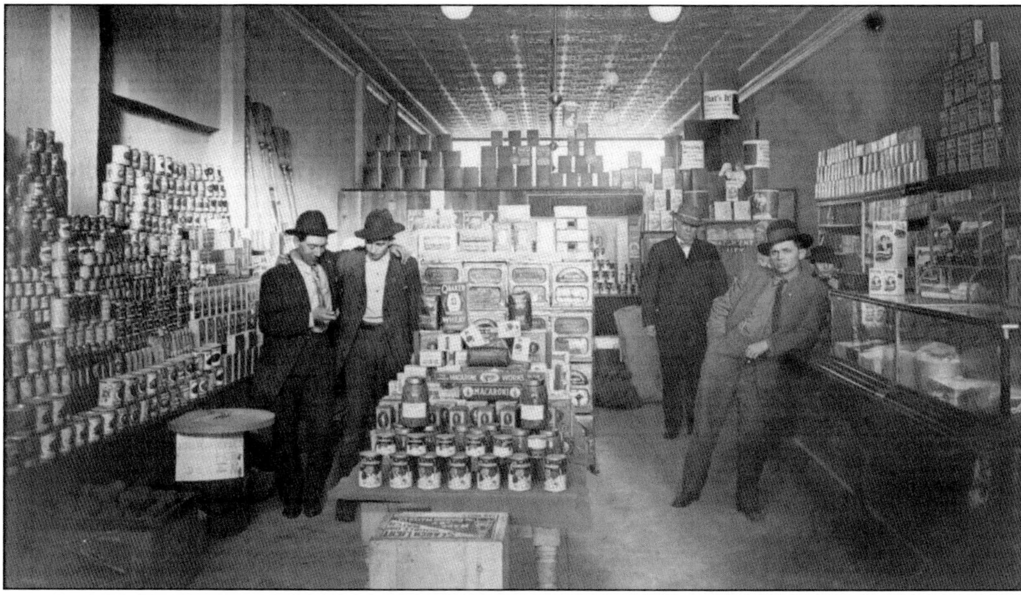

This photographic postcard shows a typical early-20th-century grocer's shop in Joplin. Stacks of canned and boxed merchandise line the walls and center aisles. Bulk items stored in bins clutter the floor space. Gaslights illumine the windowless interior. The 1910 Joplin city directory listed 125 retail grocers! Just about everyone in town could easily walk to a nearby grocery store. (Courtesy of Galen Augustus.)

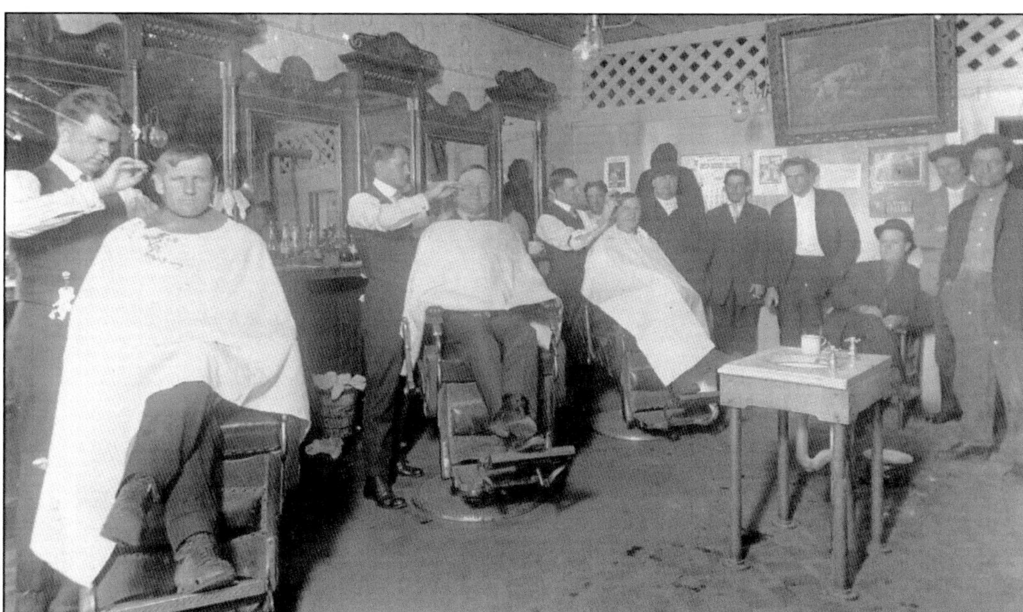

The 1916 Joplin city directory listed 44 barbershops, over half of which were located on Main Street. The major hotels and apartments housed barbershops for their residents. According to a 1916 *Joplin News Herald* article, the local barber's association set the following prices for services: 15¢ for a shave, 25¢–35¢ for a haircut, 25¢ for a beard trim, and $5 for shaving a corpse. (Courtesy of Galen Augustus.)

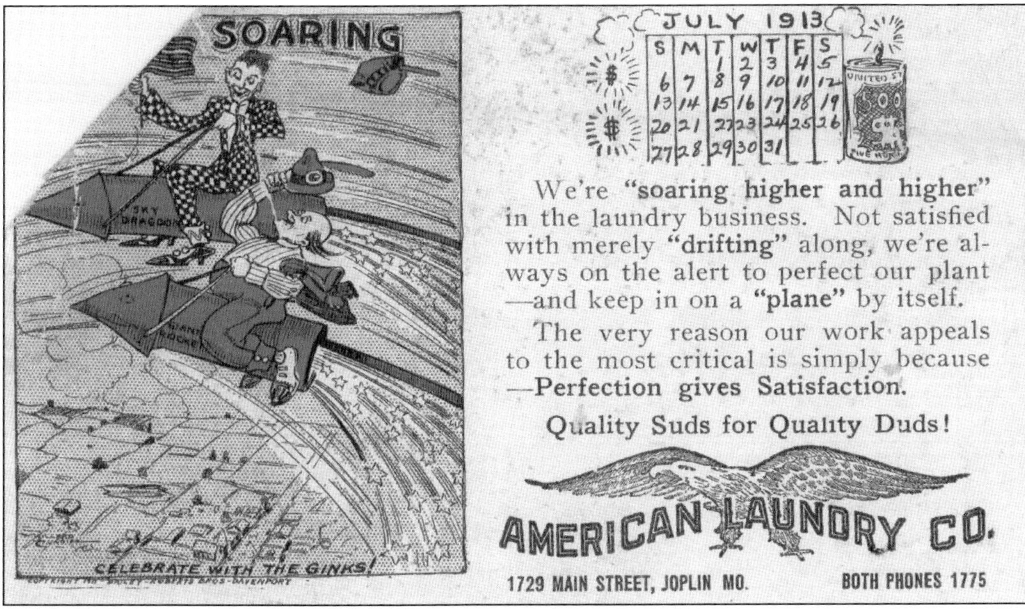

The laundry industry boomed because housewives hated the backbreaking chore. Americans were obsessed with scientific advancements and hygiene; they associated dirty clothes with lower classes and loose morals. Clean, starched, and ironed clothing represented the upper classes, urbanization, and respectability. The steam laundry picked up, processed, and delivered laundry to its customers, freeing the housewife to participate in civic and social activities. (Courtesy of Rodney Blaukat.)

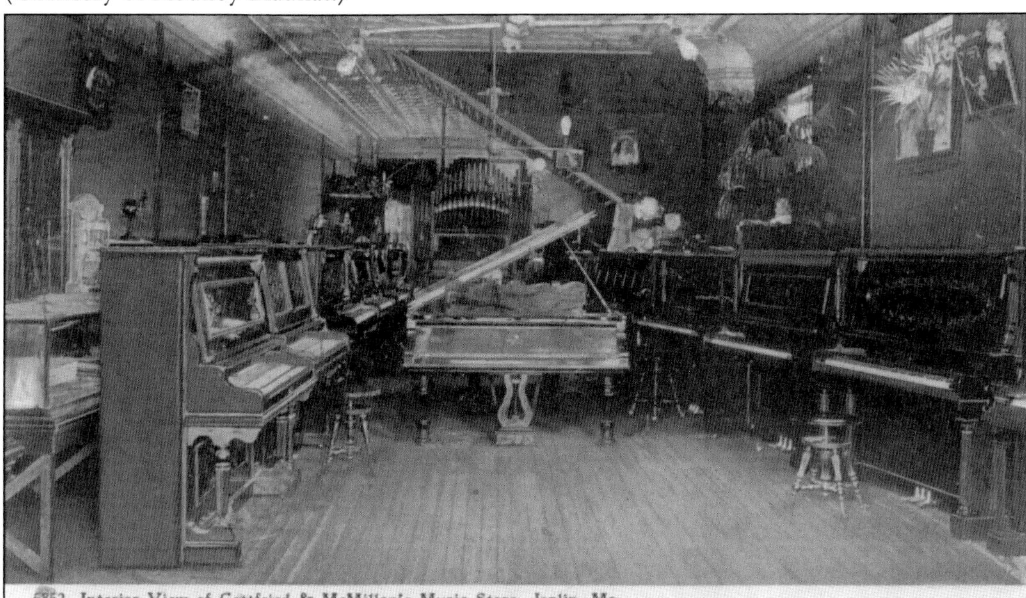

Gottfried and McMillan's Store, located at 702 Main Street, was one of four piano and organ merchants listed in the 1909 Joplin city directory. The inscription on this postcard, mailed by a store clerk reads, "I am sending you a picture of the place where I work, a fine large music store." The store also provided musical education. Upstairs, John Van Deventer ran the Van Deventer School of Music. (Courtesy of Galen Augustus.)

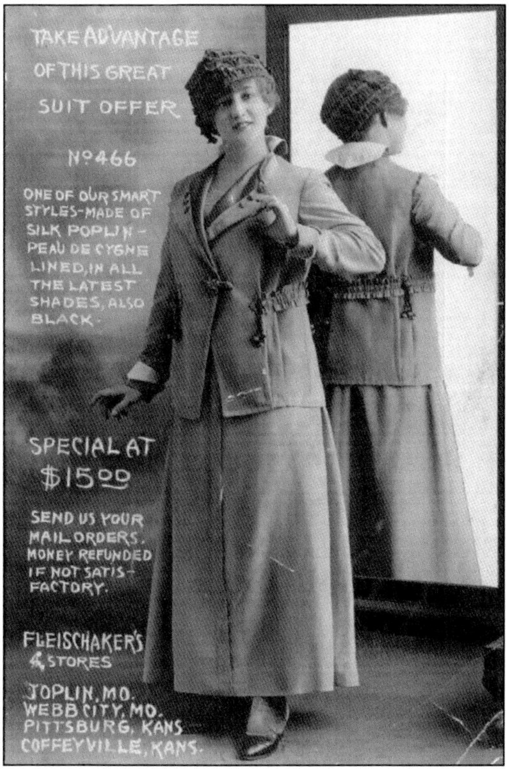

Around 1909, the Fleischaker family opened Fleischaker Dry Goods at 502–504 Main Street. The family also owned stores in Pittsburg and Coffeyville, Kansas; Picher, Oklahoma; and Webb City, Missouri. Fleischaker's remained a fixture in downtown Joplin until 1937. This card advertised the latest fashion—long loose jackets, smaller hats, formfitting skirts, and shorter hemlines offering a tantalizing glimpse of the formerly hidden female ankle. (Courtesy of Galen Augustus.)

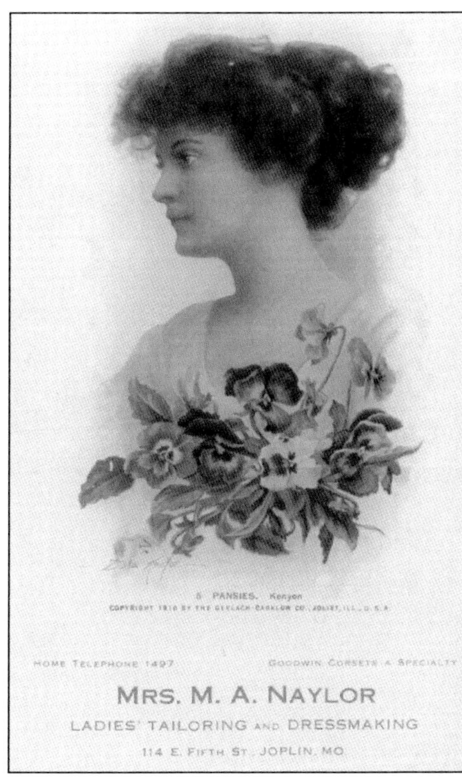

The dressmaking and tailoring trade provided one of the few respectable career options open to women in the early 20th century. The 1909 Joplin city directory lists 35 dressmakers. By 1914, that number had dwindled to only nine, revealing the toll that Newman's, Ramsay's, and other retailers had taken on the custom-made clothing trade. (Courtesy of Galen Augustus.)

The Joplin Overall Company originated in 1906 at 421 West Third Street. The model shown here was a factory seamstress; she could complete a pair of overalls in 21 minutes. In August 1916, the *Joplin News Herald* reported a run on sales of men's overalls by women who were wearing them for dirty jobs such as window washing and gardening. Retailers announced that they would start stocking women's overalls the following year. (Courtesy of Rodney Blaukat.)

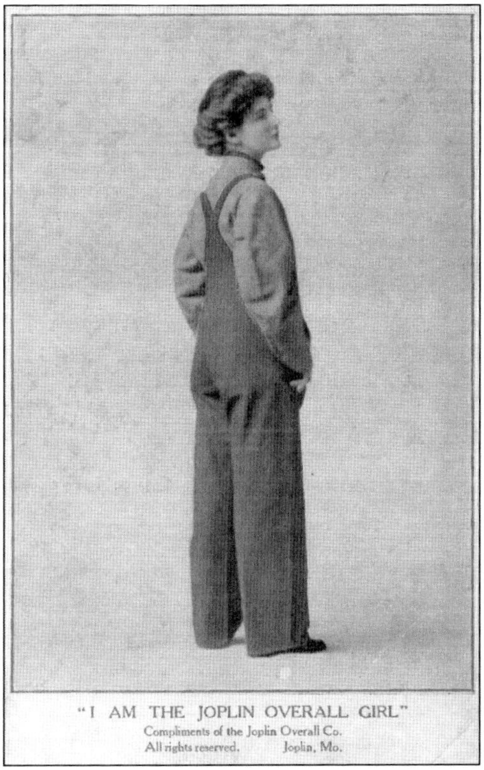

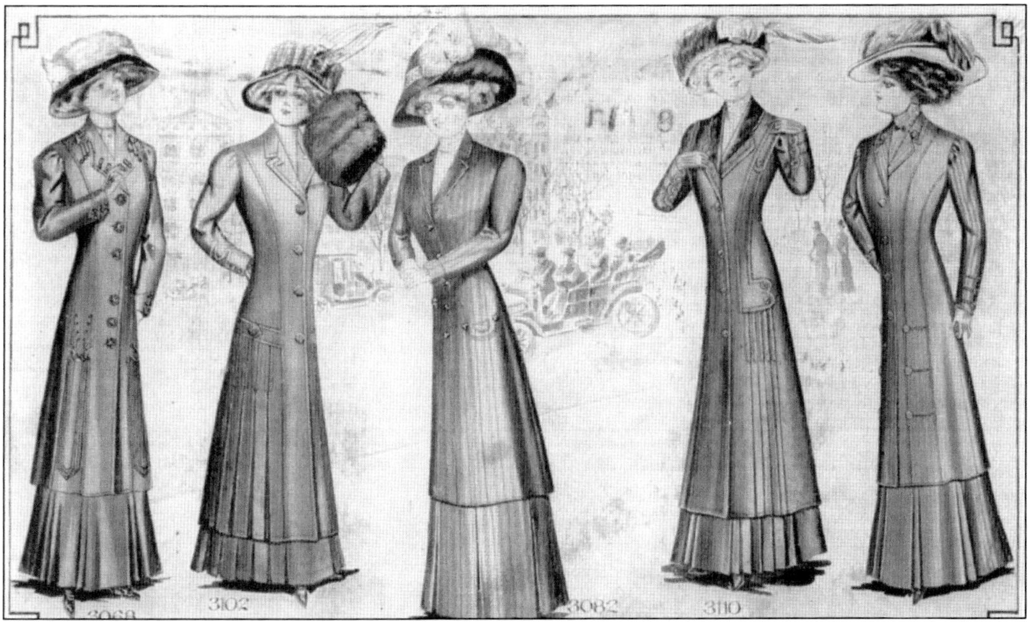

Leopold Pam specialized in ladies outer garments. The store at 410 Main Street offered fine quality cloaks, suits, and furs for women and children. The models' attire heralds a major transition in American fashion design in 1909—away from bulky sleeves and skirts and toward slender, more tailored profiles. Popular colors for suits and coats at that time included black, navy, tan, castor, brown, blue, and gray. (Courtesy of Galen Augustus.)

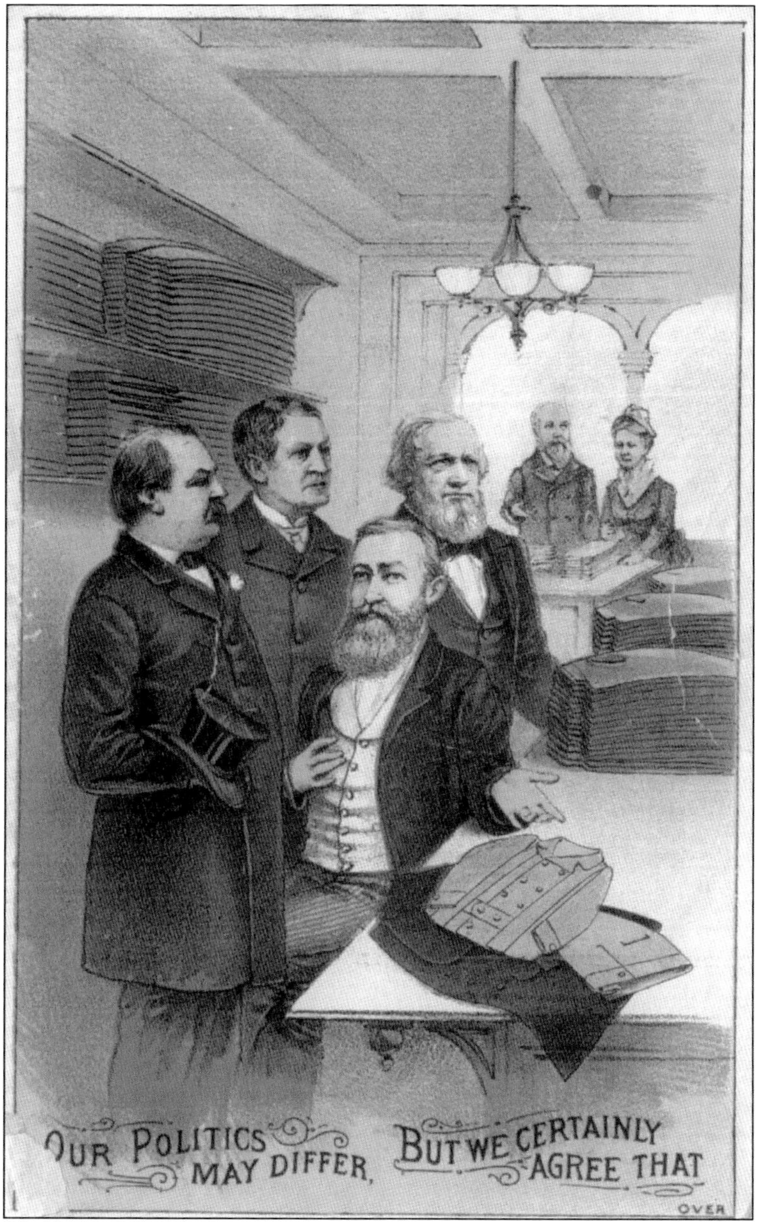

German-born Mose Weiler opened Great Western Clothing shortly after arriving in Joplin in 1874. Joplin's first telephone company, established in 1881, had offices on the second floor of Weiler's store at 305 Main Street. A charter member of the United Hebrew Congregation, Weiler nonetheless came to the aid of Episcopalian rector Charles Weed when St. Philip's Church was unable to secure financing. Weiler offered to loan the money himself; the reverend gladly accepted. After completion of the Gothic Revival masterpiece in 1911, Weed quipped, "The Jews built St. Philip's." In the early 1890s, Great Western Clothing relocated to 422 Main Street, where it continued outfitting gents until Weiler retired in 1928. This postcard illustrates how advertisers have long used celebrities to sell merchandise. The shoppers include Grover Cleveland, Benjamin Harrison, William Jennings Bryan, and Rutherford and Lucy Hayes. (Courtesy of Galen Augustus.)

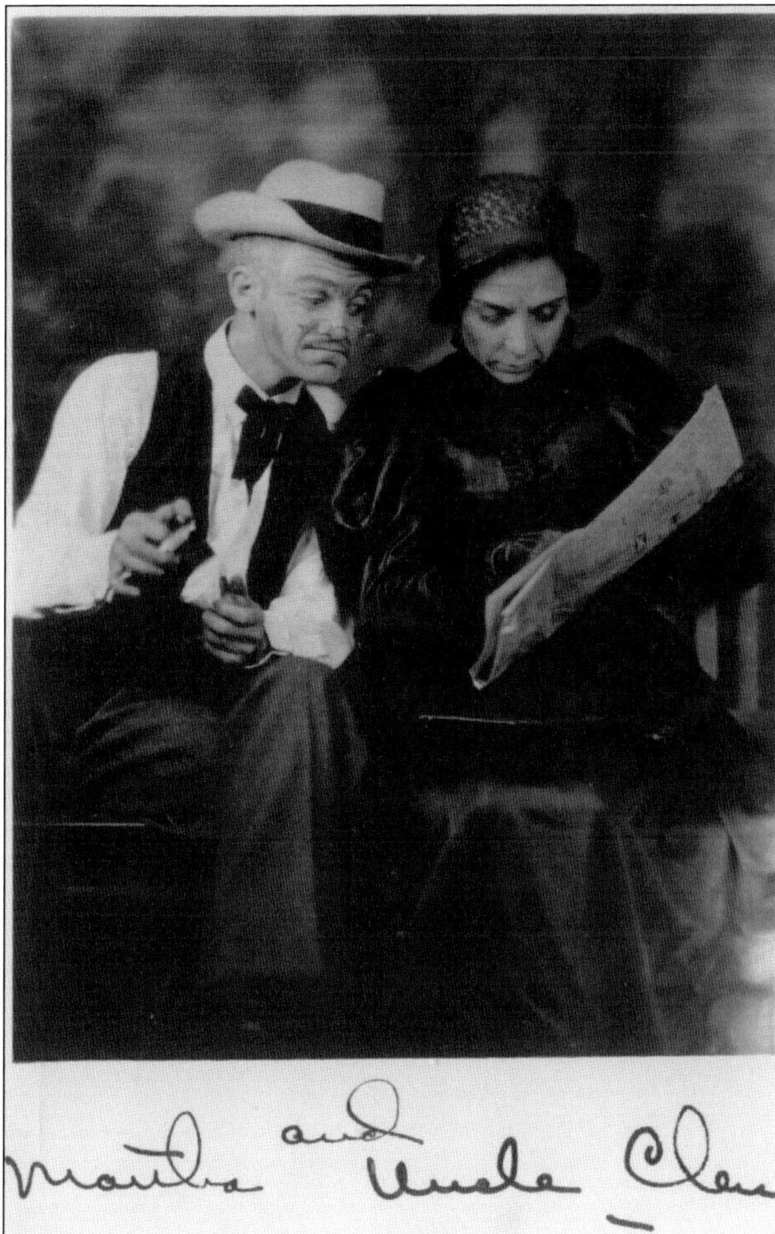

This card advertises WMBH, which claimed to be Joplin's first radio station. However, WHAH was broadcasting from Joplin's Hafer Radio Supply Company in 1922. For the first time, during the presidential campaign of 1924, Joplin residents clustered around radios and listened to the voices of the candidates. In order to reduce interference to the broadcast's reception, the city had to turn off all its streetlights! WMBH began servicing the Joplin area in 1926 with a studio in the Keystone Hotel. In 1942, the station moved into the lobby of the Frisco Building. Other stations began competing with WMBH in 1946, when CBS-affiliate KSWM broadcast from studios in the Connor Hotel. In 1948, KFSB aired from the Interstate Grocery Company at 1027 Main Street. By the 1960s, KODE, KQYX, KOAM, and KSYN stations had cropped up. (Courtesy of Galen Augustus.)

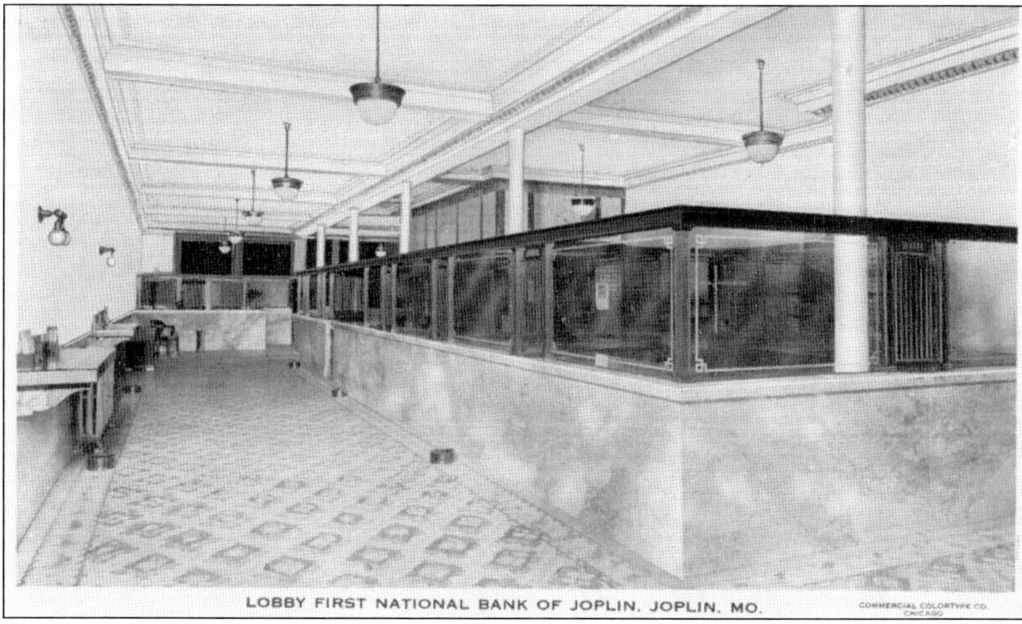

The history of the First National Bank of Joplin is so complicated with moves, name changes, and mergers that it is impossible to summarize here. By 1892, there were three large banks in the 400 block of Main Street—Bank of Joplin at 405 Main Street, First National Bank at 411 Main Street, and Joplin National Bank in the Keystone Building. In 1913, First National Bank moved to 522 Main Street. (Courtesy of Rodney Blaukat.)

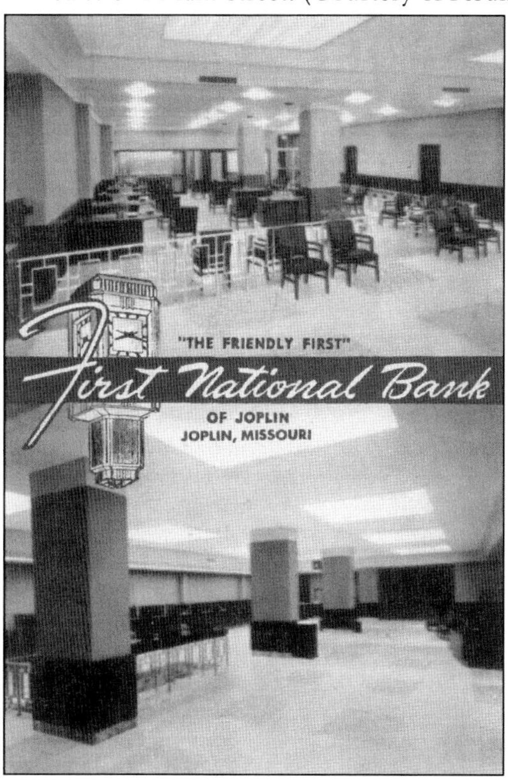

In 1917, the Bank of Joplin merged with First National Bank and moved to 522 Main Street. Liberty Bank was constructed at 402 Main Street in 1924. The following year, it was renamed Joplin National Bank. In 1952, these two banks merged under the name First National Bank at 402 Main Street. This postcard shows the lobby in about 1955. (Courtesy of the Joplin Public Library.)

Five

Places to Go

People love to be entertained; the diversions available throughout Joplin's history certainly confirm that premise. The *Joplin Mining News*, published in the summer of 1875, reported that the city had 75 saloons open day and night. Joplin leaders, dismayed at the disreputable image the town had acquired during its bonanza days, took steps to transform it into a refined city. One of the town's earliest attractions was the Joplin Exposition, built southwest of the city. One of the most spectacular buildings was an octagonal-shaped art and floral hall, which was two stories high, topped with an observatory that offered a panoramic view of Joplin and the surrounding countryside. Civic and social organizations, such as the Germania Society, Masons, and Odd Fellows, were established. Hutchinson Hall offered lectures, literary meetings, and concerts. Theater was very important in Joplin's social life; townspeople could watch everything from vaudeville acts to opera to Shakespearean plays at the Club Theatre, Haven Opera House, Blackwell's Opera House, Shubert Theatre, and Memorial Hall. Grand movie palaces, such as the Fox, Paramount, Orpheum, Electric, and Hippodrome, superseded them. Food and drink establishments represented another component of the entertainment scene. Many of Joplin's restaurants and bars were known all over the United States. This chapter also demonstrates how ordinary people had fun going to dance halls, roller rinks, carnivals, and museums.

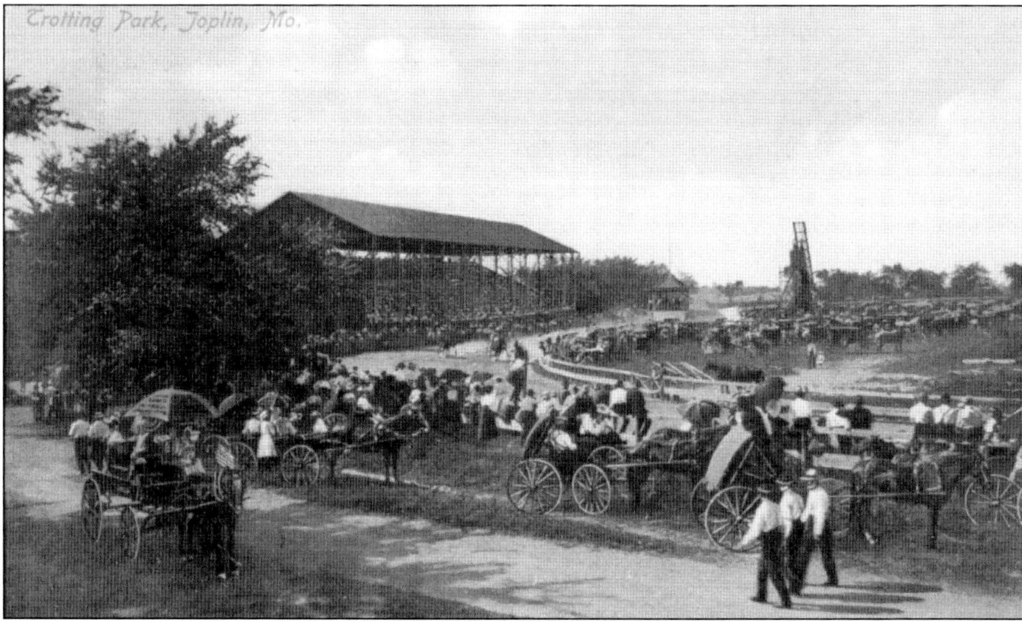

In the 1870s, the Joplin Exposition grounds stretched from Seventeenth to Twentieth Streets between Murphy Avenue and Maiden Lane. They boasted a racing track, stables, a grandstand, and a 3,000-seat amphitheater. After the Exposition wound down in the late 1890s, Gilbert Barbee purchased the site, renamed it Barbee Park, and kept the racetrack going for several more years. (Courtesy of Rodney Blaukat.)

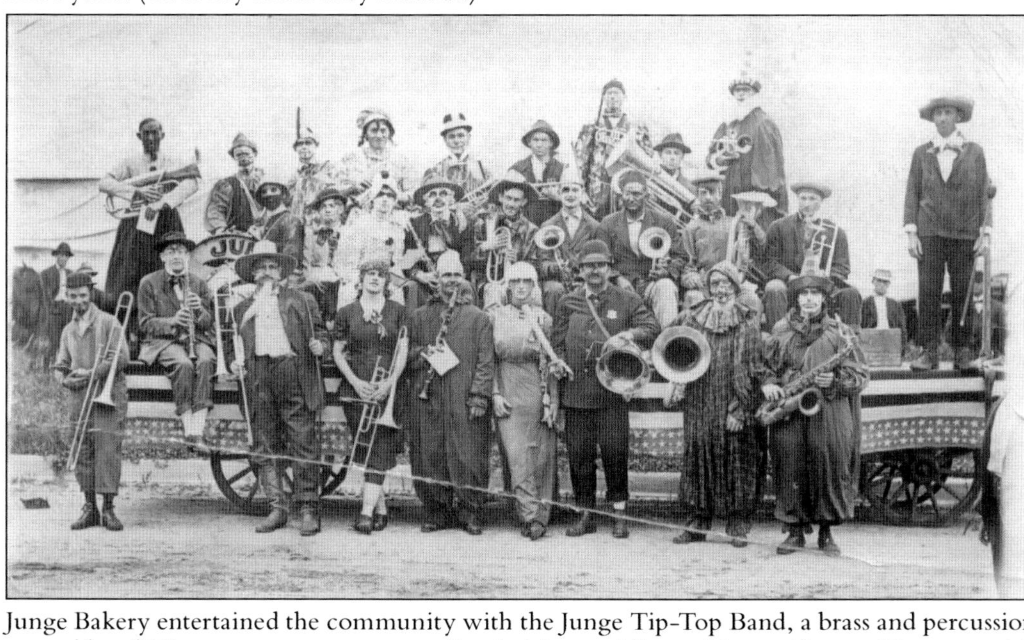

Junge Bakery entertained the community with the Junge Tip-Top Band, a brass and percussion ensemble of 30 or so young men, usually clad in sparkling white uniforms. However, this 1910 postcard shows the band in rather unusual garb for a parade performance. Notice the bizarre assortment of cowboys, Chinamen, Turks, hobos, and men in drag. The Tip-Top appellation advertised one of the brands of bread manufactured by the company. (Courtesy of Galen Augustus.)

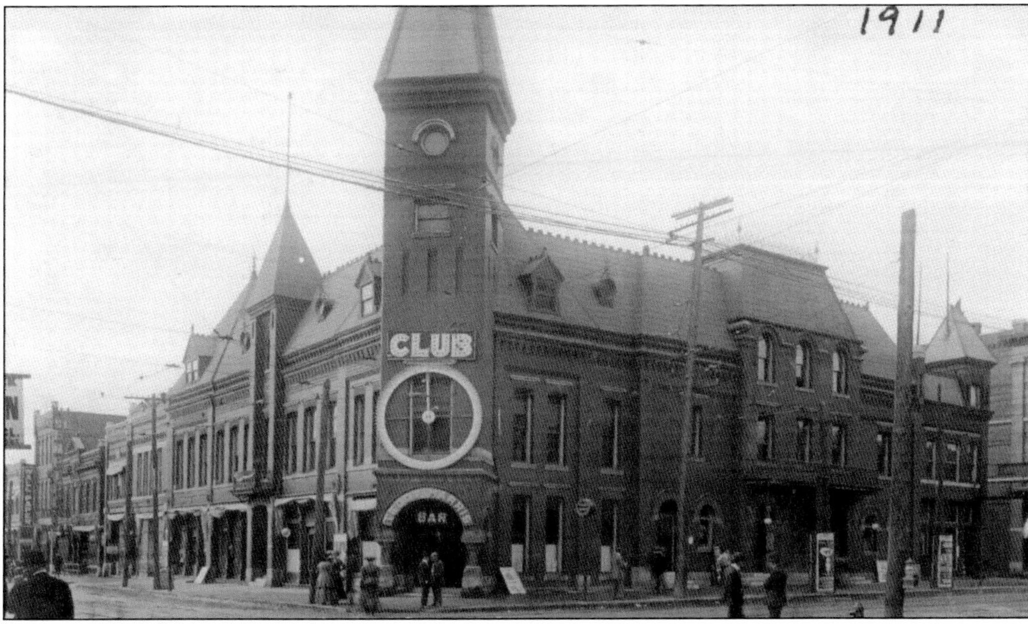

After the grand opening in 1891, the *Joplin Globe* declared the Club Theatre at 402 Joplin Avenue as perfect as a cameo. The exterior featured limestone and granite trim, four cupolas, and a mansard roof. Nothing could top the Club during its heyday. Theatergoers filled the elegant 1,400-seat auditorium to see Viennese and Italian opera, Scottish minstrels, and celebrities such as John Philip Sousa and Eddie Cantor. (Courtesy of Galen Augustus.)

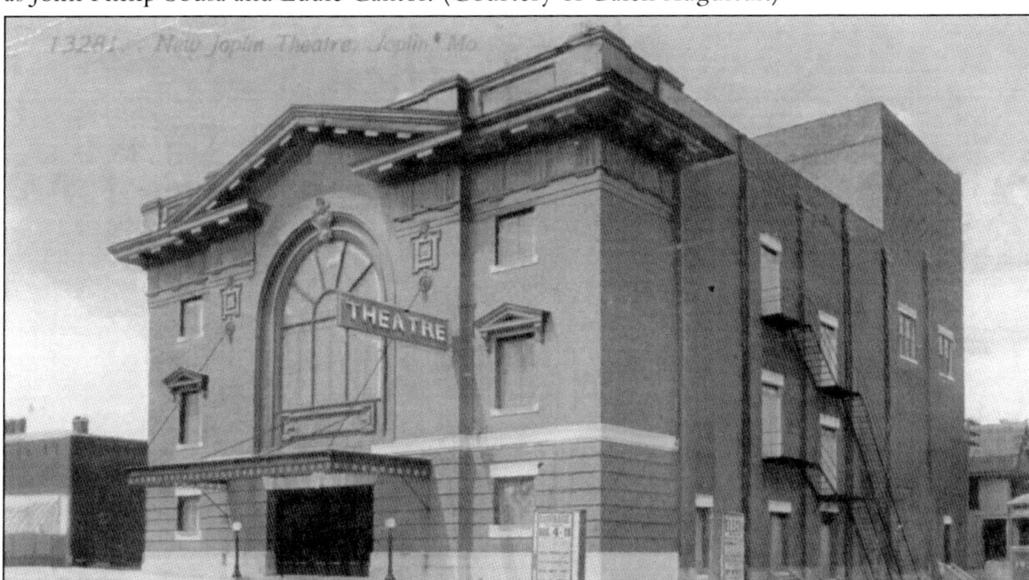

Austin Allen designed the Shubert Theatre, later renamed the New Joplin Theatre. Completed in 1908, the fashionable theater siphoned business from outmoded ones like the Club. Some highlights of its reign include a massive stage production of *Ben Hur* and the first blockbuster movie, *Birth of a Nation*. Some notables who appeared there were John, Drew, and Ethel Barrymore, Sarah Bernhardt, Will Rogers, and the notorious Evelyn Nesbit Thaw. (Courtesy of the Joplin Public Library.)

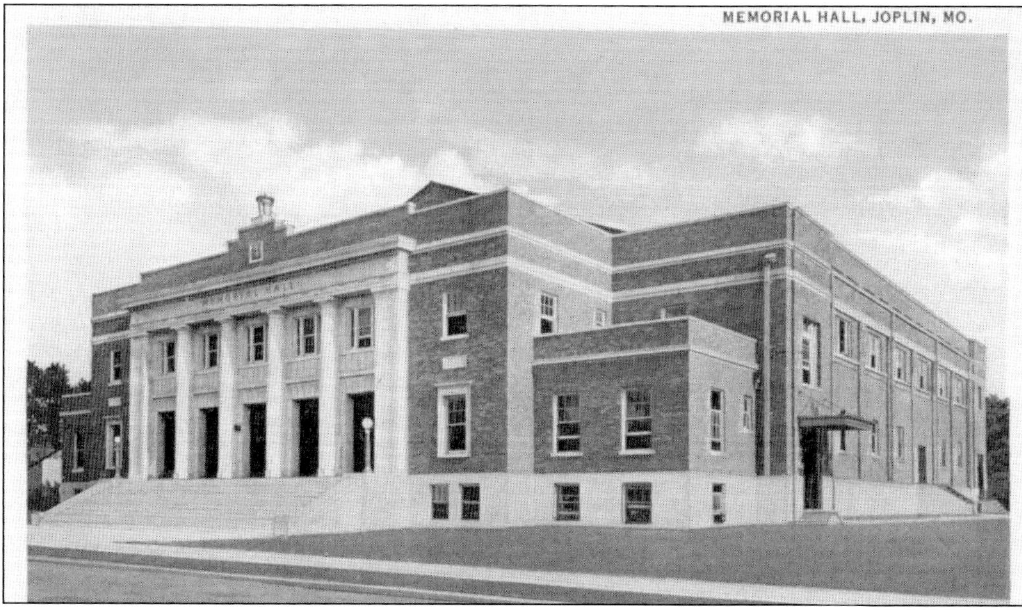

Alfred and August Michealis designed Memorial Hall as a war memorial. Unfortunately, it also became a memorial to one of them. On July 29, 1925, Alfred Michaelis suffered a fatal fall in the nearly completed building. The 4,110-seat auditorium surrounded a large stage where the finest performers and speakers appeared, including Al Jolson, Nelson Eddy, Arthur Rubenstein, the Ballet Russe, Eleanor Roosevelt, Marian Anderson, and operas such as *Aida* and *Carmen*. (Courtesy of the Joplin Public Library.)

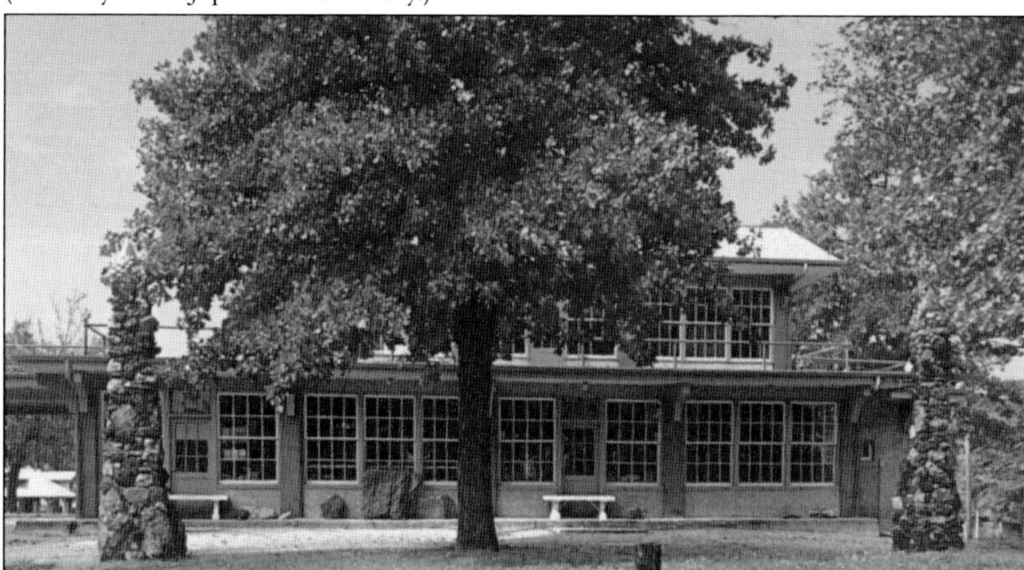

The Tri-State Mineral Museum, now named the Everett J. Ritchie Wing of the Joplin Museum Complex, opened on May 17, 1931, in a former concession building at Schifferdecker Park. The museum displayed an array of Tri-State lead and zinc ores and other local minerals. The collection also included photographs and a miniature mill to demonstrate various aspects of mining. Attendant Harry Kingsbury gave short lectures about mining and the specimens. (Courtesy of the Joplin Public Library.)

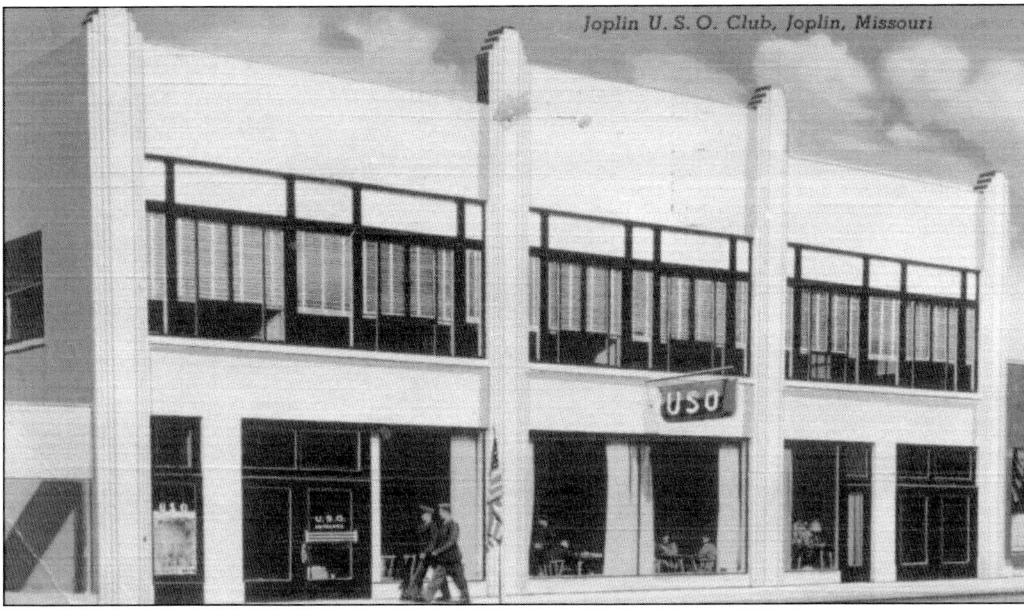

On May 10, 1941, the United Service Organizations (USO) selected Joplin for a local chapter because of the city's proximity to Camp Crowder in Neosho. By December, servicemen and officers were heading to Joplin for recreation. The club, located at 310 Wall Avenue, sponsored dances, programs, musicals, picture shows, watermelon feasts, street carnivals, and outings in the Ozarks. The clubhouse lounge, decorated in the latest style, provided a pleasant getaway. (Courtesy of the Joplin Public Library.)

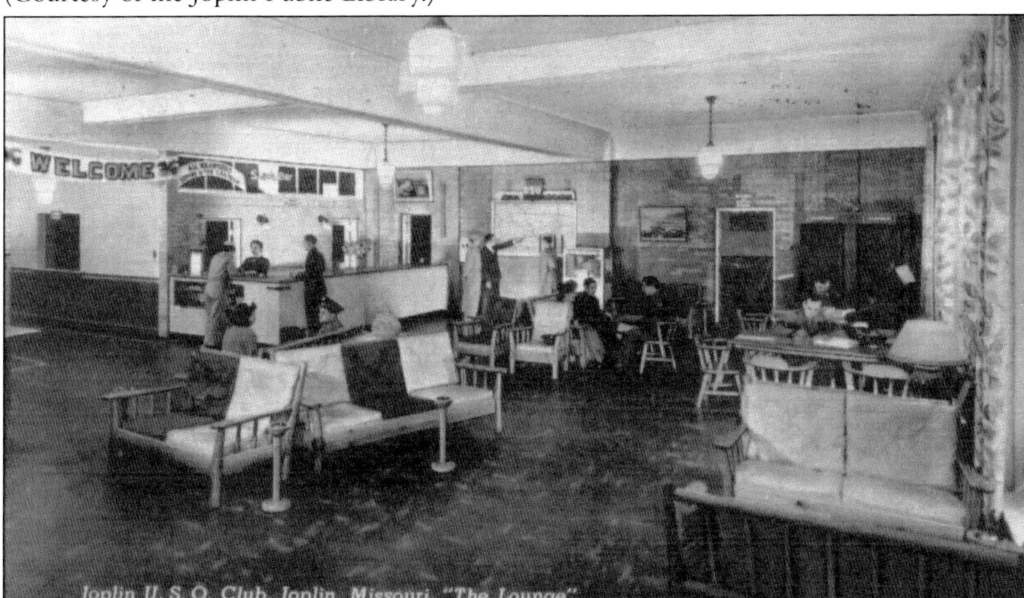

The USO Council faced an unforeseen dilemma when colored troops began arriving at Camp Crowder in 1942. After two years of debating what could be done, they opened the Negro USO Club on the second floor at 221 Main Street. By the time the war ended, over one million Camp Crowder soldiers and their families had made use of Joplin's USO clubs. (Courtesy of Rodney Blaukat.)

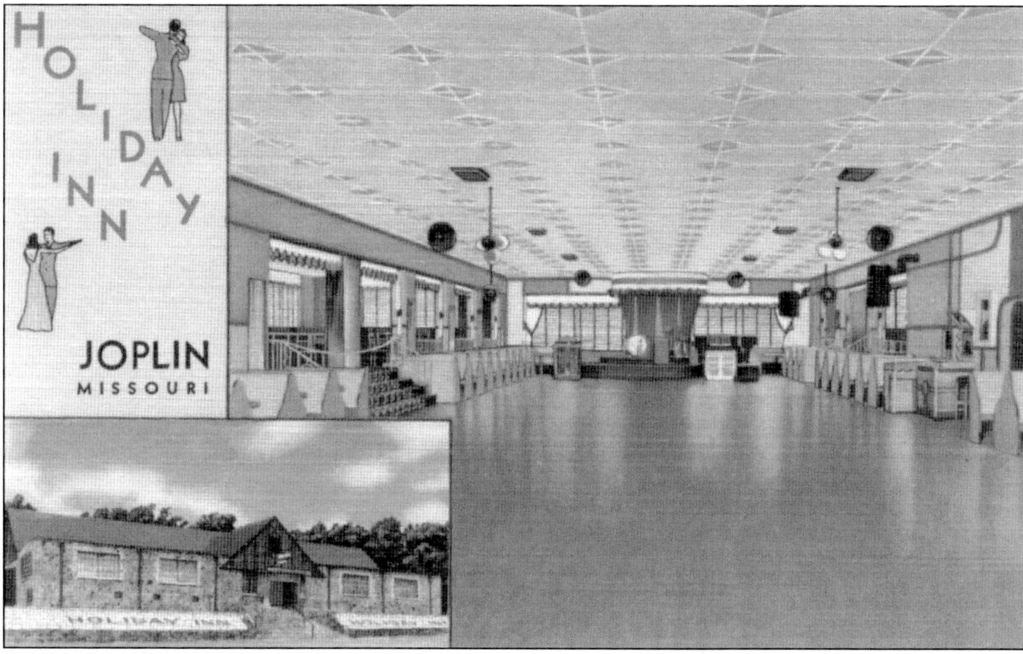

Joplinites' favorite place to dance to live band music was the Holiday Inn Ballroom on south Main Street. John R. Garrison opened the dance hall soon after World War II ended. He expected happy times and big bands to roll again. However, with the advent of television, rock 'n' roll, and other new pastimes in the late 1940s, commercial ballrooms began a steady decline. The Holiday Inn closed in the mid-1950s. (Courtesy of Galen Augustus.)

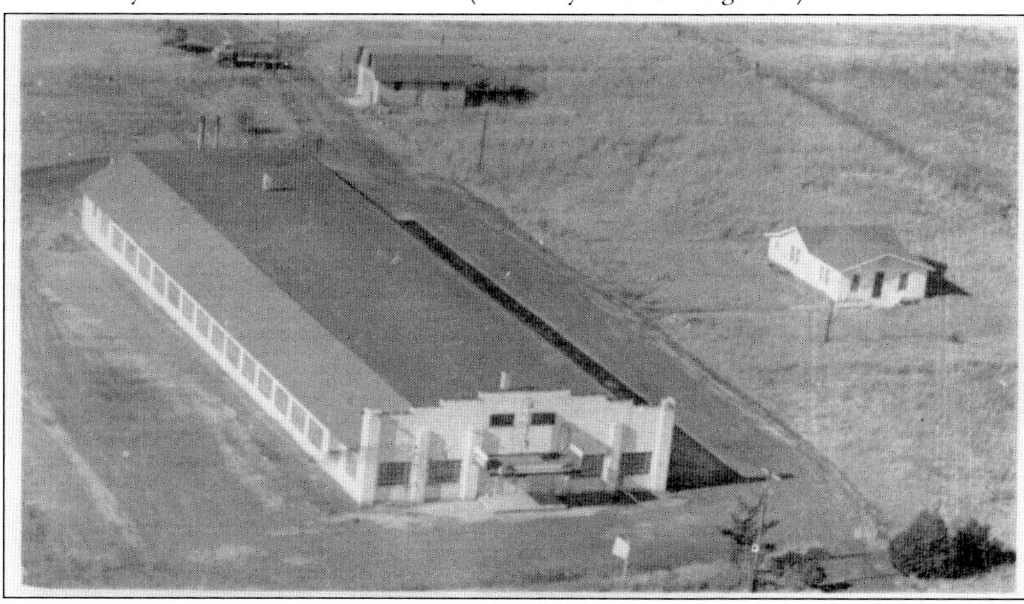

Roller skating was a national craze in the United States from the 1930s to the 1950s. Local roller rinks attracted everyone from small children to grown-ups, providing a fun place to skate and to socialize. The Greentop Roller Rink was originally located one-half mile west of Schifferdecker Avenue on Seventh Street. After that building burned in September 1949, a new one was built on North Main Street. (Courtesy of Rodney Blaukat.)

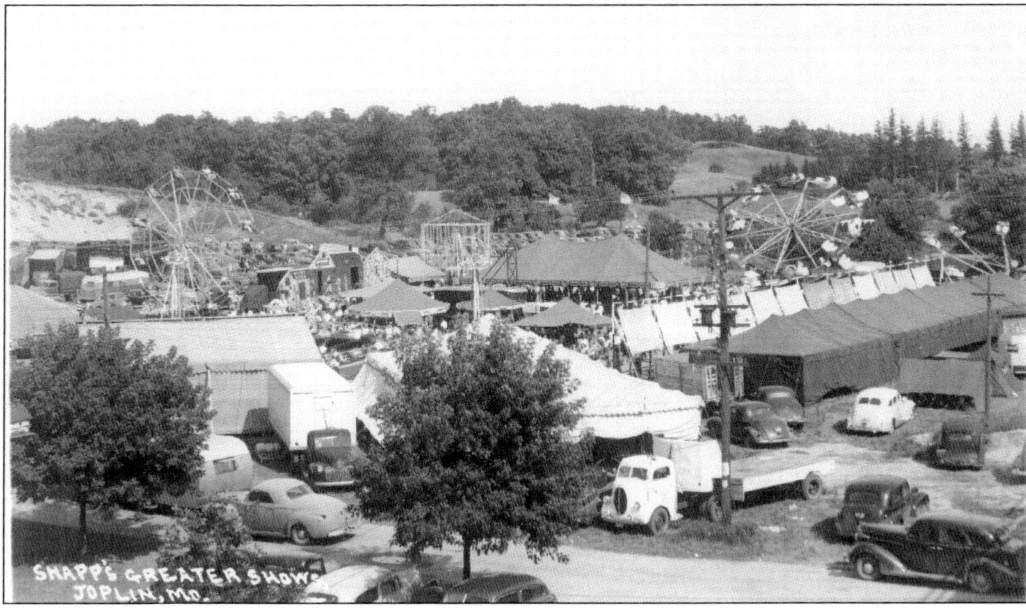

Carnivals, which had grown out of the old 19th-century medicine shows, often earned a sleazy reputation. Concerned mothers warned children to steer clear of the carnies. Nevertheless, there was great excitement when the carnival rolled in and pitched its tents at the edge of town! Barkers enticed customers to booths offering various games of chance, souvenirs, and freak shows. Grease joints supplied hamburgers, hotdogs, cotton candy, popcorn, and other food. Ferris wheels, carousels, tilt-a-whirls, and other metal contraptions provided other ways to relieve patrons of their cash, and perhaps their lunch! These two c. 1940 postcards depict the same lively scene, when the nation was on the brink of war. After rationing of food and gas commenced in January 1942, the traveling carnival went into hiatus. It emerged again after the war and flourished into the 1950s and 1960s. (Both, courtesy of Galen Augustus.)

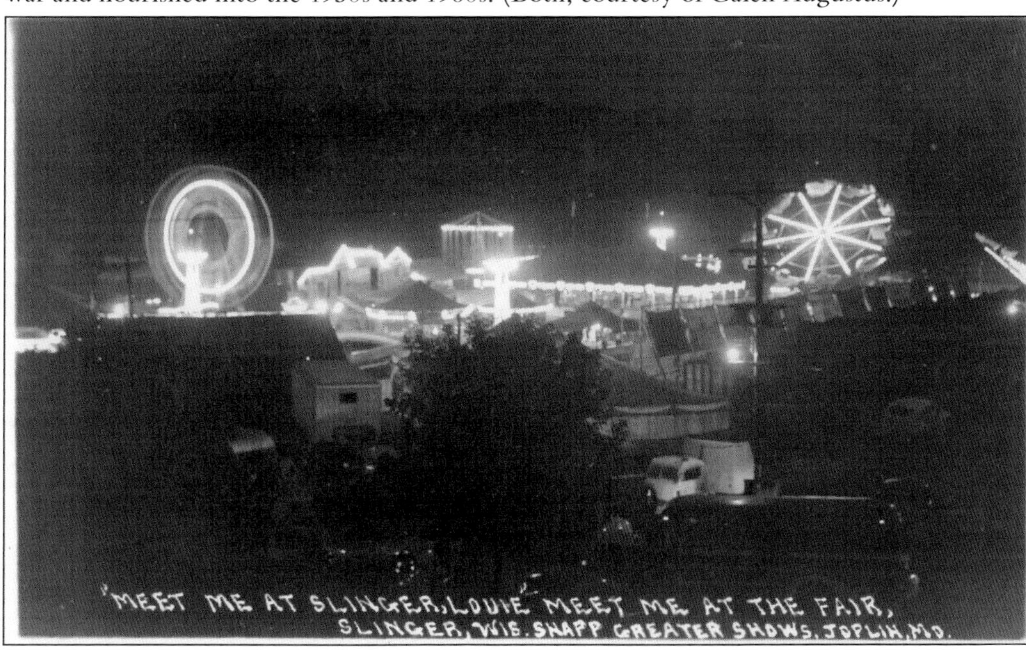

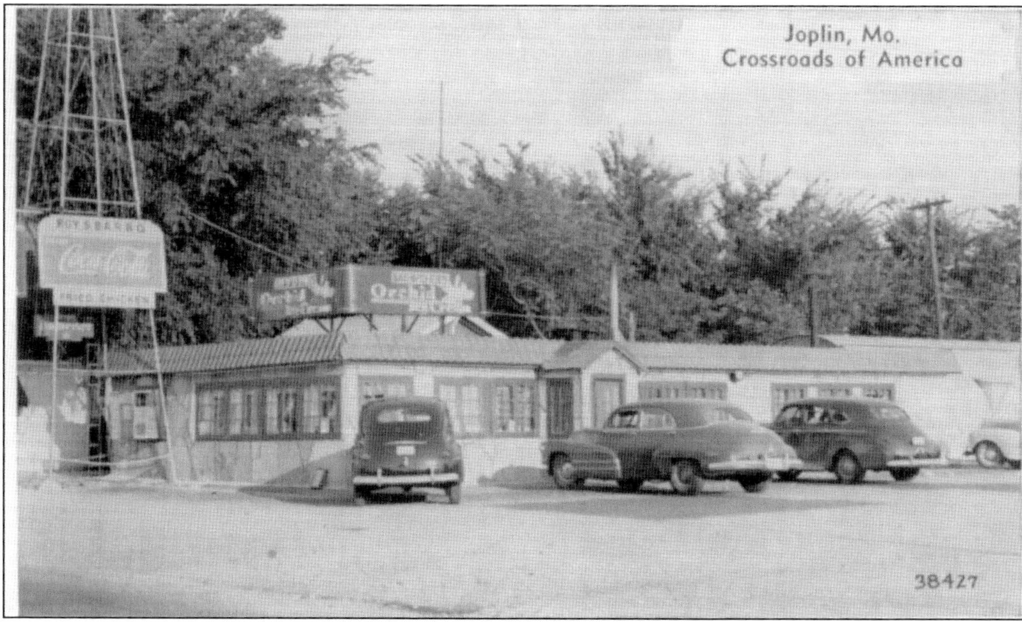

In the mid-1930s, Roy Hemphill opened his first restaurant on South Main Street. The heavy traffic on Route 66 motivated him to relocate to 1514 West Seventh Street around 1939. Roy's offered such delicacies as "golden brown fried chicken, choice barbecue ribs, sandwiches, delicious thick malts," according to a mouth-watering advertisement. Charles Keller purchased the business around 1948, and he changed the name to Keller's Bar. (Courtesy of Galen Augustus.)

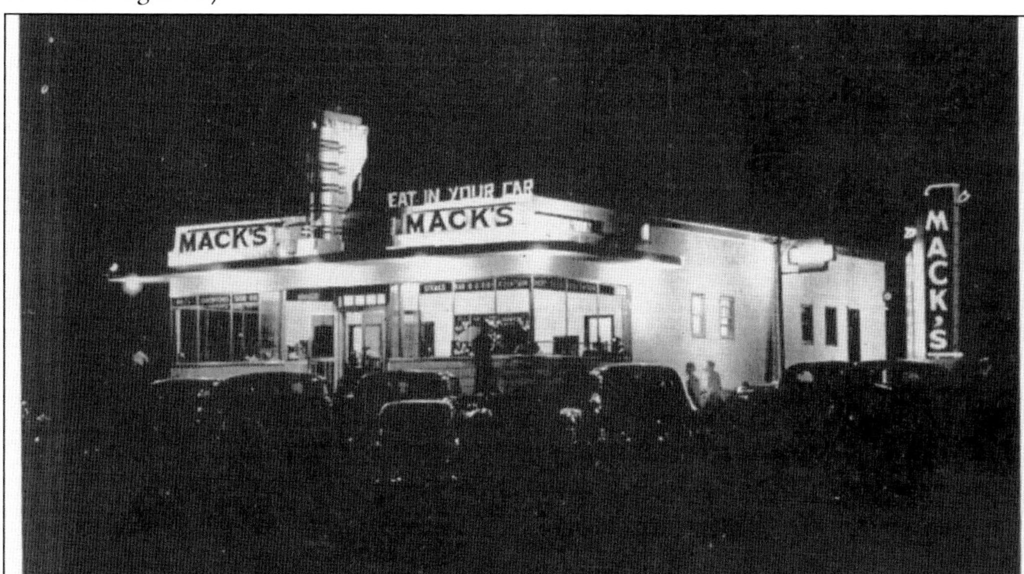

From the late 1930s through the mid-1950s, Mack's Drive-In at 3202 Main Street was a happening place. At night, Clifford "Mack" McIntyre's Art Deco–style building glowed with bright neon lights as cars crowded into its parking lot. According to Mack's advertising, the restaurant was the only Joplin drive-in approved by *66 Highway Guide and Magazine*. (Courtesy of Post Memorial Art Reference Library.)

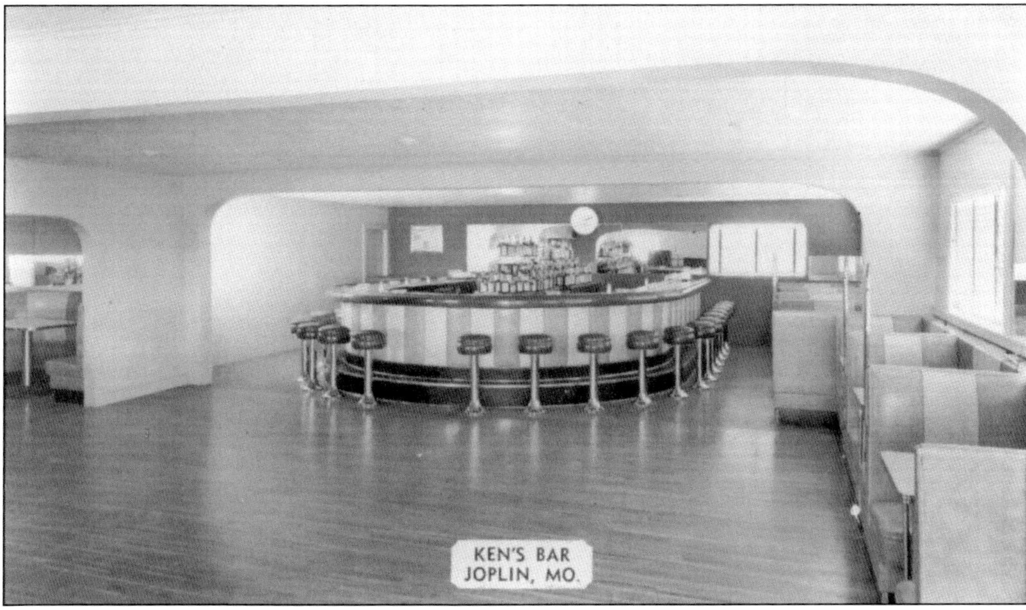

Early-day Joplin was infamous for its downtown saloons, but that changed after World War II. Taverns moved to the city's outskirts to attract motorists. Postwar drinking establishments, such as Ken's at 2409 West Seventh Street, conveyed a sophisticated image. A far cry from dingy corner taverns, these well-lit establishments boasted decorative color schemes, gleaming chrome fixtures, and hardwood dance floors. They preferred classier appellations like cocktail lounge or nightclub. (Courtesy of Galen Augustus.)

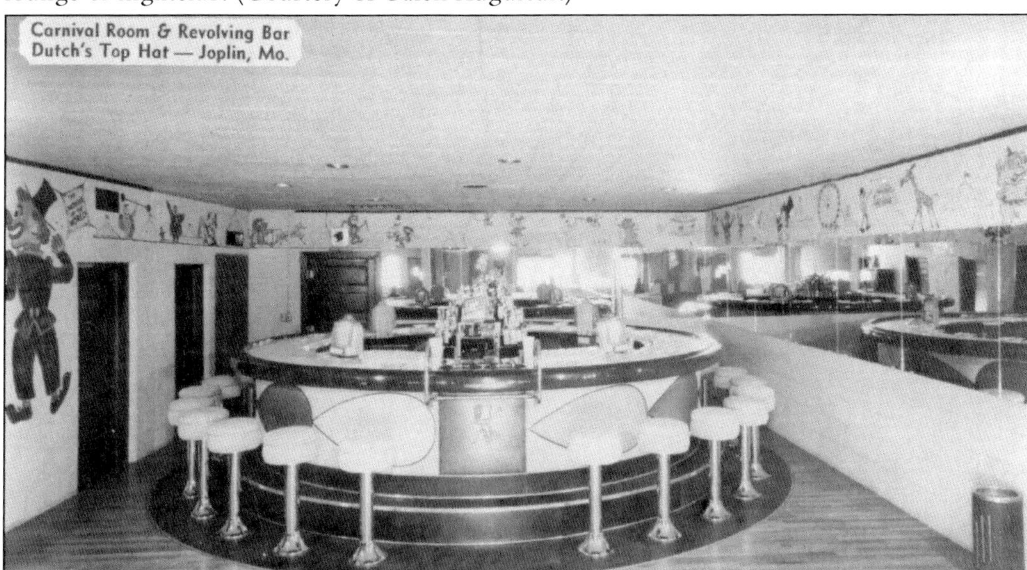

Joe Mertz opened Dutch's Top Hat Cocktail Lounge at 1818 West Seventh Street around 1950. The aptly named Carnival Room, decorated with brightly colored circus motifs, included something of a carousel ride for grown-ups. Although one might wonder about the wisdom of having a revolving bar in an establishment where the customers get tipsy anyway, Dutch's widely advertised its claim to fame as the only completely revolving bar in the state. (Courtesy of Galen Augustus.)

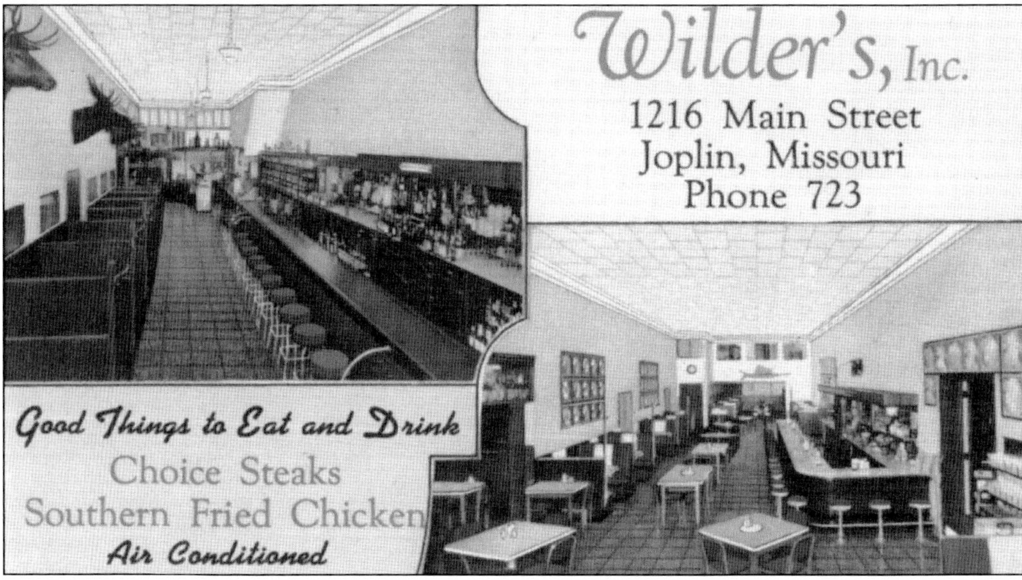

Wilder's Restaurant, which opened at 1216 Main Street in 1933, quickly gained a national reputation for fine food and fun times. The restaurant earned a four-star rating for its seafood, prime rib, pork chops, and steaks. Food was not the only attraction; Wilder's was also known for its gambling hall upstairs. That stopped in 1949, when the Jasper County prosecuting attorney raided local establishments, putting an end to such shenanigans. (Courtesy of the Joplin Public Library.)

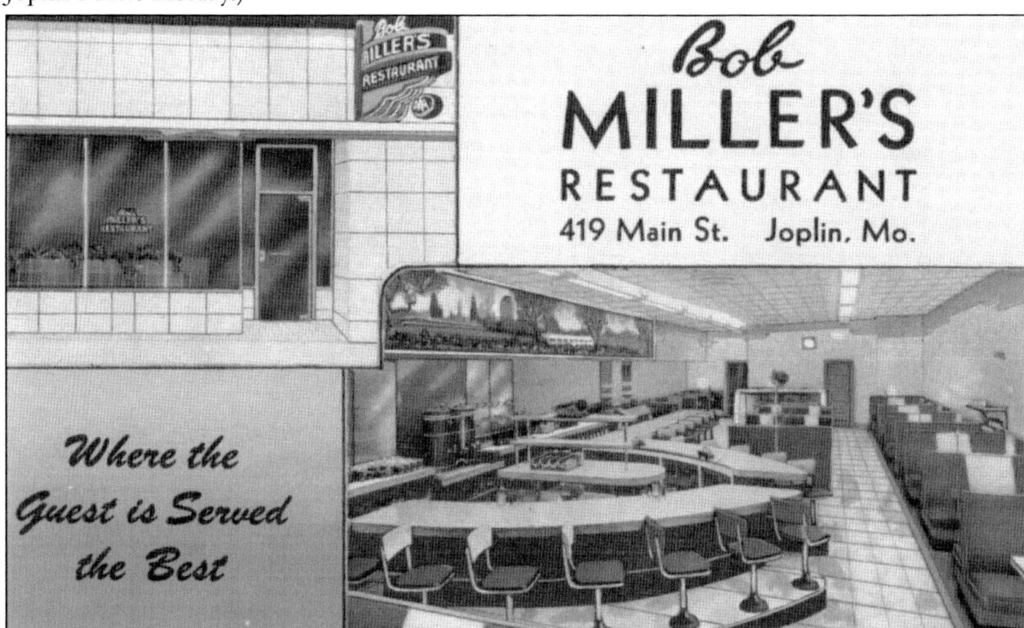

Bob Miller's Restaurant, which opened after World War II at 419 Main Street, represented the ultimate in convenient and affordable comfort food. Downtown workers could always count on a fresh pot of hot steaming coffee to go with fresh baked pies or a lunch of such hearty fare as steak and fried chicken. They could hang out in booths or swivel back and forth on stools at the counter. (Courtesy of Rodney Blaukat.)

Six

Keeping the Faith

Religion has always played a role in the lives of Joplin's citizens. Even before there was a town, the Methodist Church sent missionaries to work with the first settlers and try to convert the indigenous tribes living in the region. Joplin acquired its name, in an indirect way, from early Methodist missionary Harris Joplin, who settled beside a creek in Jasper County in 1839. He did not remain in the area for long, but the creek retained the name Joplin Creek after he left. When pioneer John Cox platted out a town beside the creek in 1871, he named it Joplin. The first church house in Joplin was the Methodist church, built at Fourth Street and Kentucky Avenue in 1872. That same year, the African Methodists established a church but met in rented rooms since they did not have a building. In 1873, the Presbyterian church was established. The Christian and Episcopal churches followed the next year. In 1876, the Baptist and Congregational churches were established. Catholic missionaries arrived on the scene that year as well. Fr. Henry O'Reilly established a parish of 12 to 15 families. In 1885, the Sisters of Mercy, 12 intrepid nuns who had come from Louisville, Kentucky, to bring religion to the heathen mining town, purchased a house for use as their convent and as a boarding school and day school for girls. This chapter, which discusses some of Joplin's churches, ends with two well-known mortuaries. After all, when the saints go marching home, they need funeral homes to escort them on their journey!

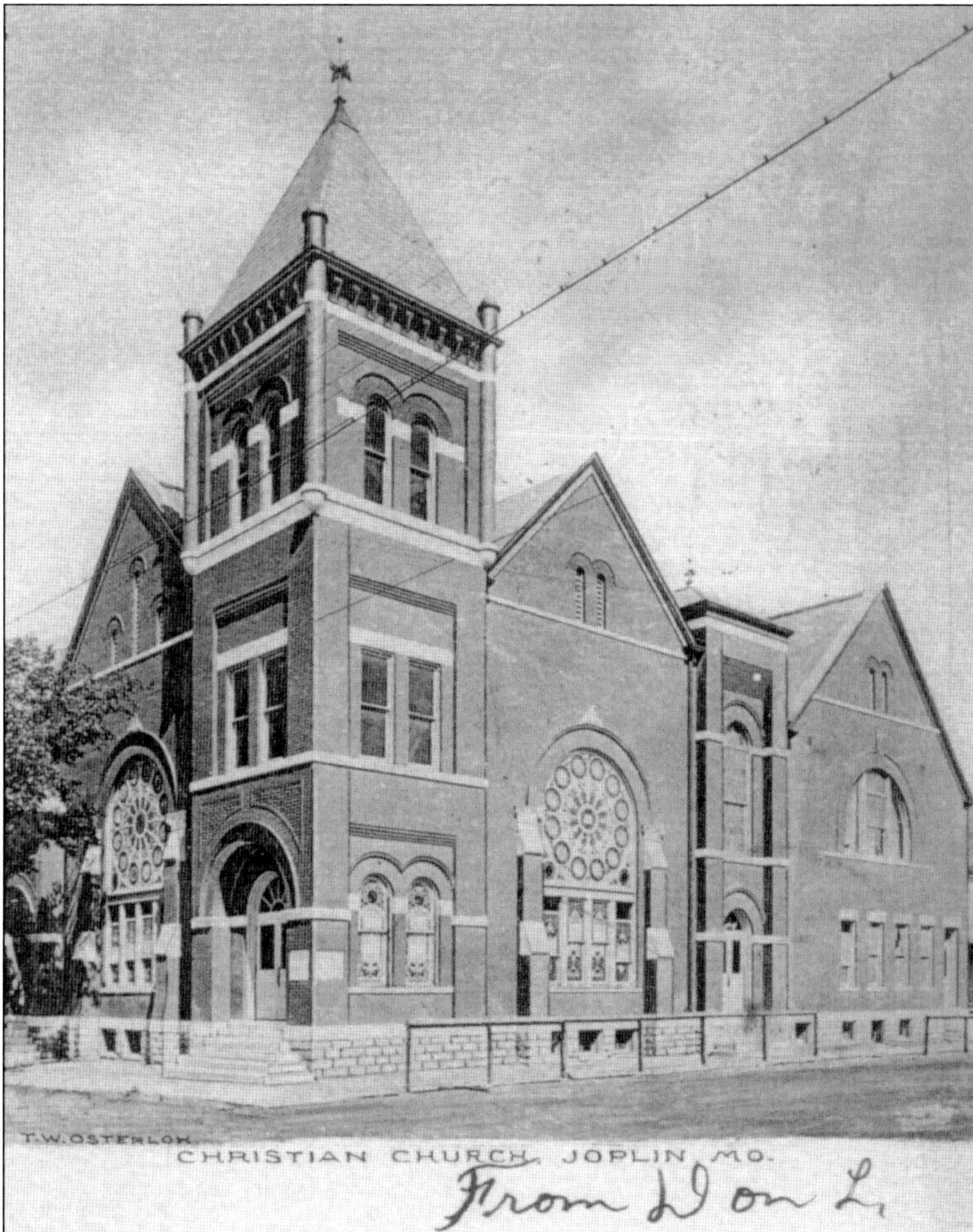

The Christian Church (Disciples of Christ) organized in Joplin in 1874. This brick Romanesque Revival church house was constructed at 401 West Fourth Street in 1901. It featured beautiful stained glass rose windows and a corner tower. The church grew rapidly; a 51-day revival meeting added 675 new members! During this exciting time, the church installed the first pipe organ in Joplin. Always evangelistic, the church sponsored missionaries to Charleston, South Carolina, and Japan and set up mission churches in Joplin in Villa Heights and South Joplin. When the local option question on alcohol came up, minister E.F. Walters helped lead the fight for prohibition. So vicious was the conflict that the minister had to hire a bodyguard. After would-be arsons made two attempts to set fire to the church building, guards were placed on duty at night. (Courtesy of Galen Augustus.)

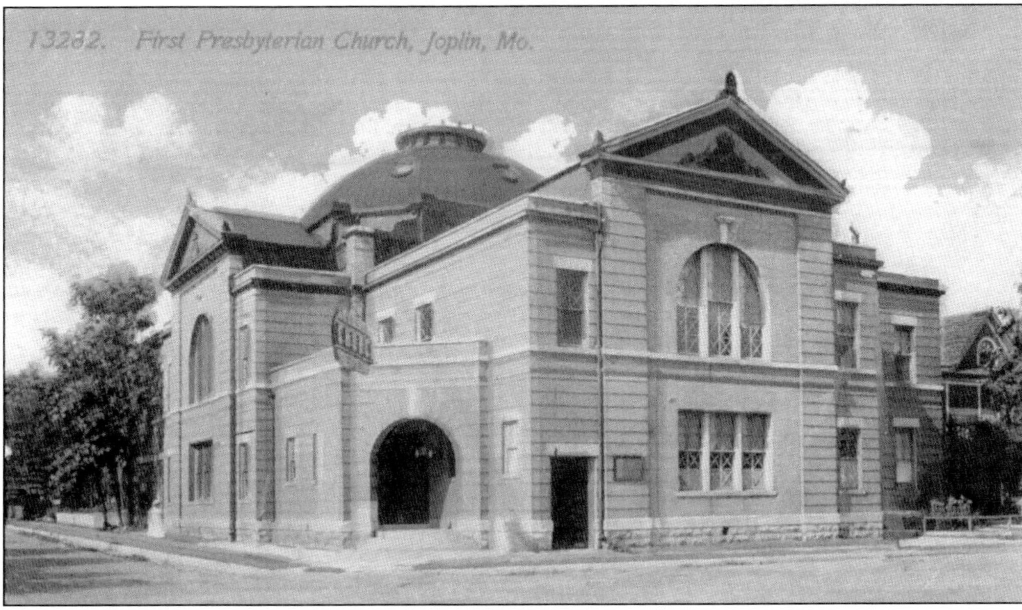

Designed by architect August Michaelis, the Grecian-style First Presbyterian Church at 319 West Sixth Street was completed in 1902. From the very beginning, the dome leaked; in 1906, it was necessary to completely repair and redecorate the structure. The worst disaster transpired in February 1923, when a horrific fire destroyed the building. Most tragic of all, a young firefighter, Robert Lee Sherwood, lost his life when the dome collapsed. (Courtesy of Rodney Blaukat.)

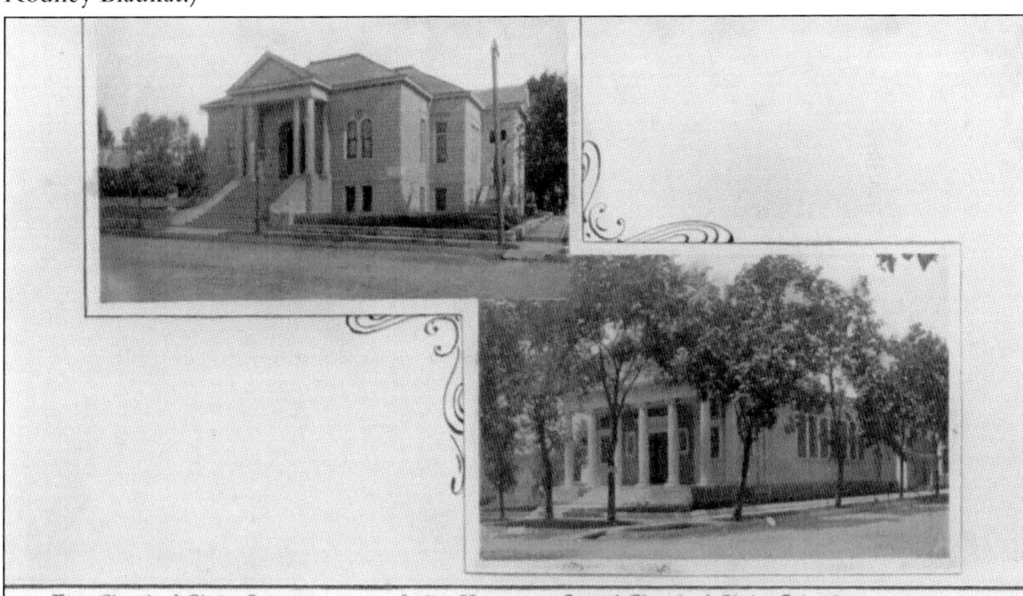

The Christian Science Society first organized in Joplin in 1894, with a handful of followers holding services in a private residence. Church membership grew by leaps and bounds, as did its coffers. In March 1906, the First Church of Christ, Scientist built a Romanesque-style church house at 218 West Sixteenth Street. The Second Church of Christ, Scientist erected this Greek Revival church at 602 Moffet Avenue in 1907. (Courtesy of Galen Augustus.)

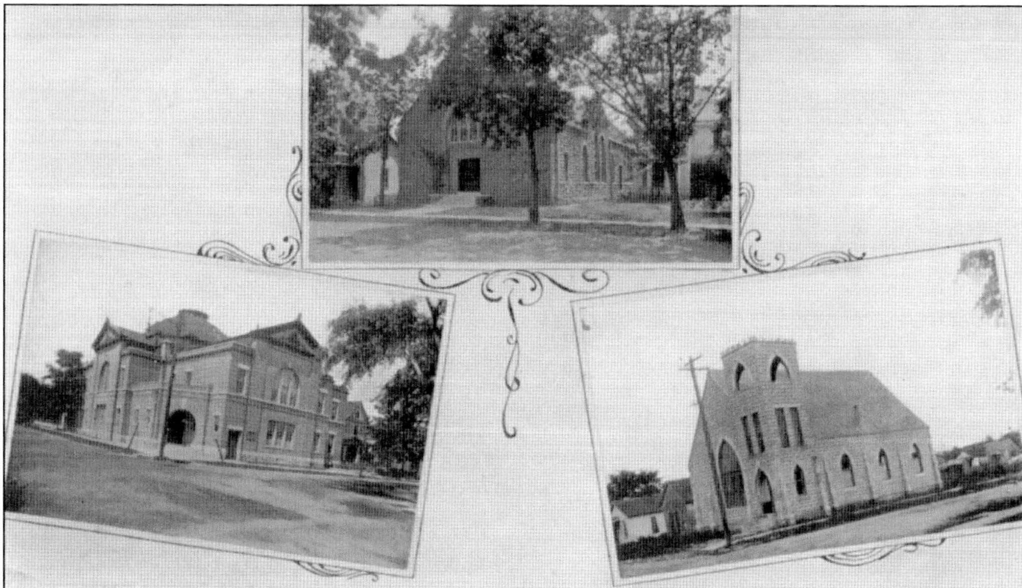

First Presbyterian Church — First Congregational Church, Joplin, Mo. — East Joplin Congregational Church 858

The Congregational church, one of Joplin's earliest churches, chose August Michaelis to design a brownstone edifice at 204 Pearl Avenue in 1899, shown above, middle. Soon after completion, the walls of the church began sinking due to the collapse of an old mine shaft beneath. They disassembled the building and moved it to 417 Pearl Avenue. East Joplin Congregational Church was constructed in 1908 at 1023 Hill Street as a mission church. (Courtesy of Galen Augustus.)

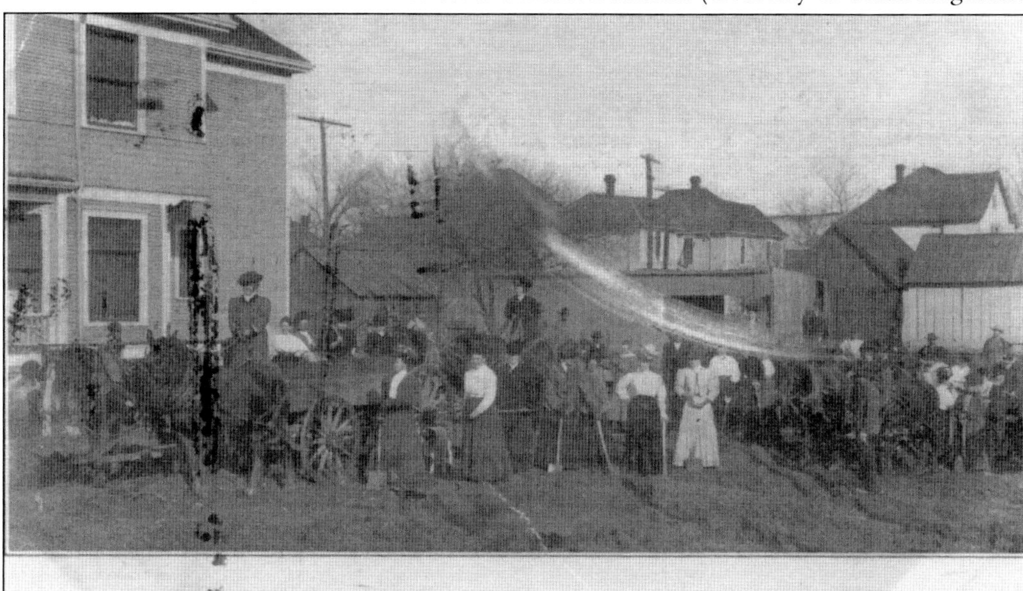

Ladies of the Central Christian Church, Joplin, Mo., Excavating for the New Church Building

On a spring day in 1908, the ladies of Central Christian Church turned out with shovels to ceremonially break ground for a new church. The Carthage limestone building at 421 West Eighth Street took a year to complete. Central Christian Church, originally an offshoot of the First Christian Church, went defunct 20 years later. The Church of Jesus Christ of Latter-Day Saints bought the structure around 1930. (Courtesy of Galen Augustus.)

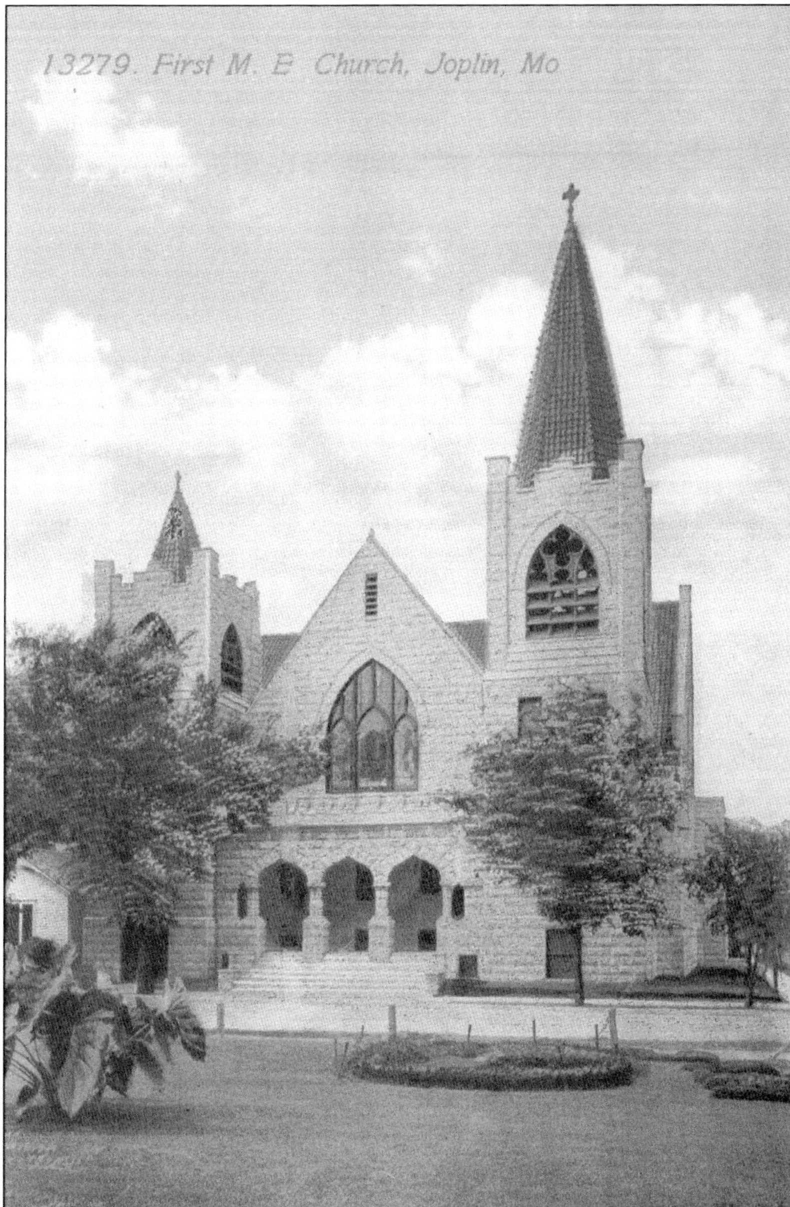

Construction of this impressive Gothic-style Carthage limestone church, designed by architects Garstang and Rea, commenced at 501 West Fourth Street in 1905 and was completed a year later. The majestic edifice featured large stained glass windows, a triple arched entry, and two bell towers. The sanctuary seated 1,200 people, although church membership at the time totaled only 440. Known for its evangelism and successful Sunday school, the optimistic church obviously expected to need room for future growth. In 1912, the Reverend Harvey Jones announced that the church would install a motion picture machine and begin showing wholesome movies. He wanted to counter the negative influence of the nickelodeons frequented by young people of the day. First Methodist Church was the mother church to many mission churches in the Joplin area. These included Central Avenue, East Joplin, Byers Avenue, Epworth, and Chitwood. (Courtesy of the Joplin Public Library.)

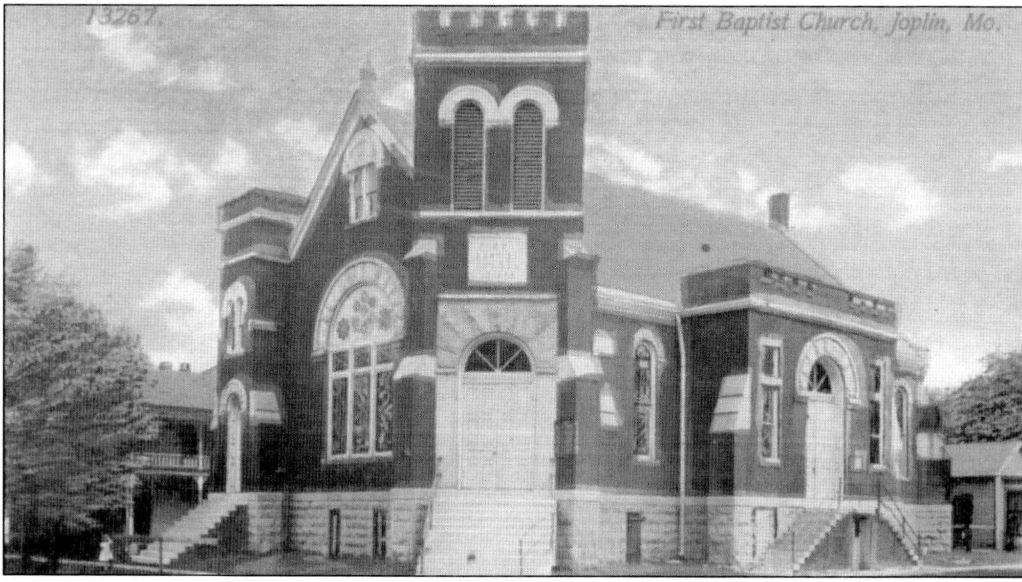

On August 24, 1890, First Baptist Church broke ground for a new building at 633 Pearl Avenue. Construction began in 1893 but was not completed until 1895. The redbrick structure featured a 40-foot-tall tower, arched stained glass windows, and buttress supports. Very evangelistic in focus, First Baptist planted several mission churches. There was Gregg Mission, East Joplin Baptist, Empire Street Baptist, Bankers Chapel, and Second Baptist. (Courtesy of Galen Augustus.)

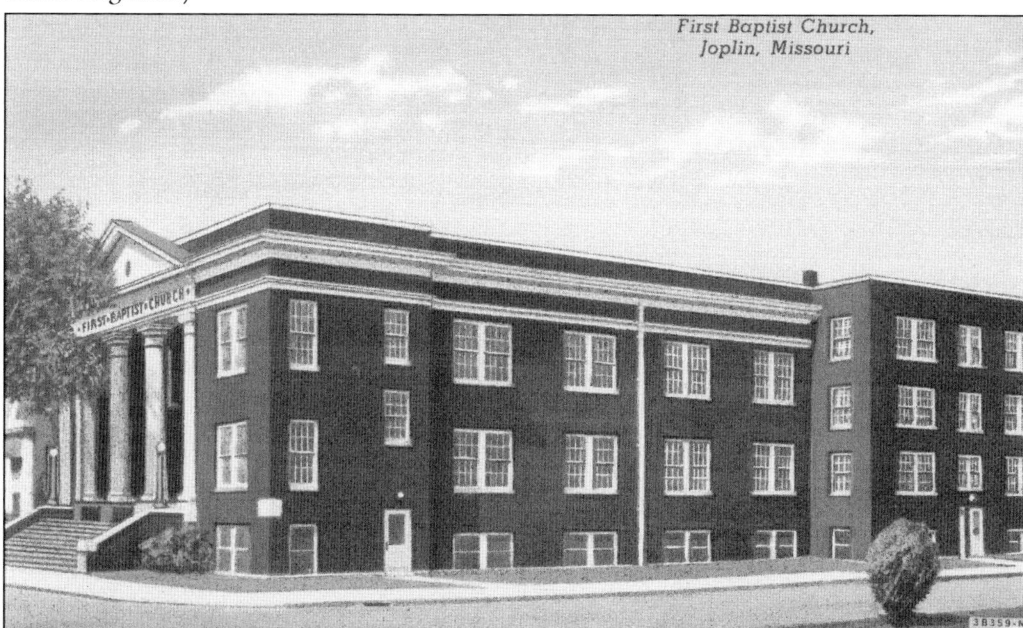

In 1925, First Baptist Church demolished its 30-year-old home in order to build a new one on the same site. During the construction, the congregation met in the YMCA at 510 Wall Avenue. Completed in April 1926, the large brick building could accommodate 1,200 people in its sanctuary. In 1980, the church facade was remodeled extensively, replacing the steps and columned entry of the original. (Courtesy of the Joplin Public Library.)

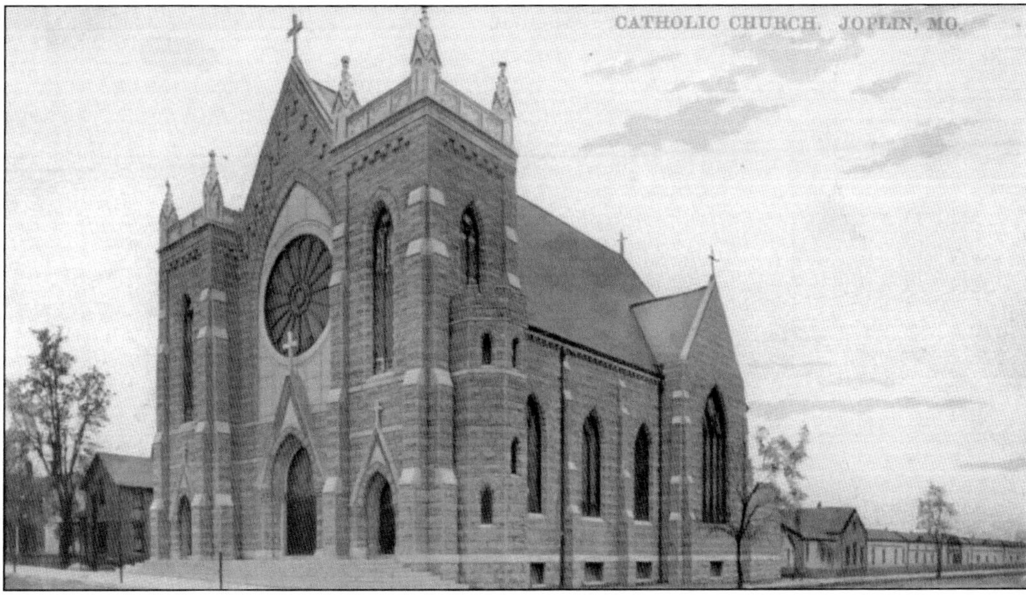

Begun in 1906 and completed the following year, St. Peter's Catholic Church transformed the southwest corner of Eighth Street and Pearl Avenue. Architect Austin Allen looked to the Gothic Revival style for inspiration. Rich and poor, Catholics and Protestants, all enthusiastically contributed to the fund drive. On the day of the dedication, the *Joplin Globe* stated that the edifice was "the handsomest structure within the limits of the town of Joplin." (Courtesy of Galen Augustus.)

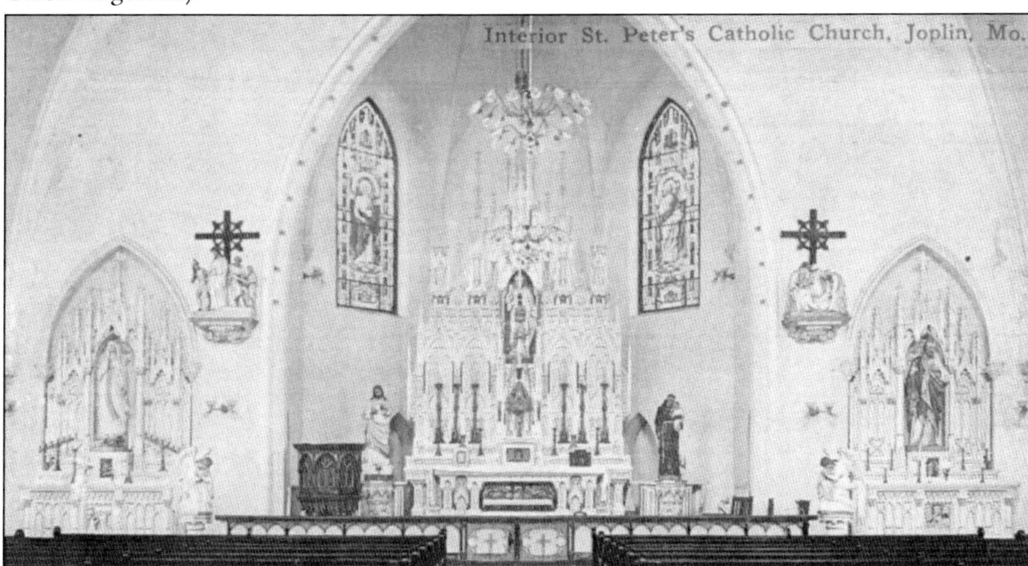

During the day, St. Peter's luminous interior shimmered with multicolored light coming in through stained glass windows. A plaster ceiling featured oak ribs that fanned out and terminated in decorative motifs. Five chandeliers were suspended from the ceiling. The dazzling high altar was embellished with onyx and gold ornaments and topped with 46 spires. A large pipe organ and carved wood confessionals, pulpits, and statuary elegantly furnished St. Peter's sanctuary. (Courtesy of Rodney Blaukat.)

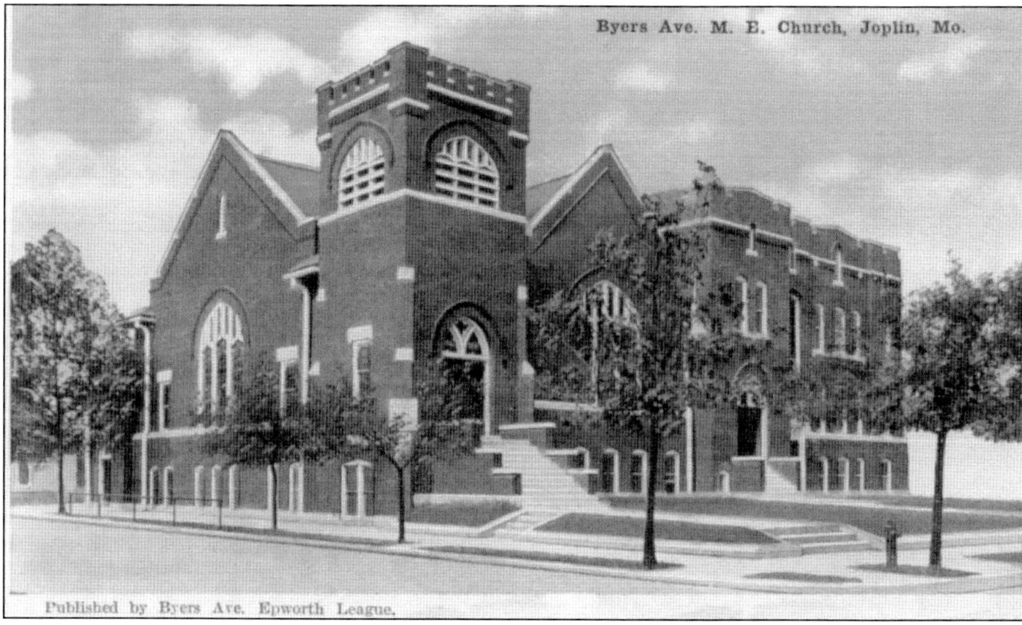

Byers Avenue Methodist Church formed as an outgrowth of the First Methodist Church. It dedicated its Gothic Revival brick building on Thanksgiving Day, 1899. The church featured a 30-foot-tall, square-towered entry and a 300-seat sanctuary with luminous stained glass windows. The church actively supported missionaries in China and India as well as local efforts such as the Woman's Missionary Society, which worked with the poor people of Joplin. (Courtesy of Galen Augustus.)

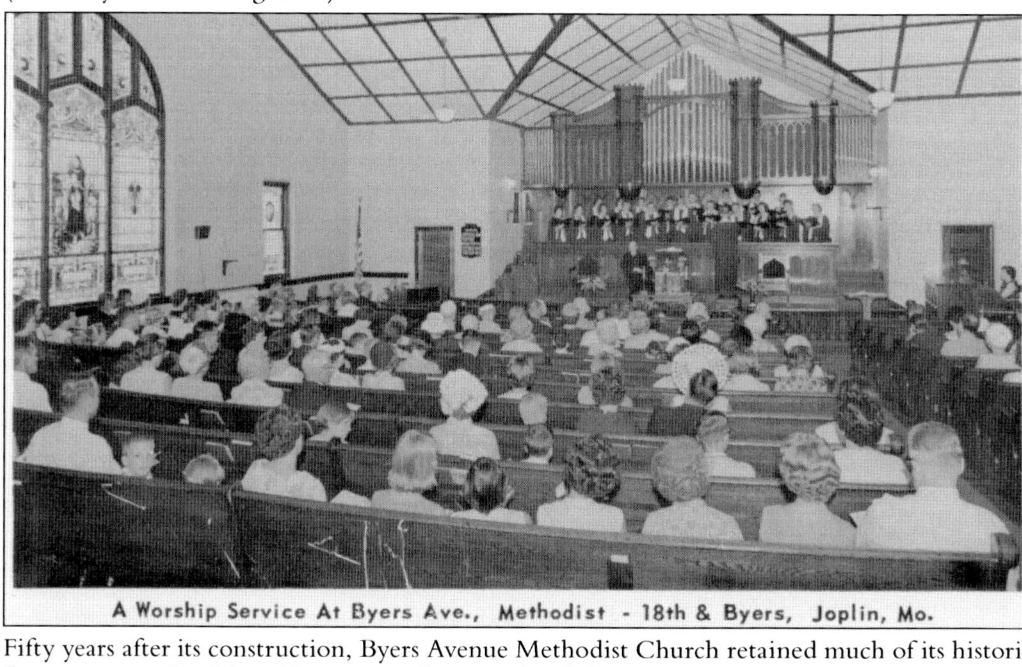

Fifty years after its construction, Byers Avenue Methodist Church retained much of its historic flavor, as seen in this mid-century photograph of the sanctuary interior. The outstanding Himmer pipe organ originally cost $10,000 but is worth considerably more than that today. It was installed in 1928 and refurbished in 1964. (Courtesy of the Joplin Public Library.)

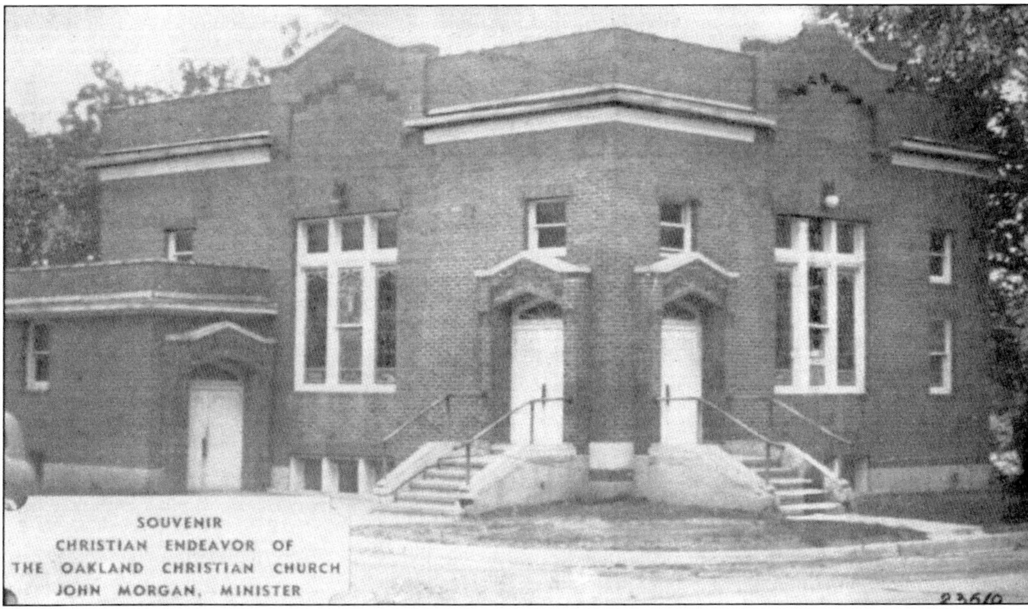

Oakland Christian Church dedicated its new building at 2930 Zora Street in 1926. Although the auditorium seated 250, it could easily accommodate 500 by opening up six adjoining classrooms. The basement included an auditorium with stage, a parlor, a kitchen, and a modern heat and ventilation system. The church sat on a half-acre plot surrounded by trees. The congregation held picnics, sporting events, and various gatherings in the park-like setting. (Courtesy of Post Memorial Art Reference Library.)

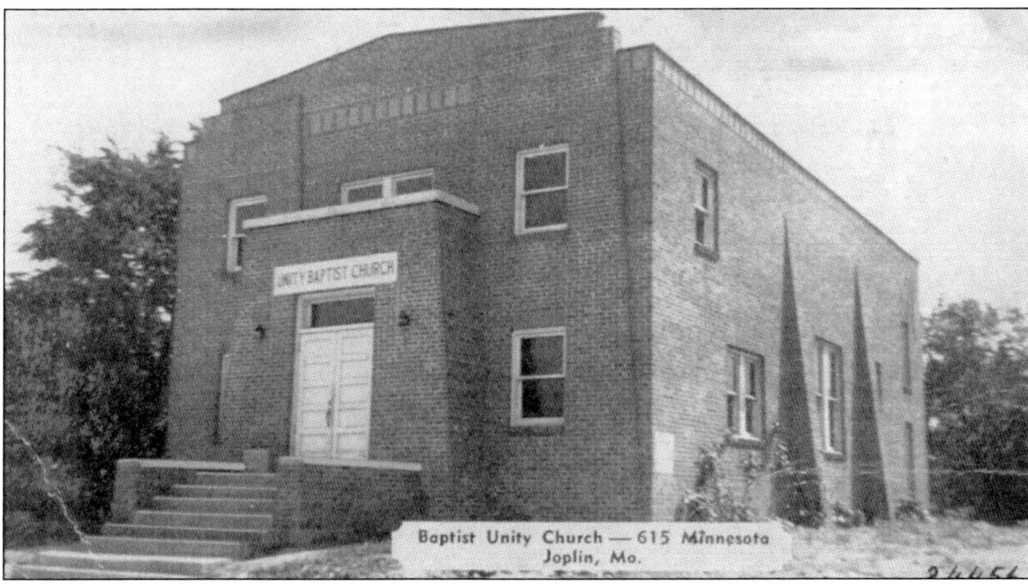

Unity Baptist Church, a fellowship for African Americans, formed in 1901. Two years later, a tornado destroyed its church house at Seventh Street and Kentucky Avenue. Philanthropist Thomas Connor donated $5,000 for the church to rebuild at 511 East Seventh Street in 1904. This structure was demolished to make way for construction of the East Seventh Street viaduct. Unity Baptist built the church shown here at 615 Minnesota Avenue in 1939. (Courtesy of Post Memorial Art Reference Library.)

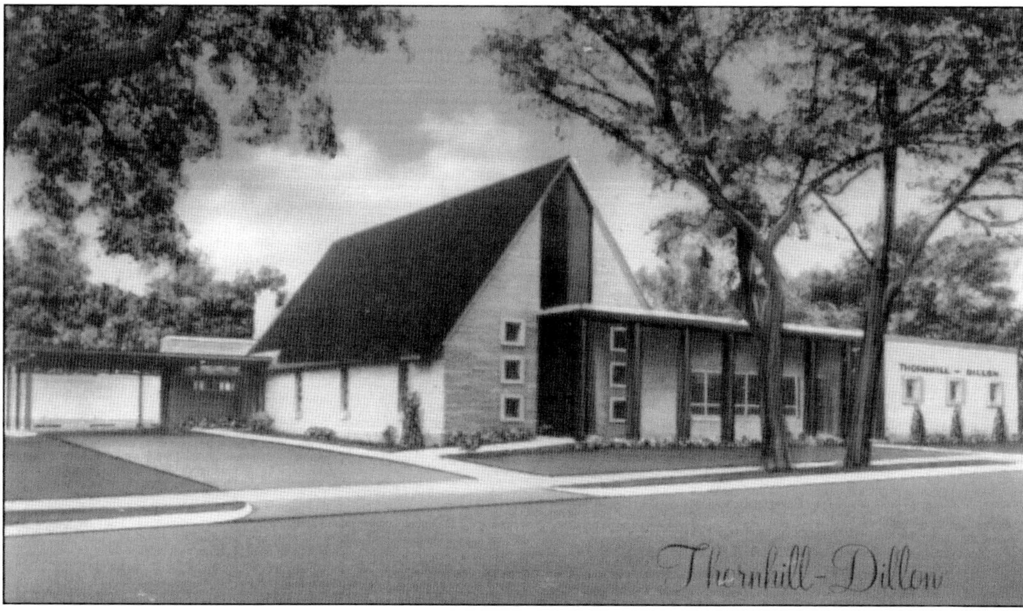

In 1938, Cecil A. Thornhill and David Dillon purchased the old Frank-Sievers Mortuary, located on the northwest corner of Fourth Street and Wall Avenue. The mortuary had been established in 1890, making it the oldest undertaking business in Joplin. The new owners continued the legacy but changed the name to Thornhill-Dillon Mortuary. The firm built this up-to-date funeral home at 602 Byers Avenue in 1955. (Courtesy of the Joplin Public Library.)

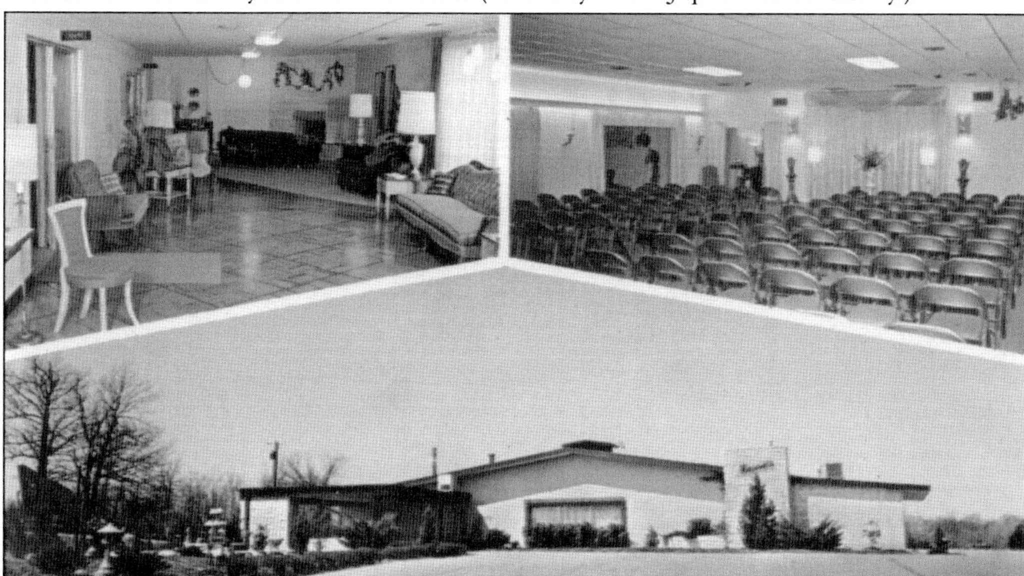

Lee and Ann Mason moved from Springfield, Missouri, to establish Mason Chapel and Mortuary in 1961. They built this modern structure just north of Forest Park Cemetery on Range Line Road. In 1976, Wayne Woodard purchased the firm and renamed it Mason-Woodard Mortuary; two years later, it burned to the ground. By that time, Range Line was experiencing vigorous commercial development, so Mason-Woodard decided to rebuild on East Seventh Street. (Courtesy of the Joplin Public Library.)

Seven

Home Sweet Home

In the early 1800s, southwest Missouri was populated by Native Americans and a few hardy white settlers, most of whom came from Kentucky, Virginia, Tennessee, and the Carolinas. They built simple log cabins using readily available timber. As they prospered, they built more substantial houses using bricks made of clay from nearby creeks. The events of the Civil War devastated the area. Entire settlements were burned to the ground; many residents fled, and some never to return. The US government enacted the Homestead Act of 1862 to encourage settlement of the Great Plains. After the war ended, a wave of settlers, many of whom were Europeans, began arriving from the northeastern states. Migration intensified after lead and zinc were discovered, and of course, people needed places to live. Investors built downtown lodging, from the simple Burnett and Forney hotels to the grand Keystone, Connor, and Clarketon. In the meantime, real estate developers platted out residential areas. Once the electric railway system came into existence in the 1890s, the building boom took off in earnest. Houses could be built outside the urban center. European designs were wildly popular during the Victorian period. Prosperous Joplinites built extravagant mansions in such styles as French Second Empire, Gothic Revival, Greek Revival, and Romanesque Revival. The Olivia Apartments and Robertson Apartments offered fine lodging for those who wanted to live close to downtown. The least fortunate were not overlooked; Joplin Children's Home provided a good home to hundreds of abandoned children. In addition to houses, hotels, and apartments, this chapter also surveys Joplin's tourist lodging from the 1930s through the 1960s.

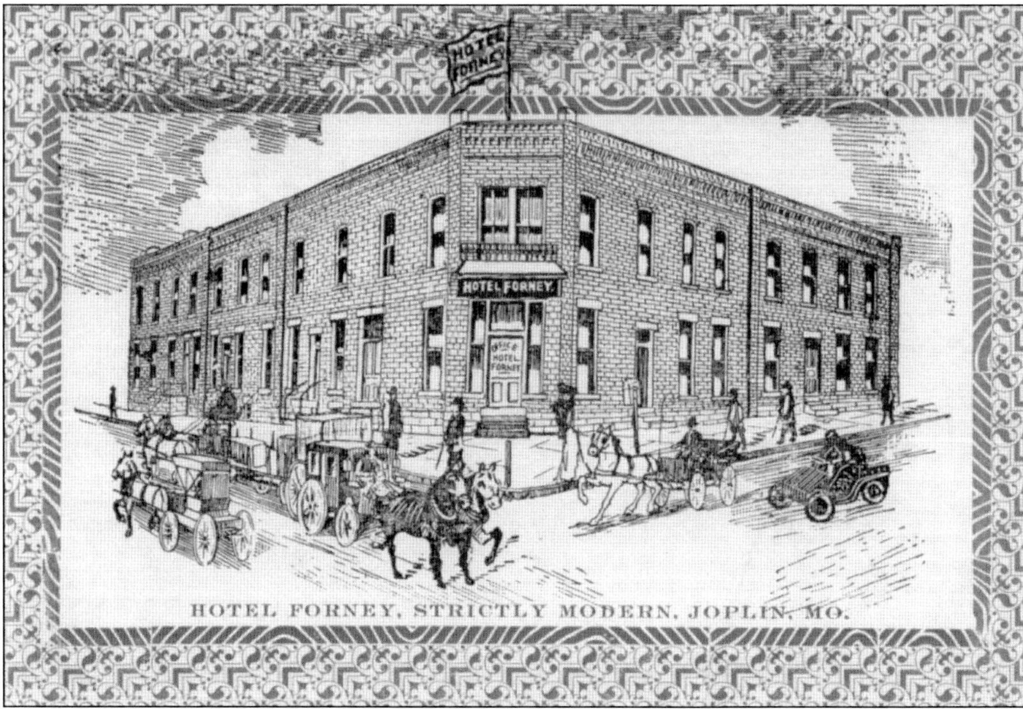

The Forney Hotel at 424 Pennsylvania Avenue remained a downtown fixture from 1890 until 1925. A 1909 newspaper ad called it "Joplin's modern popular price hotel." Forney's boasted a dining room, gas and electric lights, steam heat, and baths, all for a mere $1 per night. That was quite a bargain compared with the rates at the new Connor Hotel, which ranged from $2.50 to $4 depending upon the amenities. (Courtesy of Galen Augustus.)

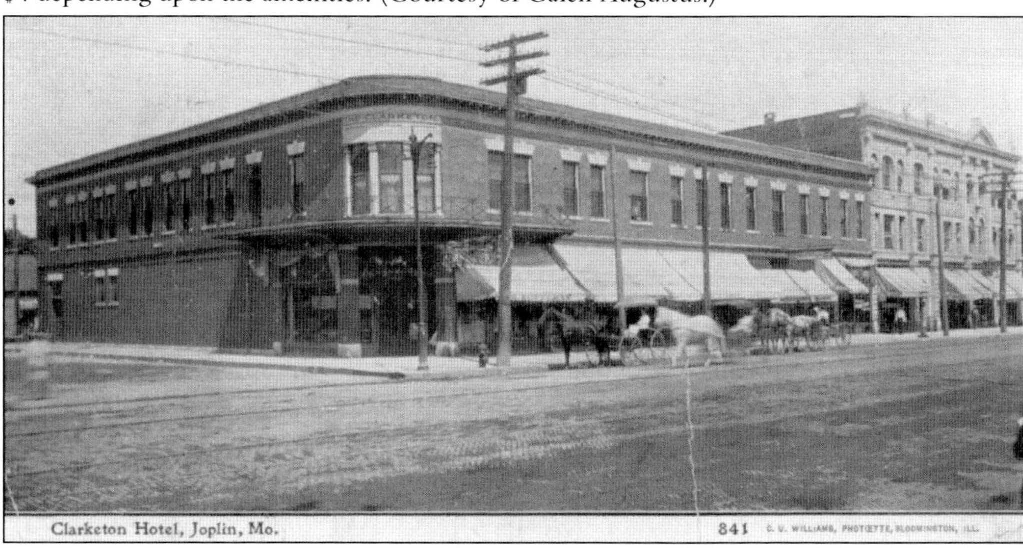

The Clarketon Hotel occupied most of the 700 block of Main Street on the west side. The original building was a three-story stone-faced structure designed by Joplin architect August Michaelis in 1899. A two-story brick addition expanded the hotel all the way to Eighth Street a few years later. In 1918, in a burst of wartime patriotic fervor, the Clarketon's owners changed its name to the American Hotel. (Courtesy of Rodney Blaukat.)

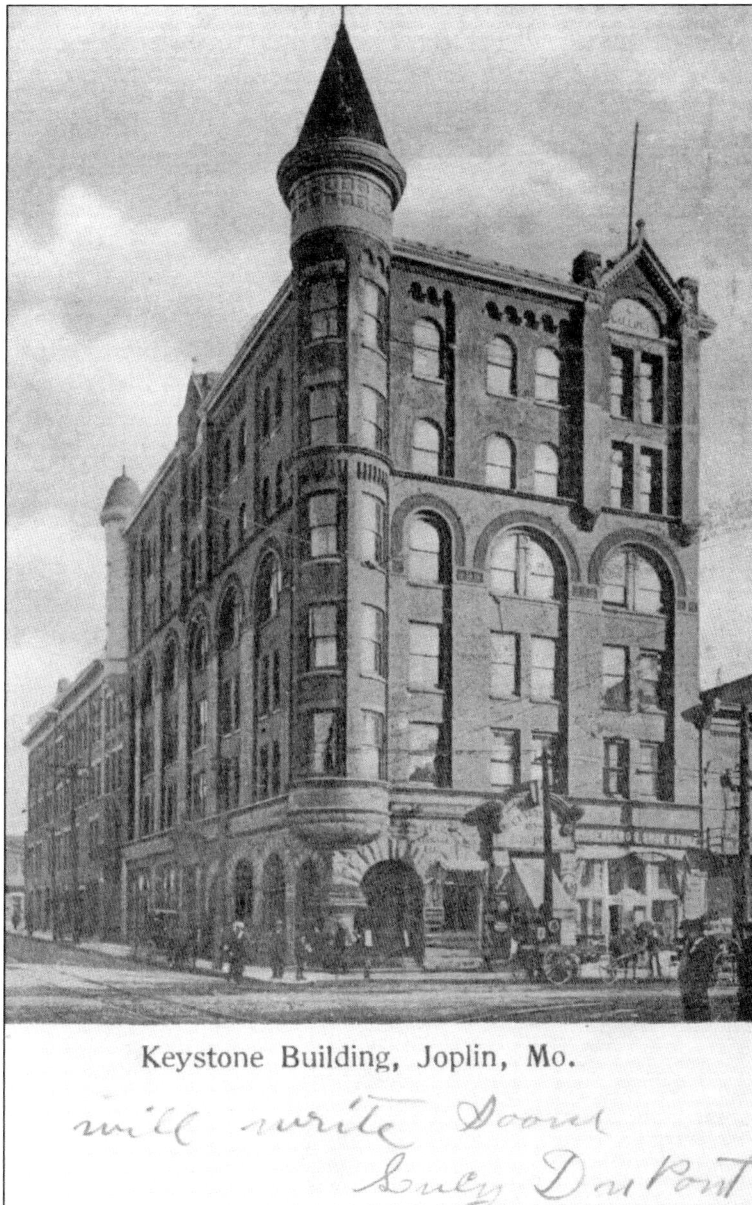

Pennsylvania newspaperman E.Z. Wallower erected this magnificent six-story hotel, which he named the Keystone Hotel in honor of Pennsylvania, the Keystone state. The pinnacled Victorian-style edifice at 401 Main Street once dominated both the skyline and the development of Joplin's business district; investors scrambled to build their businesses nearby. The Keystone opened with great fanfare in the fall of 1892. Its lavishly furnished parlors, reception halls, offices, and dining rooms were "marvels of the decorator's art," according to the *Joplin Globe*. Joplin National Bank, Era Rose's jewelry store, and the hotel lobby occupied the first floor. The Keystone persevered through the good times and the bad. As train travel declined and motorists flocked to motels along the highways, Joplin's once grand hotels met ignoble ends. The Keystone was demolished during the urban renewal programs of the late 1960s. (Courtesy of Rodney Blaukat.)

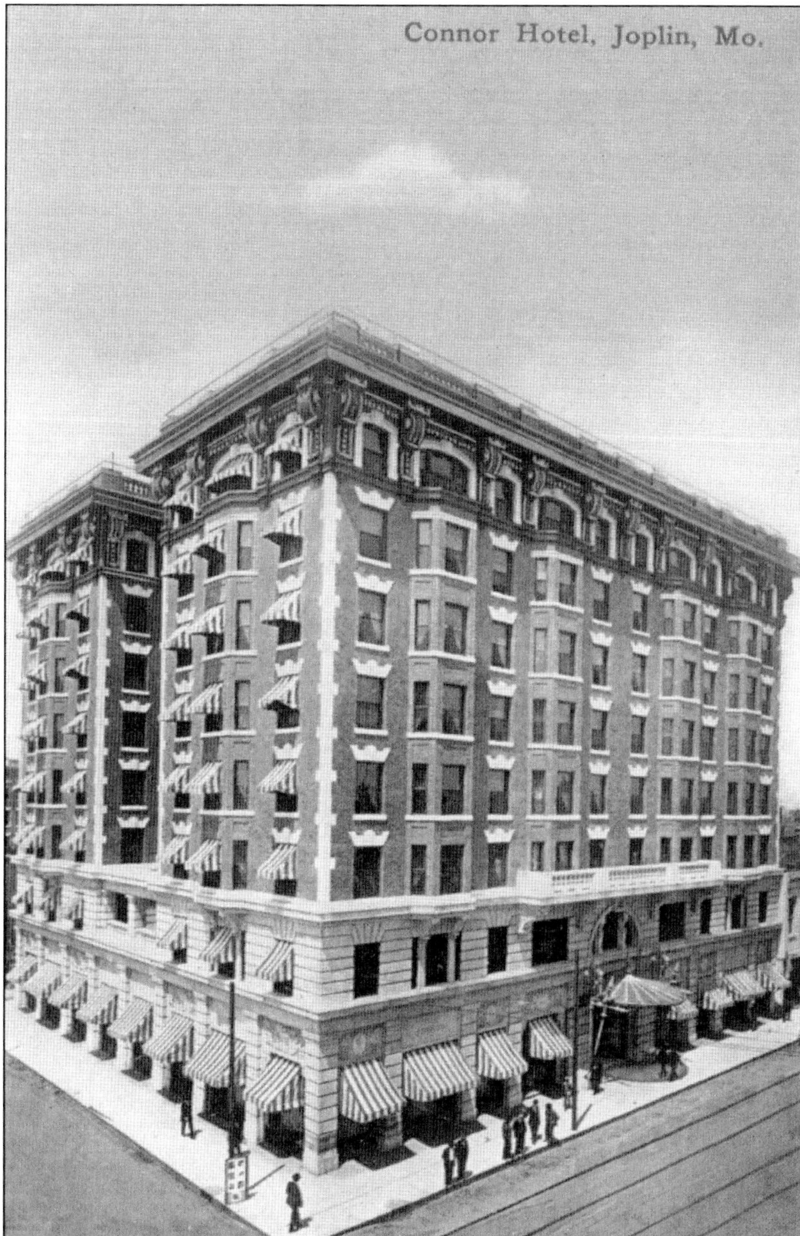

In 1906, Thomas Connor contracted with St. Louis architects Barnett, Haynes, and Barnett and the Joplin firm of Dieter and Wenzel to build an eight-story brick and stone hotel. Unfortunately, Connor died in 1907, a year before its completion. Above the regal hotel, an open-air roof garden overlooked the city; in 1912, the roof garden was enclosed so that it could be open all year. In 1929, an annex was completed, bringing the hotel's room capacity to 400. Dining pleasure was a high priority; two huge kitchens served the Kit-Kat Club, the University Club, and the spectacular Marie Antoinette dining room. Not only did the Connor cater Joplin's most prestigious social and business functions, but it also provided lodging for an impressive roster of celebrities, such as Joan Crawford, Bob Cummings, Ronald Reagan, Eleanor Roosevelt, Nelson Eddy, and Dennis Weaver. (Courtesy of the Joplin Public Library.)

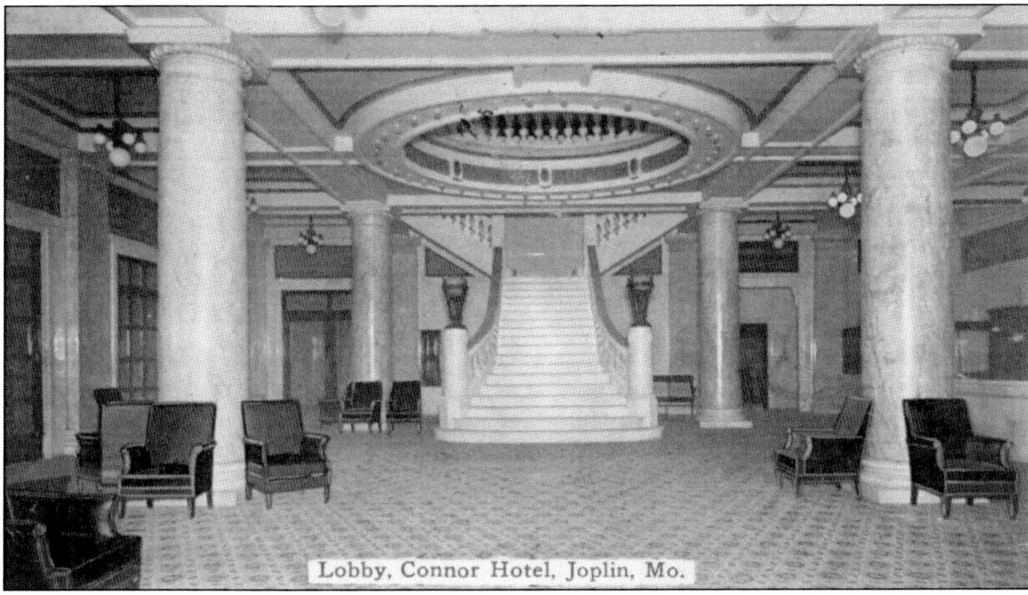

The dazzling lobby featured a crystal chandelier suspended from the rotunda. A grand white marble stairway swept up to the mezzanine. Guest amenities included handsomely furnished rooms, a billiard room, fine dining facilities, a gleaming barbershop, a tobacconist, and other retail establishments on the ground floor. Although claims that the Connor was the greatest hotel west of New York were probably exaggerations, the sheer elegance of the Connor cannot be disputed. (Courtesy of Rodney Blaukat.)

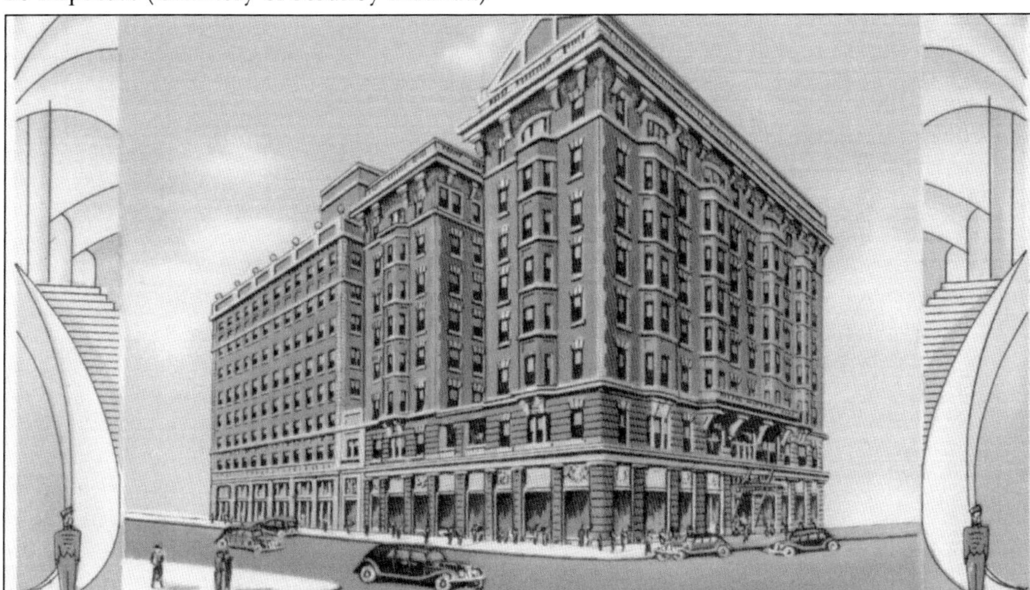

As rail service declined in the 1960s, so did occupancy in the Connor. In 1970, the hotel's contents were auctioned off for back taxes, leaving a boarded-up shell. The city hired a demotion crew to raze the hotel on November 12, 1978. The structurally weakened Connor came crashing down a day ahead of schedule. Three workers were trapped under the rubble for 82 hours; only one of the men survived. (Courtesy of the Joplin Public Library.)

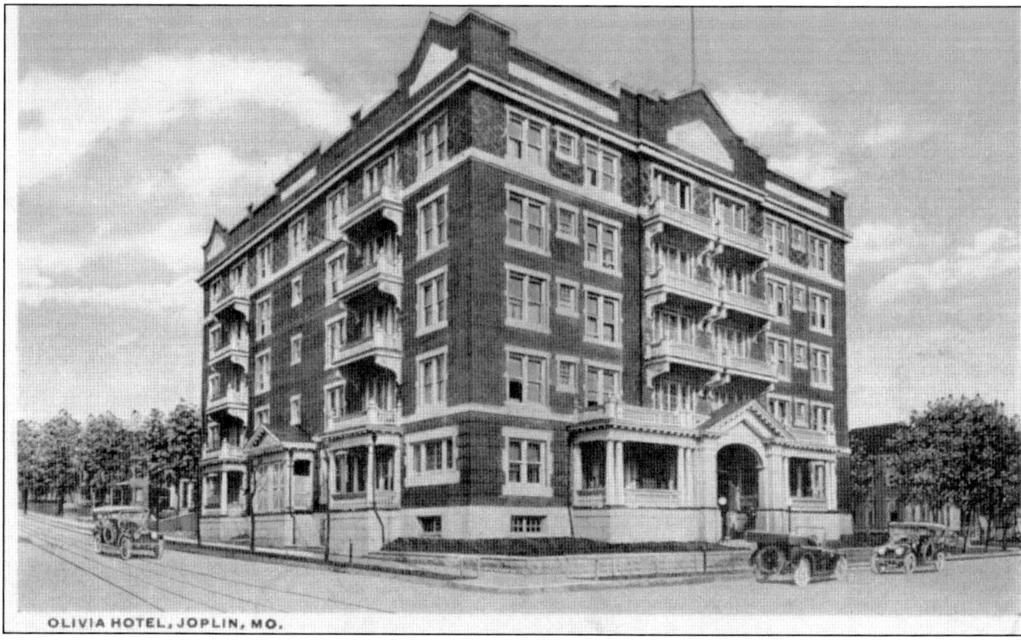

In 1906, Canadian mining engineer Arthur Bendelari commissioned Austin Allen to construct an elegant apartment house at 320 Moffet Avenue. Each of the 110 apartments opened onto a private balcony; a roof garden overlooked the city. No kitchens were needed, as a world-class chef prepared meals on the fifth floor, in the formal dining room, and in the grillroom. Other amenities included a game room, a barbershop, and a manicure shop. (Courtesy of Rodney Blaukat.)

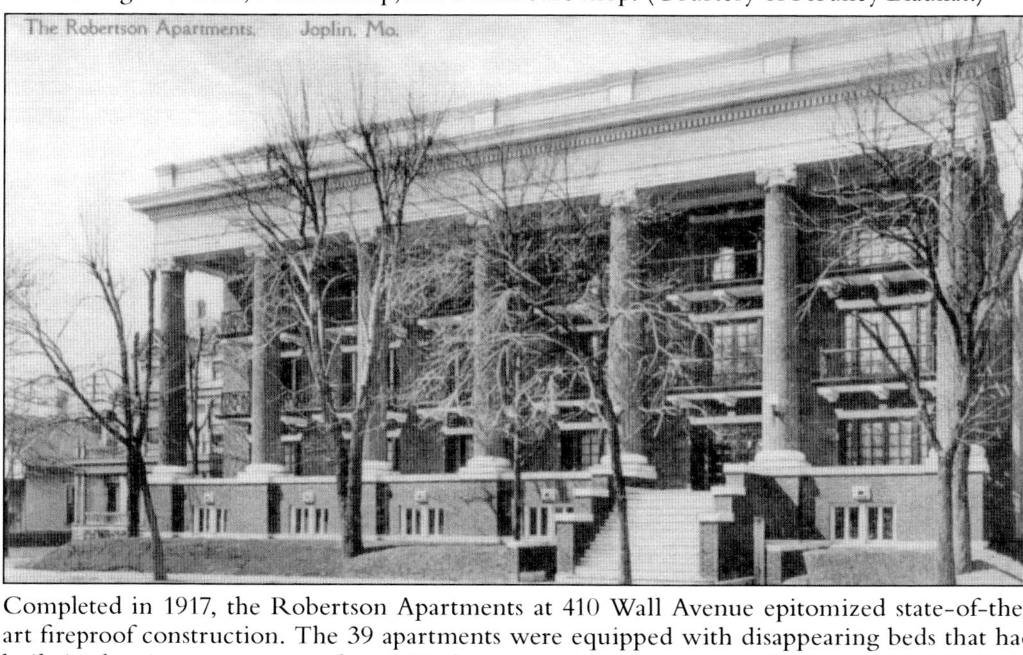

Completed in 1917, the Robertson Apartments at 410 Wall Avenue epitomized state-of-the-art fireproof construction. The 39 apartments were equipped with disappearing beds that had built-in dressing rooms over them. Kitchenettes with gas ranges, refrigerators, and built-in cabinets made for convenient meal preparation. A telephone system allowed tenants to make direct calls. The imposing appearance, splendid location, and admirable manner of planning the apartments attracted a long waiting list of prospective tenants. (Courtesy of Galen Augustus.)

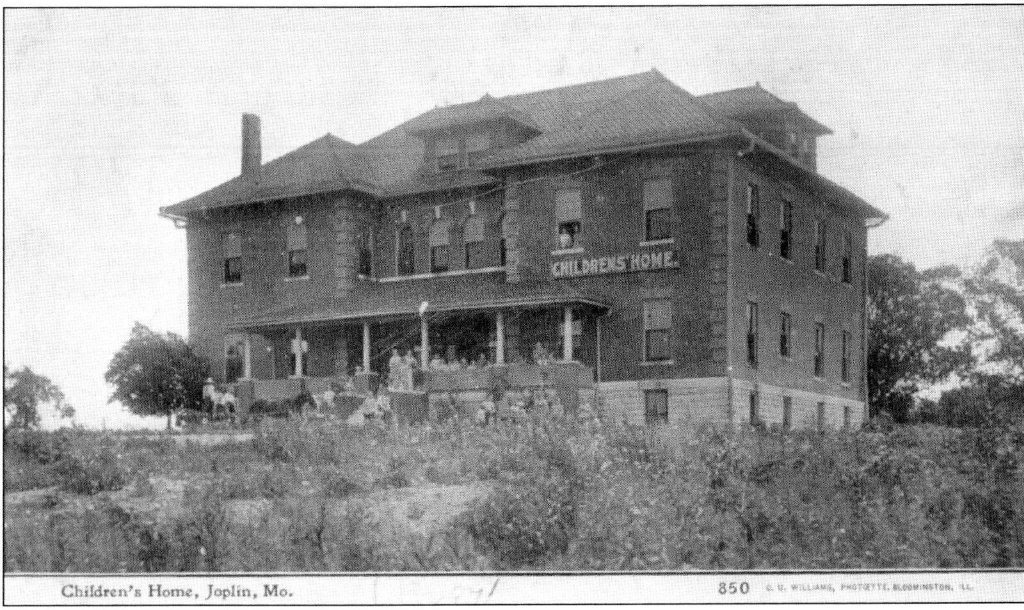

Joplin leaders faced a social crisis in the late 1800s. Due to mine-related deaths and high mortality rates, there were many orphaned children. In 1905, the architectural firm of Garstang and Rea designed the Joplin Children's Home at 301 Comingo. Nine years later, it became a city-run institution. The Boys' Club acquired the building in 1957, after the city closed the orphanage, which sheltered almost 5,000 children during its operation. (Courtesy of Rodney Blaukat.)

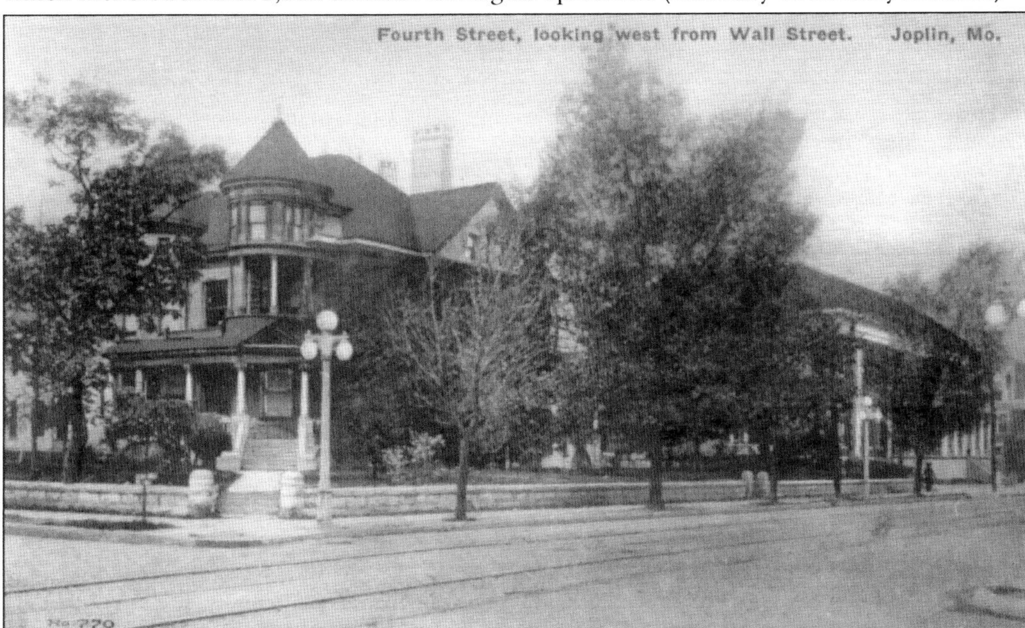

Born into a life of poverty in Ireland, Patrick Murphy's story was truly rags to riches. He commissioned August Michaelis to design this mansion at 404 Wall Avenue in 1898. Murphy died less than two years later. Although he chose to live near the business district, that proximity led to the demise of this spectacular house. His widow sold it in 1913; the owner demolished it for commercial development of the site. (Courtesy of Galen Augustus.)

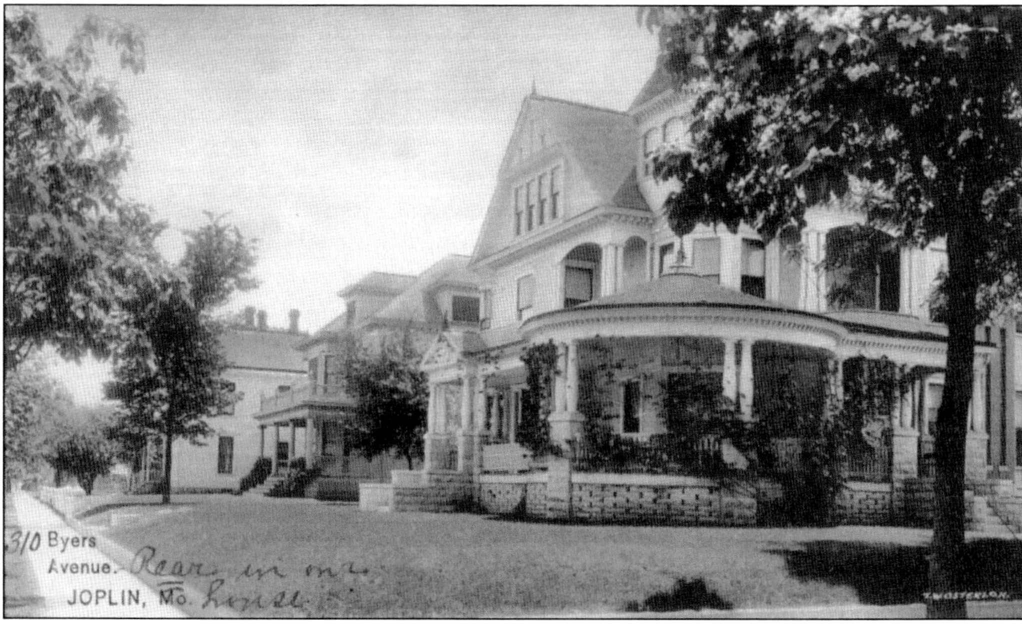

Pioneer hide and grain merchant John Wise made his fortune in mining. In 1898, he commissioned architect August Michaelis to design this fanciful abode at 504 Byers Avenue. Several years later, Mrs. Wise, who was active in civic concerns, convinced her husband that their home would make a good boardinghouse for girls who came to Joplin to work. The new YWCA could lodge up to 40 young women. (Courtesy of Post Memorial Art Reference Library.)

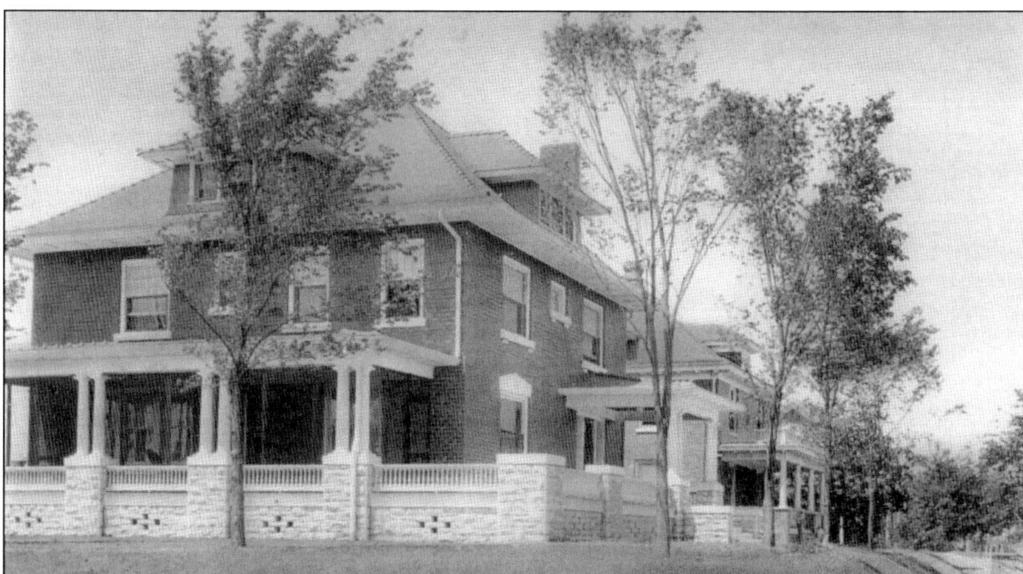

Alba Thomas moved with his family to Carthage, where his father operated a flour mill. In 1898, he established a Joplin firm, Thomas Fruit Company, with branches in Webb City and Carthage. It quickly became the largest commission brokerage in southwest Missouri, making Thomas a wealthy man. In 1908, he built this Prairie-style house at 404 North Byers Avenue in the newly developed North Heights addition. (Courtesy of Galen Augustus.)

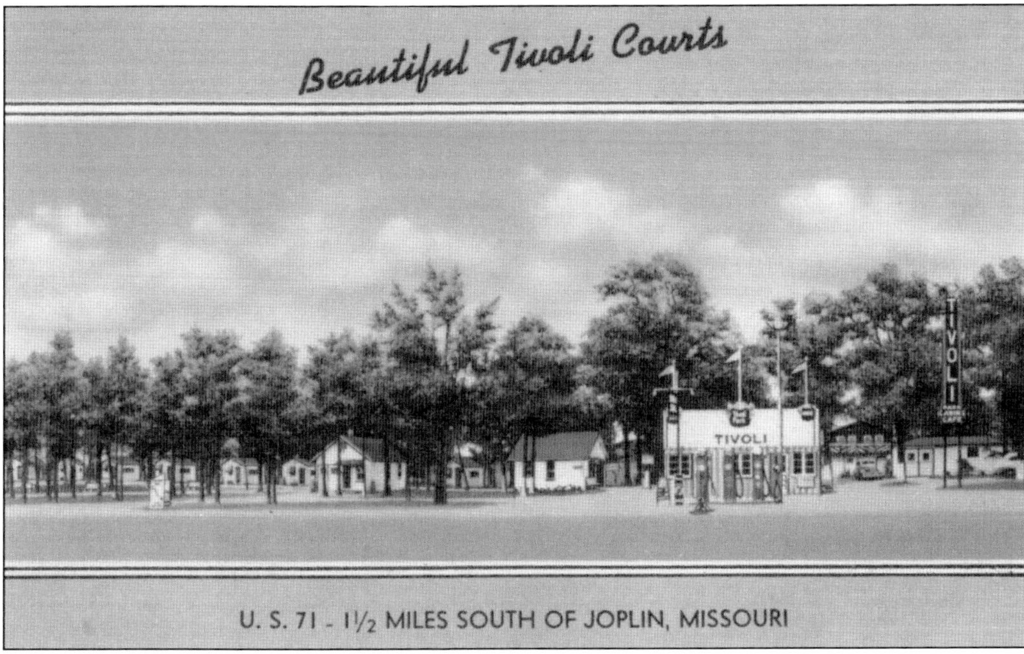

At the beginning of the 20th century, hotels were located downtown, and the railroad provided a steady stream of customers. As automobile ownership increased and more highways were built, motorists had difficulty finding convenient places to stay. As a result, a new hospitality industry arose to accommodate their needs. Tivoli Courts, located on US Highway 71 one and a half miles south of town, was one of Joplin's earliest motor courts. (Courtesy of the Joplin Public Library.)

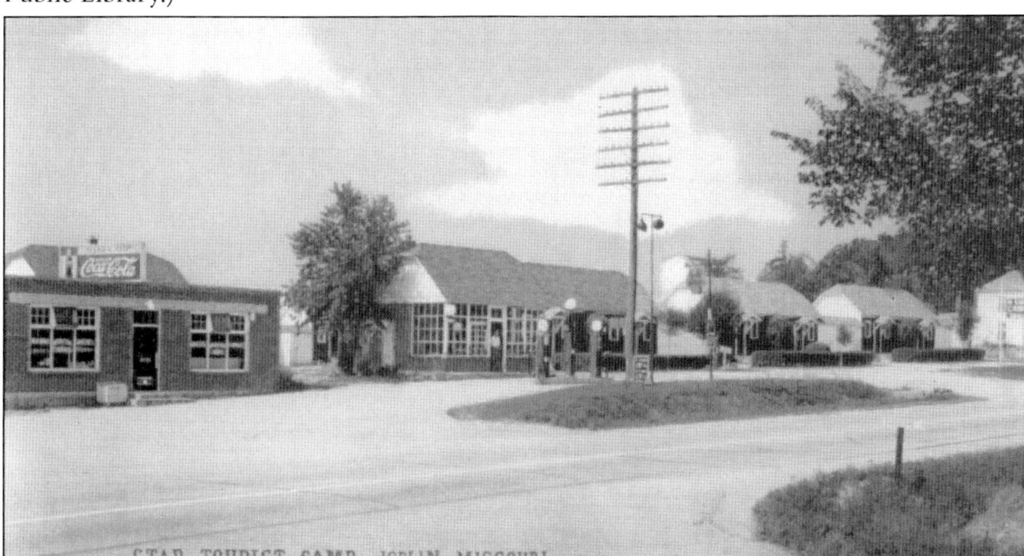

At first these automobile camps were merely clusters of tents or rustic shacks positioned around a common bathroom area. But as the tourism industry evolved, the facilities, also known as tourist, cabin, or motor courts, offered well-constructed picturesque cottages surrounded by landscaped grounds where children and family pets could play. The Star Tourist Camp at 702 Duquesne Road offered comfort as well as privacy. (Courtesy of Galen Augustus.)

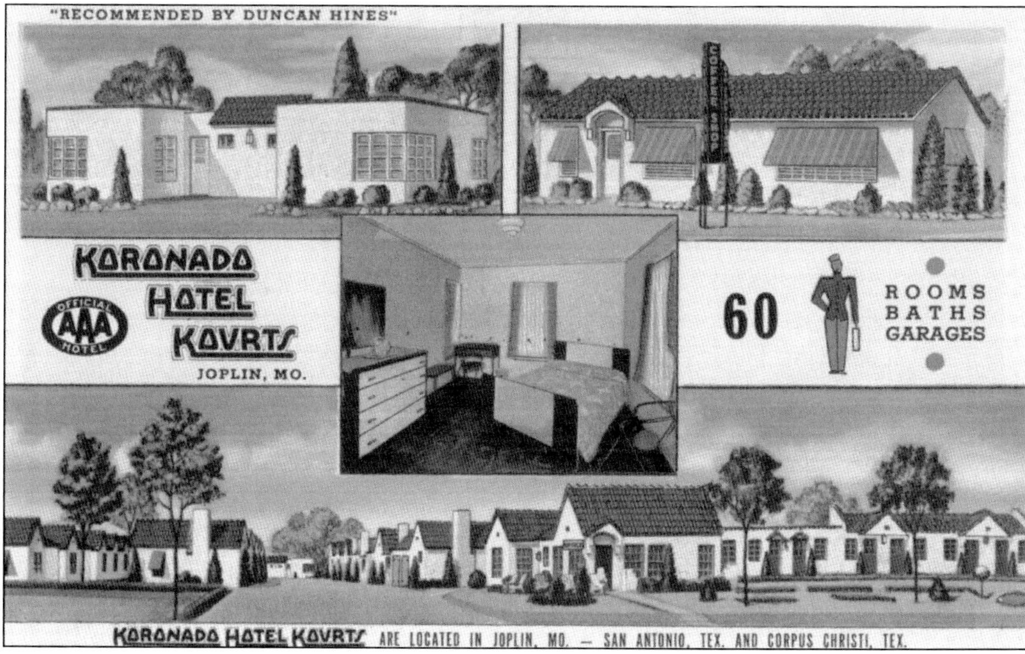

In 1928, the federal government began constructing a paved highway that meandered from Chicago to the Los Angeles basin. Paving of the Missouri stretch of this famous highway, US Route 66, was completed in 1932. It ran right through the heart of Joplin. Koronado Kourts at 1717 West Seventh Street claimed to have the finest and most up-to-date tourist cabins in the entire southwest on US 66. (Courtesy of Rodney Blaukat.)

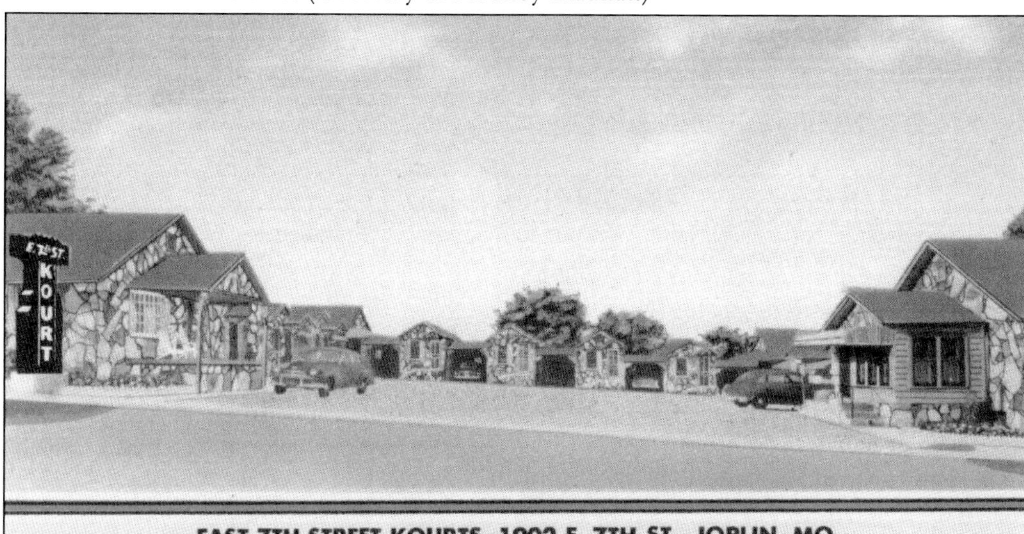

A 1933 Automobile Association of America (AAA) report proclaimed tourist cottages and camps as one of the few features of the American landscape that the Depression was causing to grow by leaps and bounds. Joplin's tourism industry confirmed those statistics. The 1931 Joplin city directory listed five tourist camps; six years later, there were 11. East Seventh Street Kourts at 1902 East Seventh Street featured 14 tourist cabins plus indoor parking. (Courtesy of Galen Augustus.)

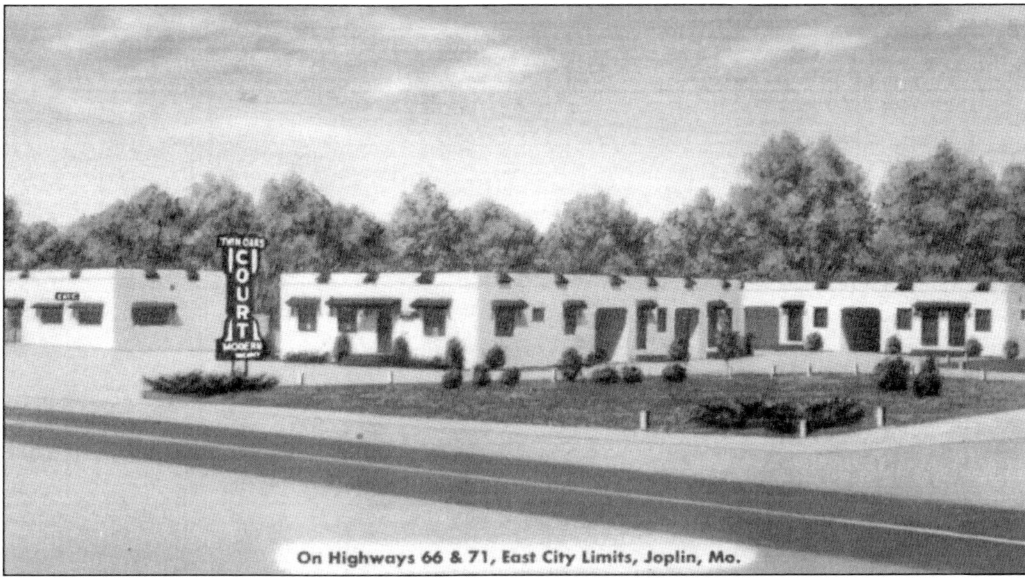

Competition was fierce among the popular cabin courts, and owners tried to attract guests with whimsical themes and fantasy architecture. Styles in the Joplin area ranged from Cape Cod cottages and rustic stone or log cabins to pseudo-adobe haciendas. Amenities included bathrooms, heat, radios, innerspring mattresses, and private garages. The hacienda-style Twin Oaks Court at 401 Range Line Road offered tasty food as well. (Courtesy of Galen Augustus.)

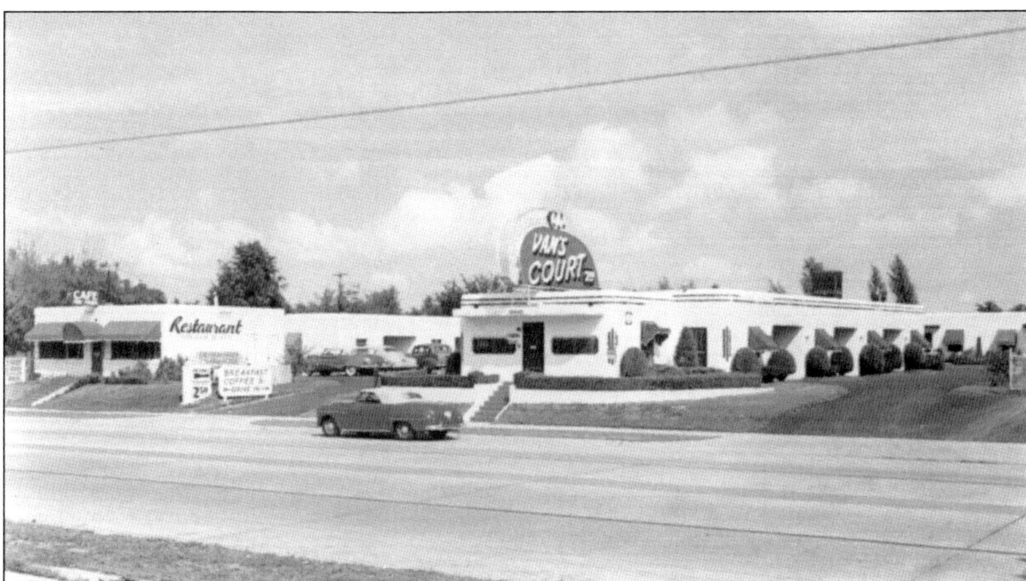

During the gas rationing of World War II and the subsequent curtailment of automobile production, business at the motor courts declined as well. They rebounded briefly following the war, although another major development in the evolution of temporary housing would take place within the next decade. Van's Court, later renamed the Villa Motel, was located at 2627 East Seventh Street and featured 17 units, garages, and a café. (Courtesy of Galen Augustus.)

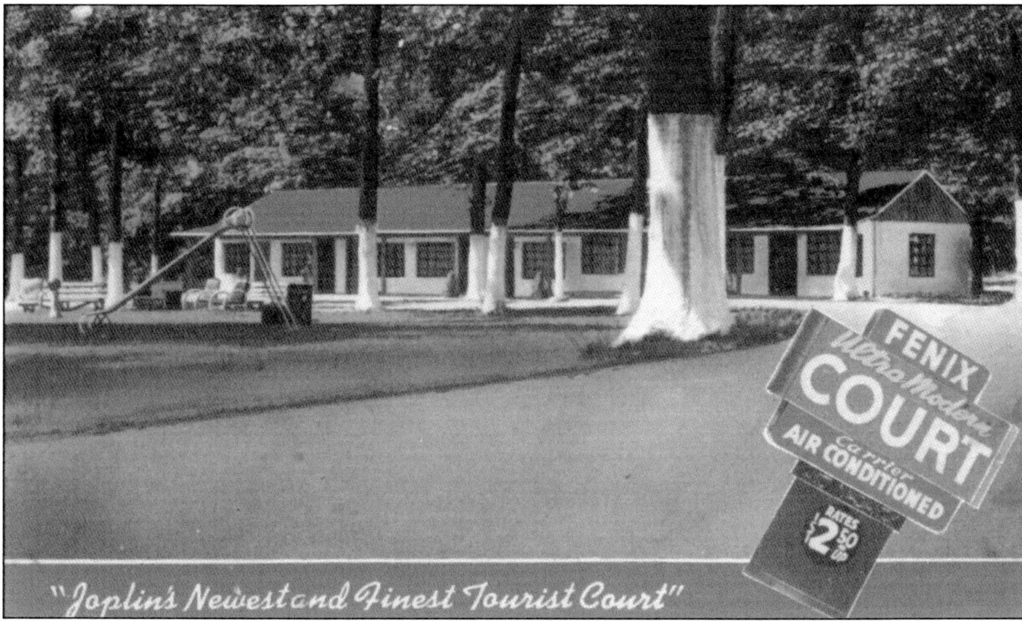

As cabin courts fell out of favor, a new form of lodging took their place. The sleek motel, with its series of rooms, was cheaper to construct and to maintain. Travelers found them clean, modern, and economical. Fenix Ultra Modern Court at the intersection of US Highways 66 and 71 had it all—air-conditioning, a playground, and 15 acres of shady lawn in the heart of the Ozark Playgrounds. (Courtesy of Galen Augustus.)

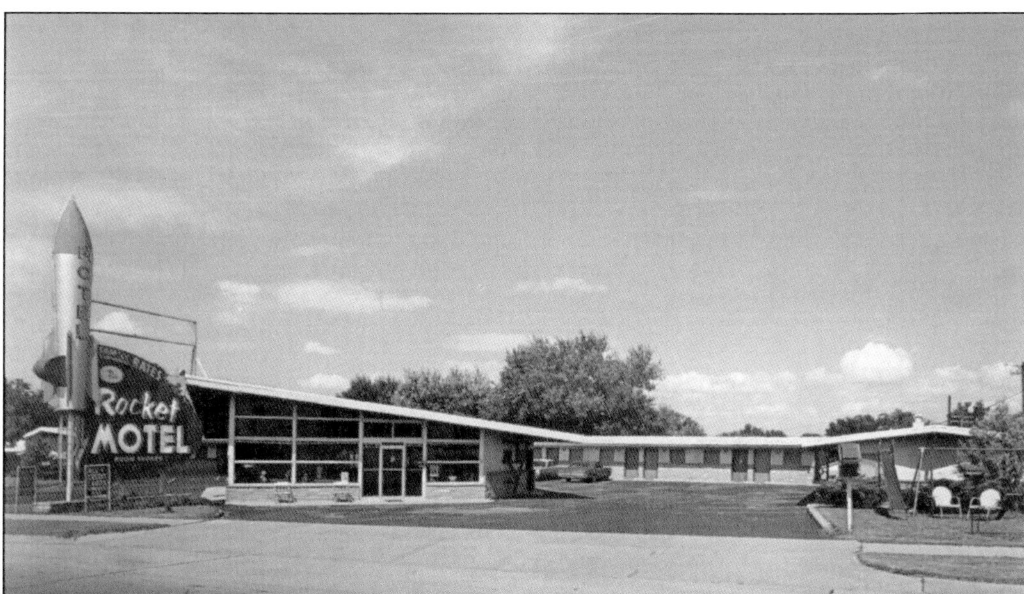

The proliferation of motels helped bring about the demise of Joplin's downtown hotels. Motels were located on the outskirts of town, on US Highways 66 and 71 and Missouri 43. Like their tourist court forerunners, motels used exterior ornamentation and gimmicks to attract guests. The Rocket Motel at 1001 Range Line Road, for example, fit right in with the 1960s fascination with space travel. (Courtesy of Galen Augustus.)

A major factor in the phenomenal growth of the motel industry was the 1956 Federal Aid Highway Act, which called for 42,000 miles of highways linking all parts of the United States. In 1958, after the Joplin stretch of Interstate 44 opened, more motels appeared in the city. Even New York Yankees super-star Mickey Mantle, who once played for the Joplin Miners baseball team, established a Holiday Inn at 2600 Range Line Road. Such corporation-established national chains eventually replaced the independently owned operations. Endorsements from travel-related organizations, such as AAA, and advertisers accelerated the trend as well. (Right, courtesy of the Joplin Public Library; below, courtesy of Galen Augustus.)

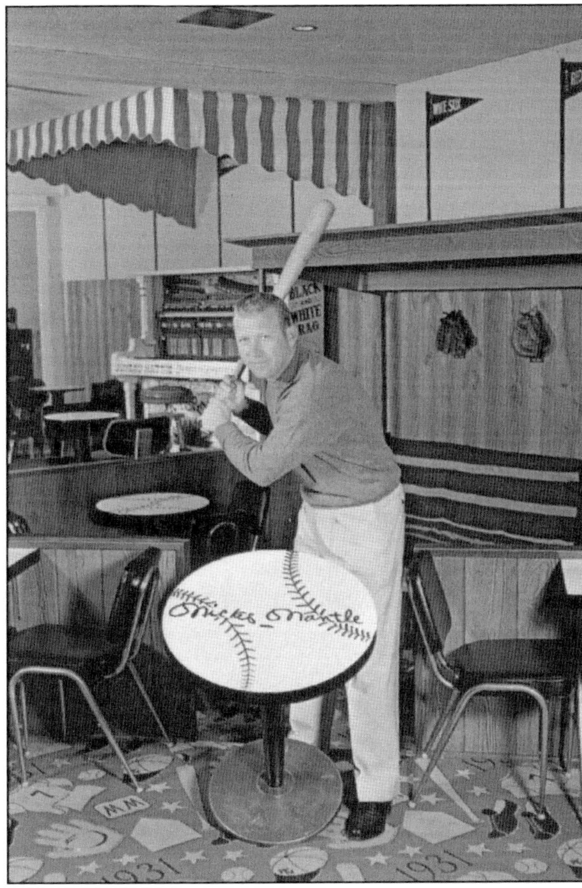

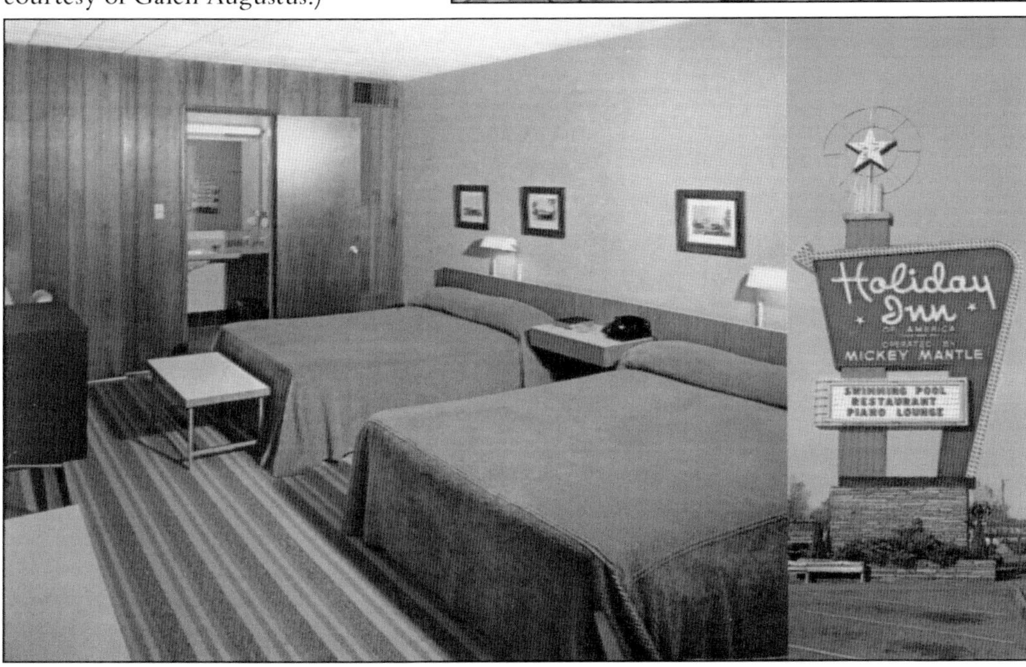

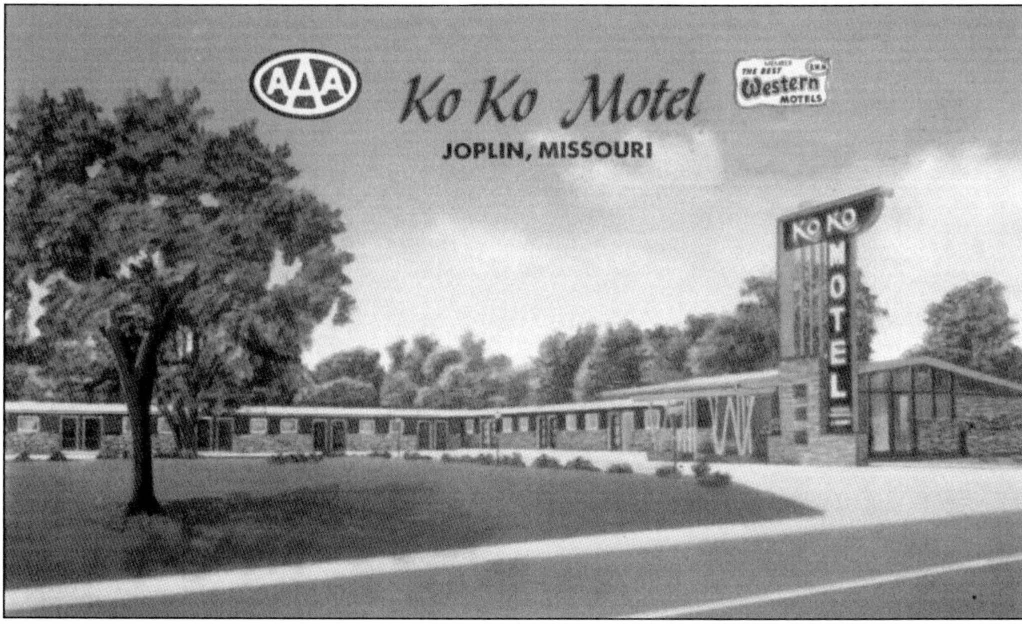

As more people traveled further distances, they demanded greater comfort, convenience, and security. Affluent travelers wanted standardized accommodations and brand names they could trust. They required amenities such as air-conditioning, television, swimming pools, restaurants, and so forth. The KoKo Motel at 3102 East Seventh Street provided all of these, plus family-friendly rates. (Courtesy of the Joplin Public Library.)

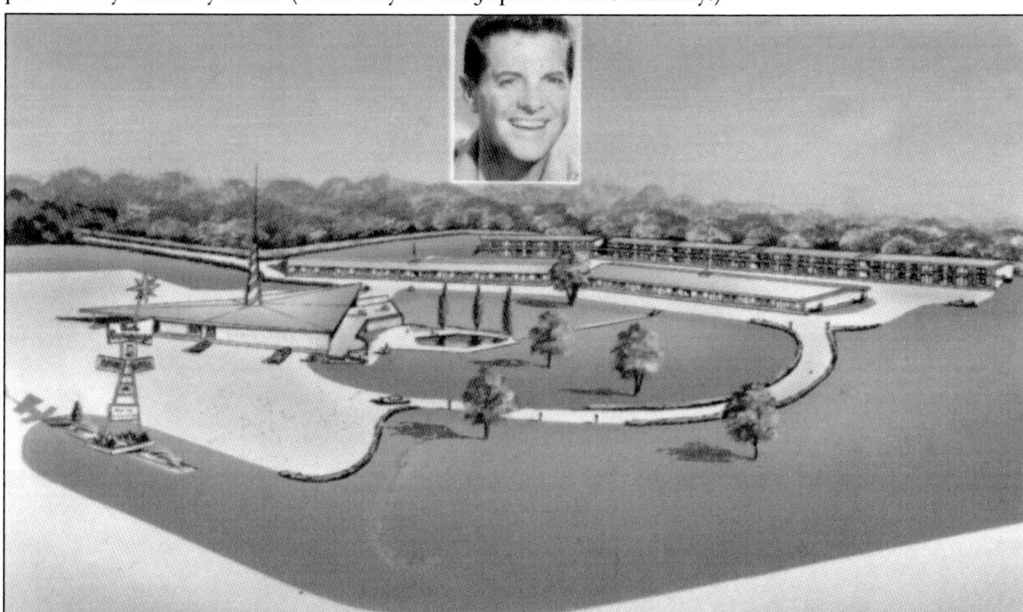

Joplin was mighty proud of native son Bob Cummings, the popular movie and television star. The Bob Cummings Motor Hotel, marketed as "Your Hollywood and Joplin host," was located at 3535 Range Line Road, near Interstate 44 on US Highways 71, 166, and 66. It boasted a restaurant, two cocktail lounges, nightly supper club entertainment, convention facilities for 500 people, and a large swimming pool. (Courtesy of the Joplin Public Library.)

Eight

Readin', Writin', and 'Rithmetic

The first school in the portion of Jasper County that would eventually become Joplin was the Franklin School, a split-log schoolhouse near Castle Rock built in the 1840s. Children from agricultural communities in the region attended school there. To the west, there was another school at the Peace Church community. Originally, these rural schools taught only the three R's. Perhaps a fourth R should be added, as teachers, who were usually men, freely used the rod. In 1873, after the mining boom put Joplin on the map, the East Joplin School was opened, thanks to the efforts of Joplin founder John C. Cox. By the end of the decade, Joplin had three school districts—East Joplin, West Joplin, and Lone Elm—14 teachers, and five school buildings. Times were so bad economically that faculty and students held fundraisers to buy coal to heat the schools. After the three districts consolidated in 1889, Joplin's school system grew into one of the best in the state. In 1908, when segregated schools were the norm, Joplin built Lincoln School for its black students; children from Carthage and other communities were bused to Lincoln as well. In the mid-20th century, the Joplin School District set the standard for smooth desegregation of formerly segregated schools. In 1954, the US Supreme Court declared as unconstitutional all state laws that established separate public schools based upon race. Fifteen days after the decision was made, the Joplin School Board ordered the immediate integration of Joplin Junior College. In June 1955, the board officially integrated the public schools. In addition to its excellent school system, Joplin has also been home to private schools, a medical college, Christian colleges, and Missouri Southern State University.

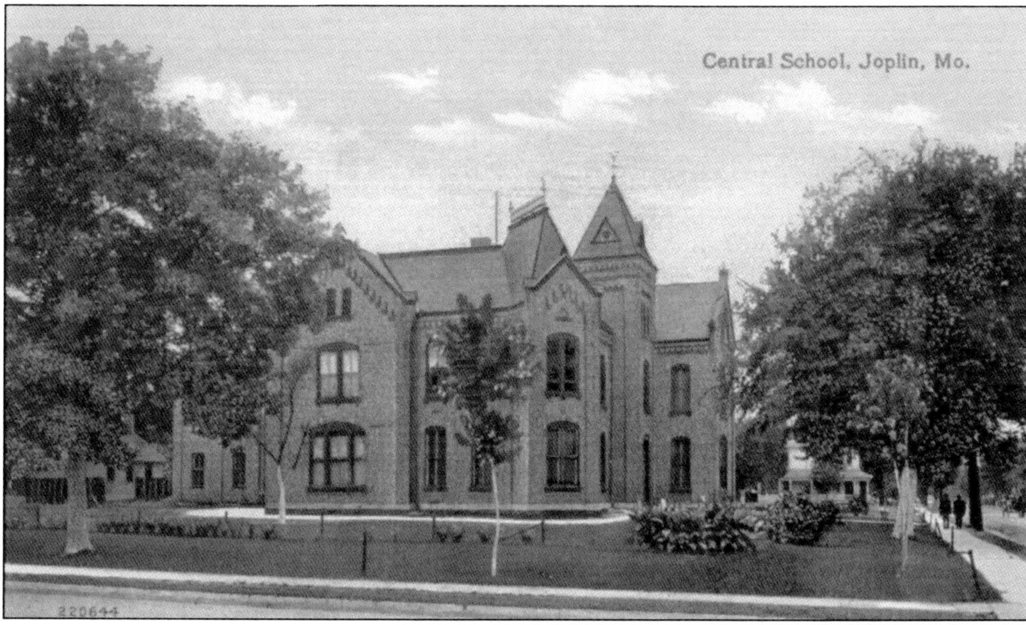

The Gothic-style Central School at 210 West Eighth Street was once the pride of the city. Joplin's first senior class of 13 students graduated from Central on May 18, 1888. In those days, schoolhouses did not have indoor plumbing. Wood-burning stoves provided heat for the drafty, high-ceilinged classrooms. In 1897, the high school moved to 424 West Fourth Street. Central was remodeled as an elementary school before being demolished in 1924. (Courtesy of Rodney Blaukat.)

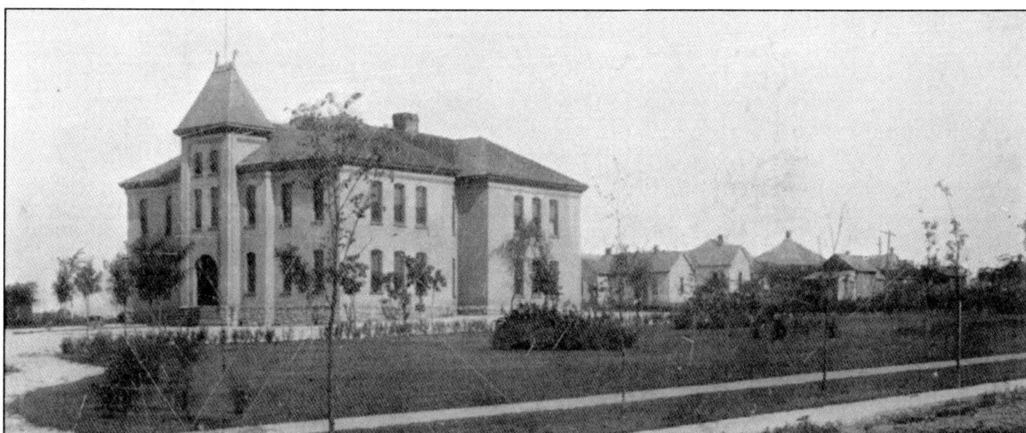

Columbia School served the children of North Heights, the area north of A Street. Built in 1892, it was named to celebrate the 400th anniversary of Christopher Columbus's historic voyage. Heated with wood stoves, the schoolhouse had only daylight for lighting. After several additions and attempts to update the Victorian-era school, it was torn down in 1927; a new Columbia School was erected on the same site. (Courtesy of Rodney Blaukat.)

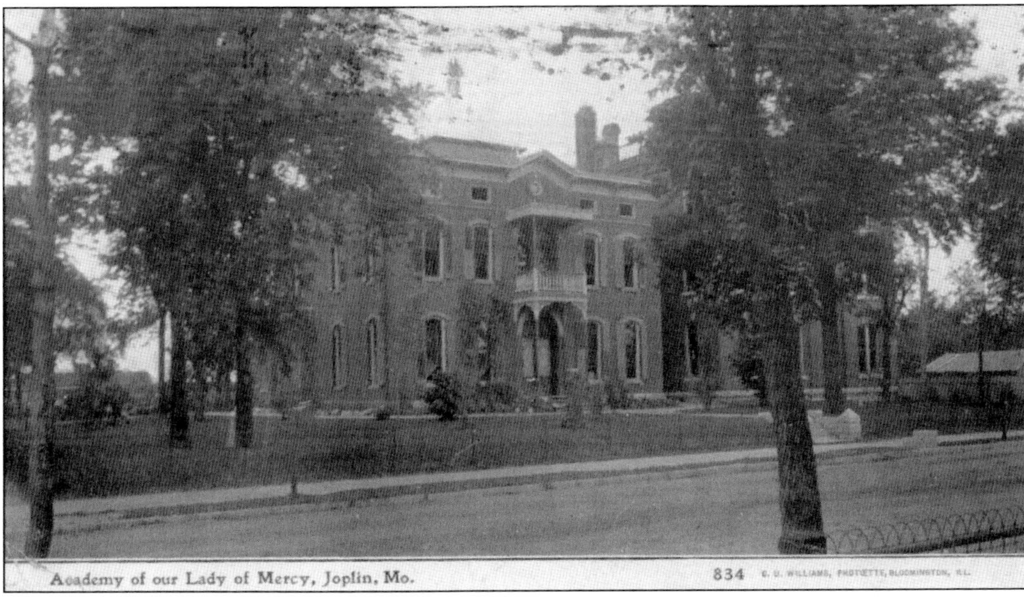

Edward Zelleken built his Italianate-style mansion at 406 West Ninth Street in 1882. Three years later, he sold it to the plucky Sisters of Mercy, who came to civilize the heathen mining town. They established an academy, the forerunner of the St. Peter's Schools. After McAuley High School was built in 1948, the old academy functioned as a convent and girls' boardinghouse until its demolition in 1985. (Courtesy of Rodney Blaukat.)

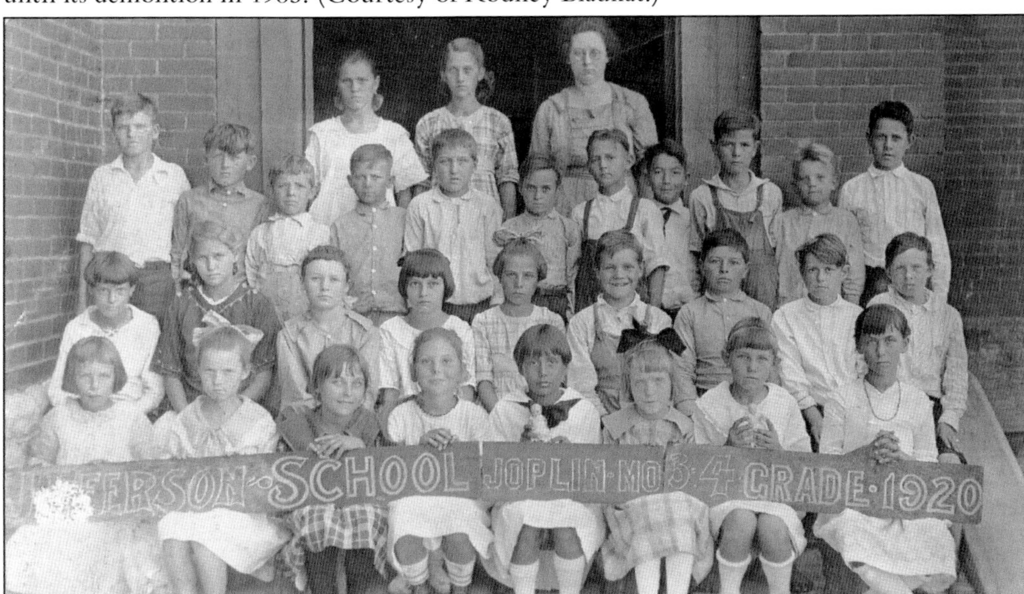

These third- and fourth-grade students attended Jefferson School at 130 McKinley Avenue. Originally known as Northwestern School, it served the mining community of Chitwood. A 1920 Joplin School District report outlined the curriculum, which included reading, spelling, composition, literature, numbers, geography, history, writing, drawing, music, elementary science, and manual training. Daily calisthenics were required, because, according to the report, "sluggish movements are not healthful and lead to bad habits." (Courtesy of Rodney Blaukat.)

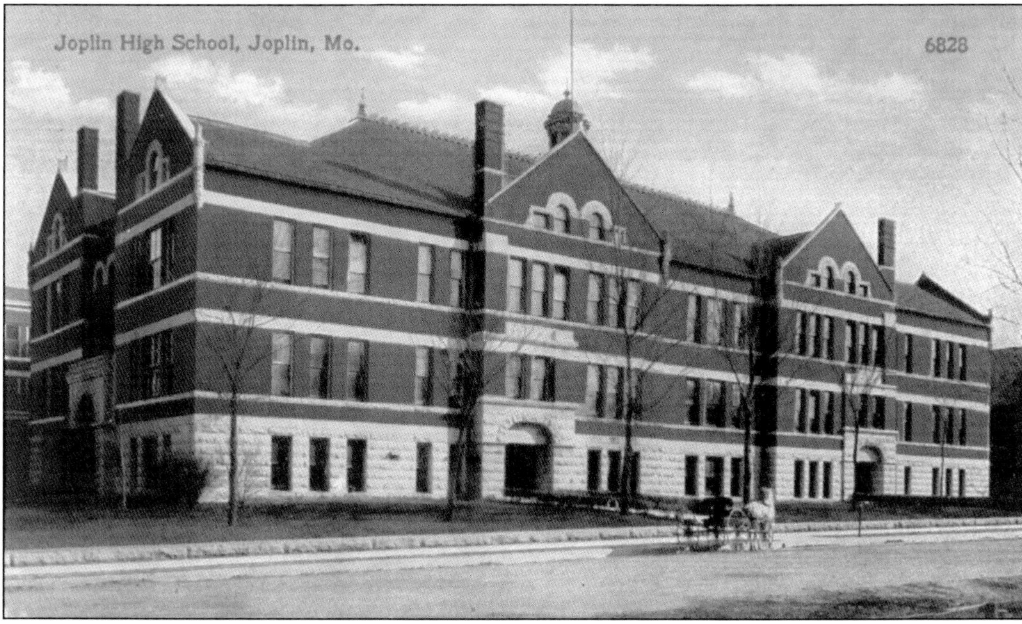

In 1896, the Joplin school district constructed a new high school designed by architect August Michaelis at 424 West Fourth Street. Phenomenal growth necessitated a sizeable addition in 1907 and a move into larger quarters at 310 West Eighth Street in 1918, leaving the old building to serve as Joplin Junior High. From 1937 until 1958, Joplin Junior College occupied the landmark, which was demolished in 1962. (Courtesy of Galen Augustus.)

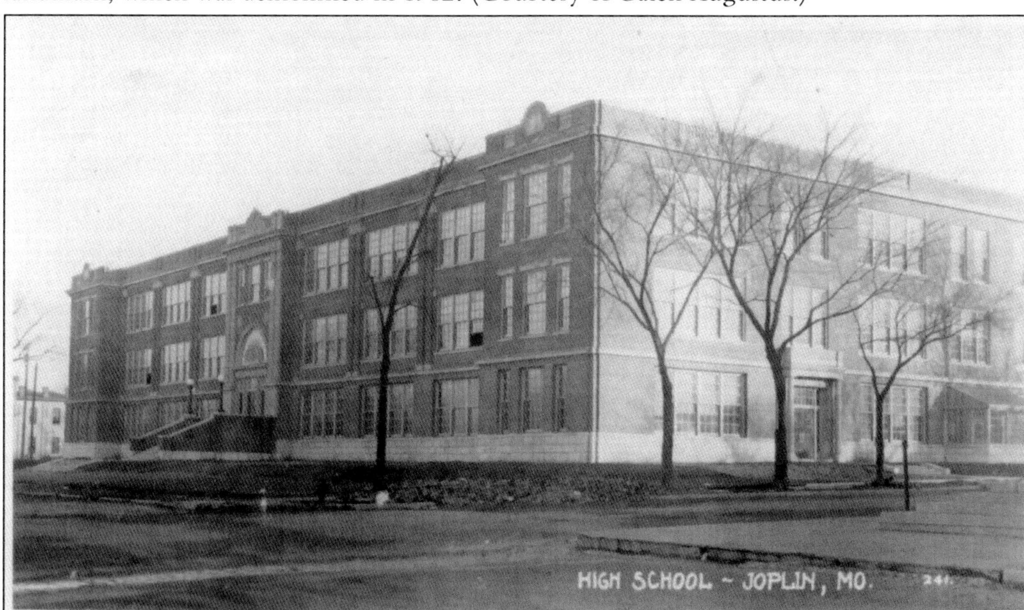

In 1918, Joplin High School at 310 West Eighth Street opened its doors. It included, for the first time, a cafeteria and innovations such as a built-in vacuum cleaning system, well-equipped gymnasiums, and scientific laboratories. By 1926, the facility could no longer accommodate its student body, which far surpassed the 1,200 students for which it was designed. Disappointed, 500 ninth-graders returned to the old building on Byers Avenue. (Courtesy of Galen Augustus.)

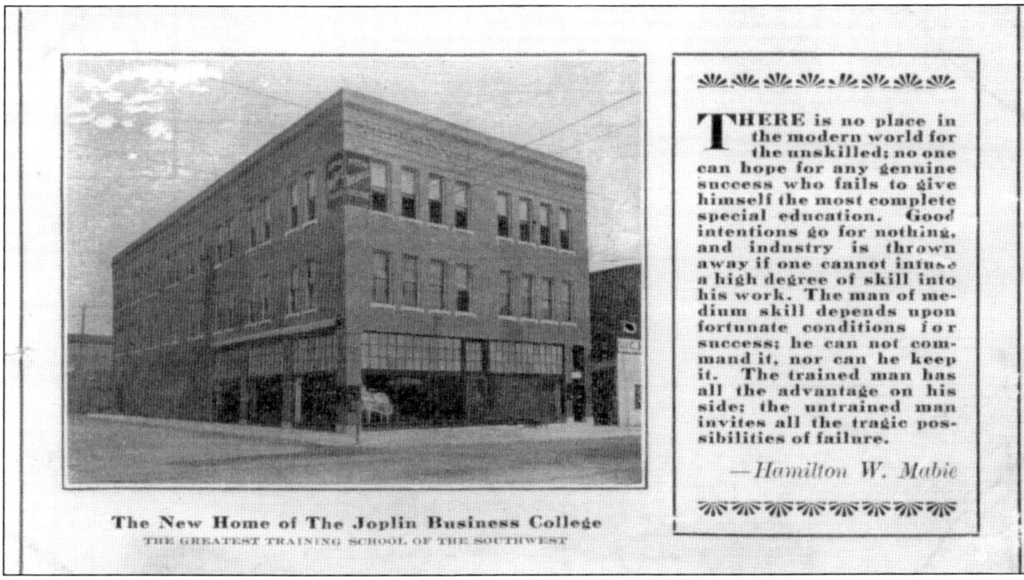

Established in 1891, Joplin Business College offered instruction in shorthand, bookkeeping, and business and commercial education. At the time of this 1908 postcard, the school had moved into the Grover Building at 532 Joplin Avenue. In 1913, the college began training telegraph operators as well. The institution continued to grow and evolve throughout the 20th century, celebrating its 100th birthday in 1991, the same year that it became Vatterot College. (Courtesy of Galen Augustus.)

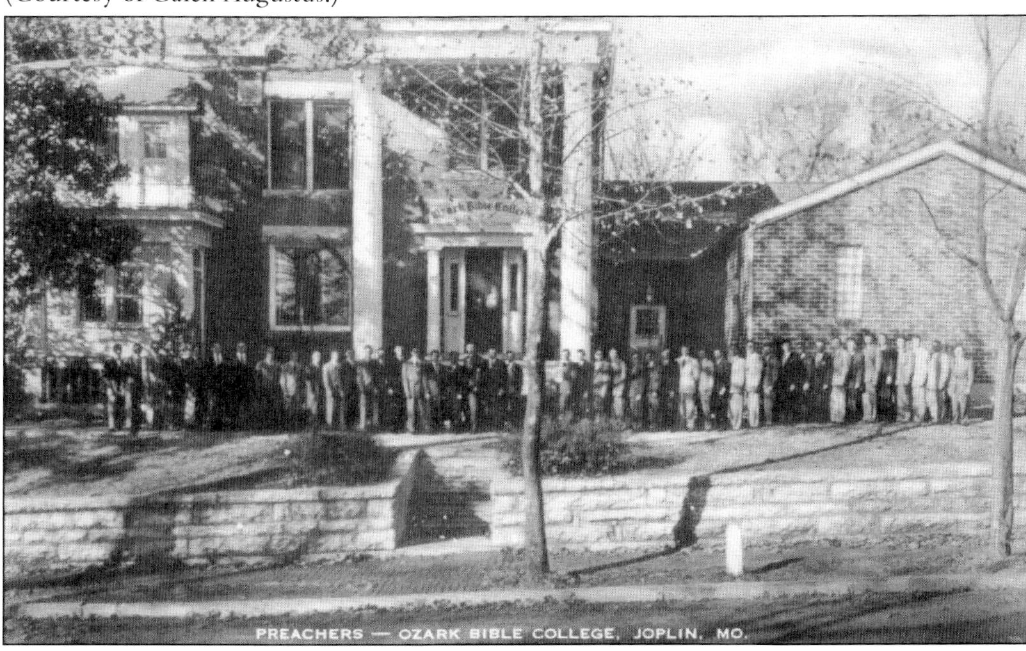

In 1938, Ozark Bible College was established in St. Joe, Arkansas, to train preachers, missionaries, and church workers. In 1944, the college moved to Joplin, settling into the Alonzo Cragin mansion at 516 North Wall Avenue. A 1948 addition to the north provided a dining room, a chapel, and classrooms. The college, now named Ozark Christian, relocated to a new 40-acre campus on north Main Street in 1963. (Courtesy of the Joplin Public Library.)

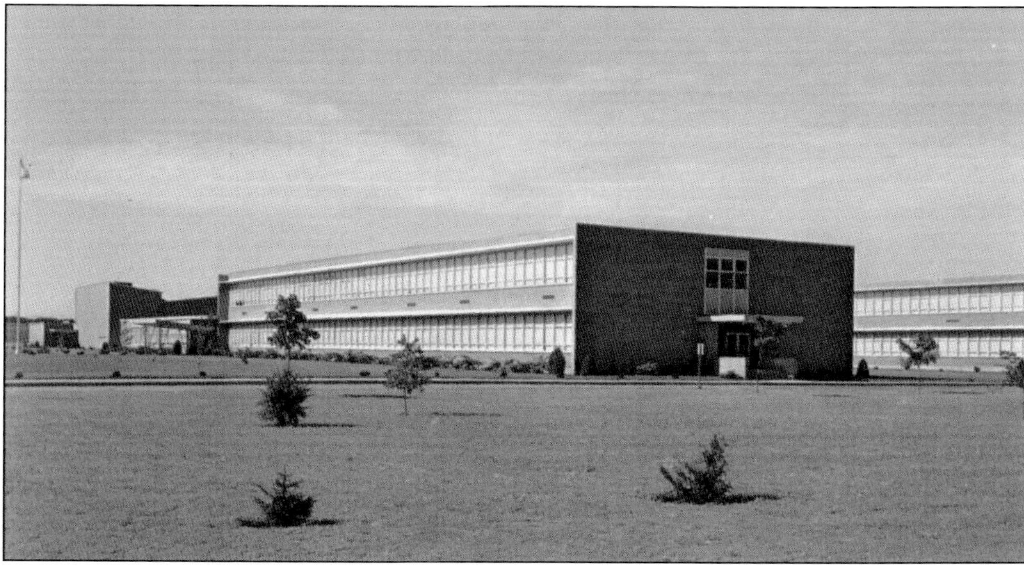

In 1956, Joplin High School occupied a new 32-acre campus at 2104 Indiana Avenue. It included a sprawling building, practice football fields, tennis courts, a baseball field, and a military drill field. A staggering change occurred in 1969 with the separation into two high schools—Parkwood at the location shown here and Memorial at 310 West Eighth Street. In 1985, the schools combined again under the name Joplin High School. (Courtesy of Galen Augustus.)

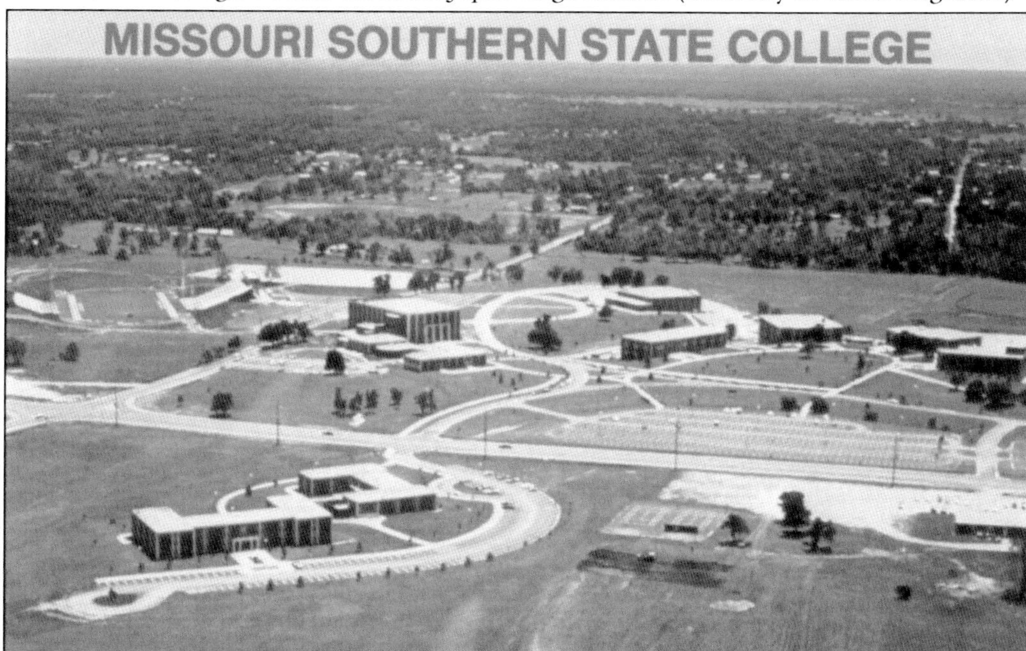

This site was once the country estate of Lucius Buchanan. Frank Wallower purchased it in 1939 and named it Mission Hills. Needing room to grow, Joplin Junior College purchased Mission Hills in 1964. The institution became Missouri Southern College in 1965, expanding to a four-year college in 1969. The Board of Regents changed its name to Missouri Southern State College in 1972, then to Missouri Southern State University in 2003. (Courtesy of Galen Augustus.)

Nine

The Call of Nature

In his 1912 opus *A History of Jasper County Missouri and its People*, author Joel T. Livingston waxed eloquent about the beauty of the region. "Here, too, nature is seen in all of its grandeur. The broad prairie with its wealth of fragrant flowers and sweet scented grasses; the hundreds of little friends in feather and fur; the forest with its monarch oak and its stately pine; the pure air and the clear waters." Not long after Joplin was founded, its citizens were attracted to the natural wonders nearby. In 1876, Charles Schifferdecker established a pleasure resort on Turkey Creek a quarter-mile east of Castle Rock. Other natural phenomena in the area drew large crowds—Castle Rock, Shoal Creek, Grand Falls, and Crystal Cave, to name a few. After the electric streetcar afforded easier travel, large amusement parks like Lakeside Park and Schifferdecker Electric Park were built outside of town. Joplin established its park system in 1897, when Thomas Cunningham donated seven acres of land to be designated as the city's first public park. The city added Mineral Park and McClelland Park next, followed by Spring Park and Schifferdecker Park. Other parks added later were Ewert, Landreth, Leonard, Roanoke, McIndoe, and Wildcat, plus numerous neighborhood playgrounds. Nature-lovers also sought out places like Saginaw Resort, Redings Mill Resort, and the Isaak Walton League. Mount Hope Cemetery, although not a park, is included in this chapter because it was designed by one of the country's leading landscape architects, Sid Hare.

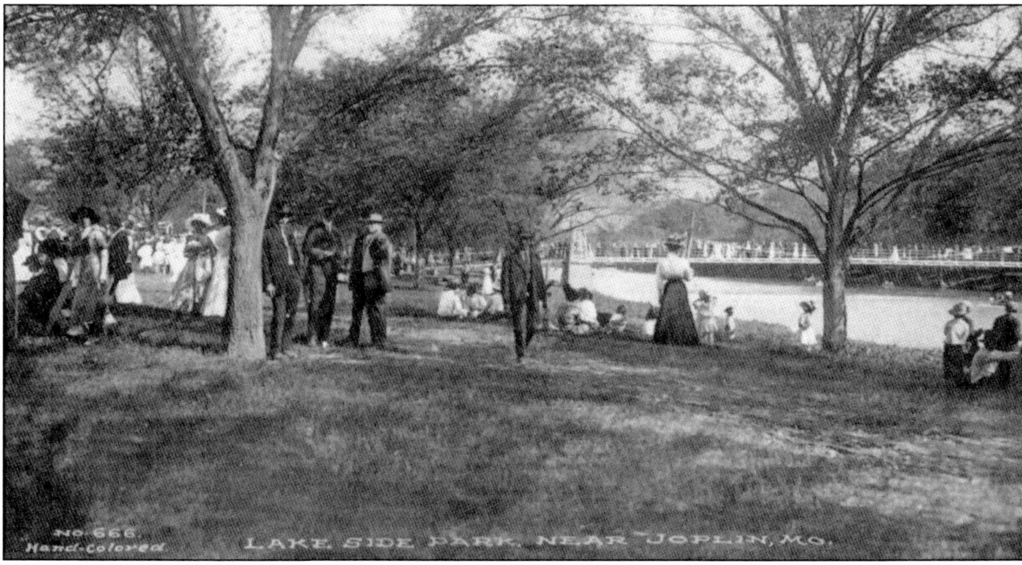

The trolley park, a unique brand of amusement parks, hit the US in the 1890s. Power companies built pleasure resorts out in the country, usually near bodies of water. Lakeside Park, located between Joplin and Carthage, opened in 1895. Patrons paid no entrance fee at the park, just the round-trip trolley fare. Each summer, Lakeside Park opened with great fanfare, announcing exciting new attractions. (Courtesy of Rodney Blaukat.)

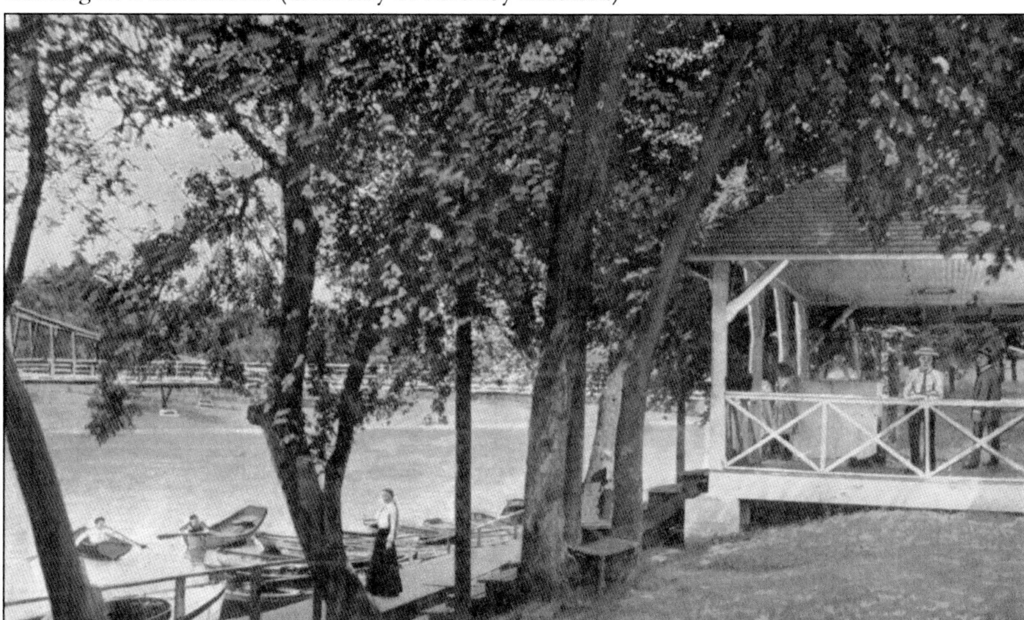

Steam calliopes played loudly throughout the day, and ragtime musicians entertained at the pavilion. During the summer, Lakeside offered daily concerts by bands and soloists. There were also shooting galleries, a huge merry-go-round, pony rides, novelty stands, and racks of canes and Kewpie dolls. At the penny arcade, patrons could plug their pennies into over 50 machines to play games, have their fortunes told, watch motion pictures, and more. (Courtesy of Galen Augustus.)

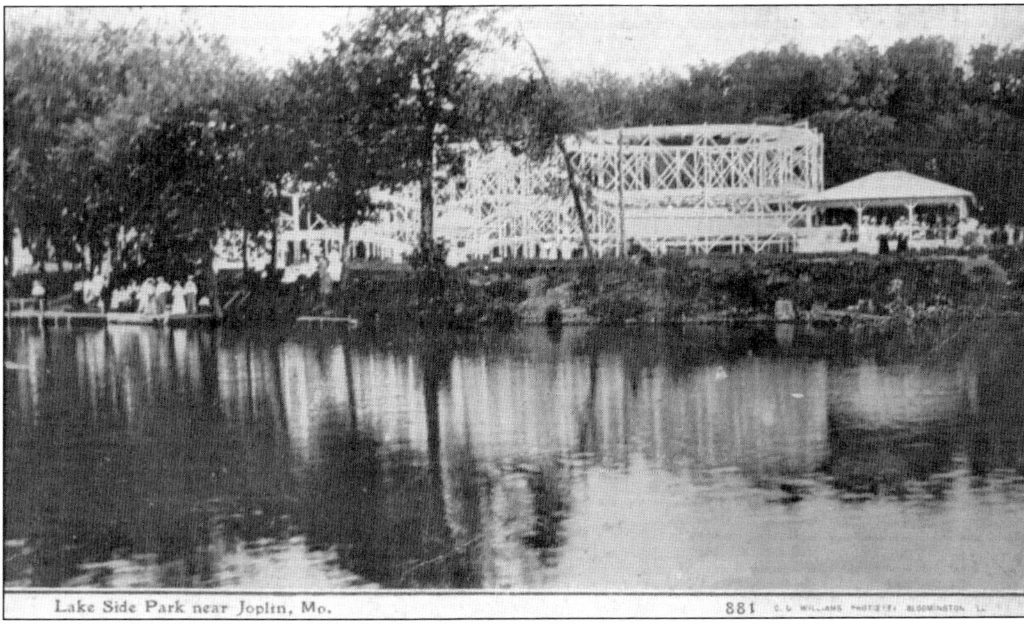

Lakeside's leading feature, the Double Figure Eight, replicated one at the 1904 St. Louis World's Fair. Unbelievable crowds crammed into Lakeside on holidays, especially on the Fourth of July, when an estimated 40,000 to 50,000 people arrived. The Southwest Missouri Electric Railway Company ran as many as 150 trolley cars to keep up with the demand. (Courtesy of Galen Augustus.)

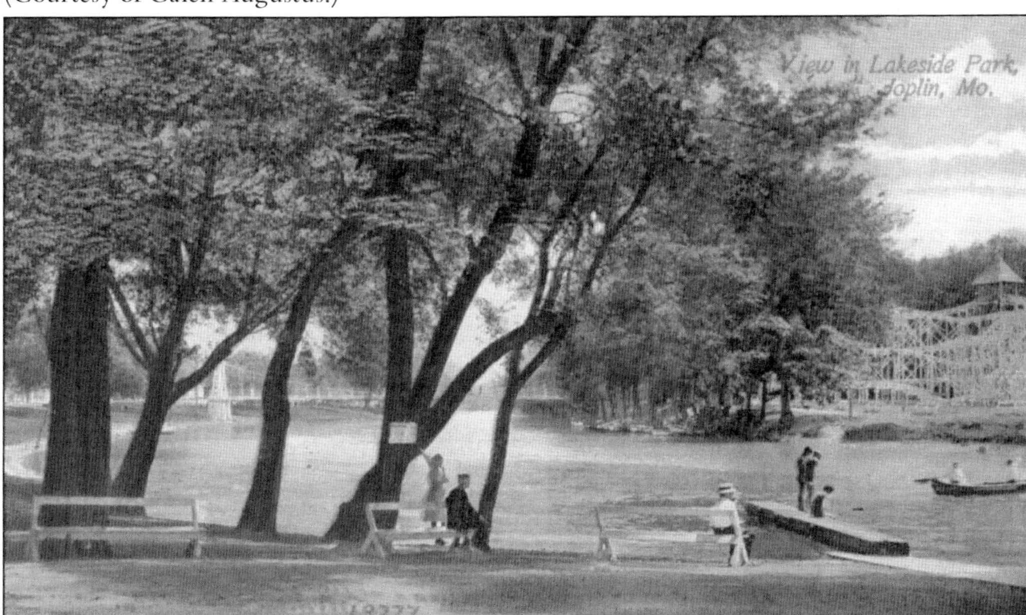

Lakeside Park spread on either side of a lake formed by damming Center Creek. Folks could rent boats for 25¢ per hour to fish or explore the lake. Boaters encountered such attractions as Three Sister Island, Lover's Retreat, Riffles, Great Dead Wood Pond, Rock Ford, and Mill Dam along the 10-mile watercourse. A steam yacht offered cruises for larger groups. (Courtesy of Rodney Blaukat.)

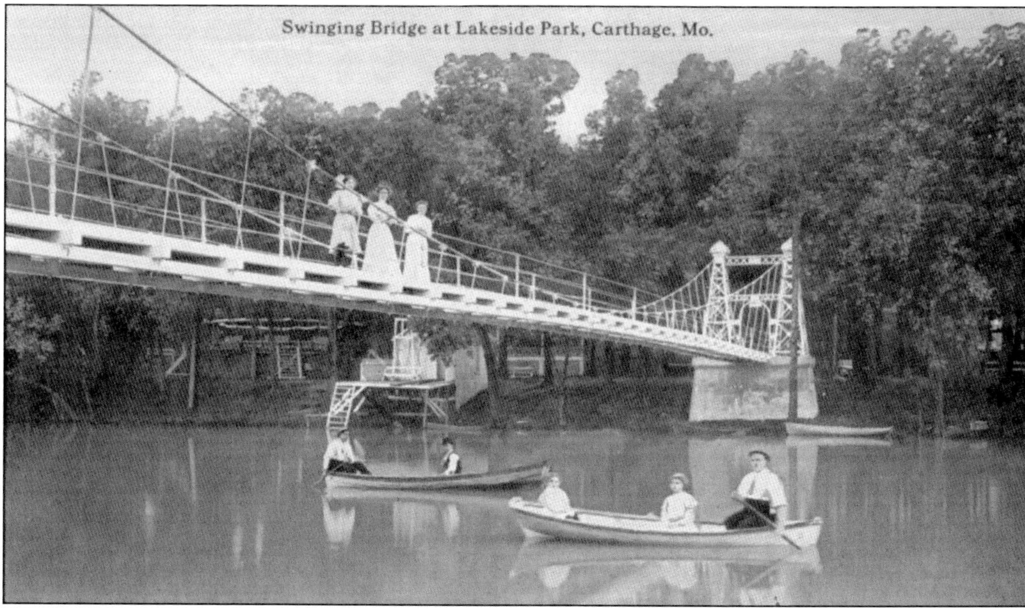

One of the most notable features of Lakeside Park was the Swinging Bridge, built in the spring of 1909. It provided access to an additional 15 acres where the baseball field and children's playground were located. The bridge provided a scenic backdrop for wedding parties, dances, and outdoor concerts, as well as a vantage point for enjoying the lake. (Courtesy of Galen Augustus.)

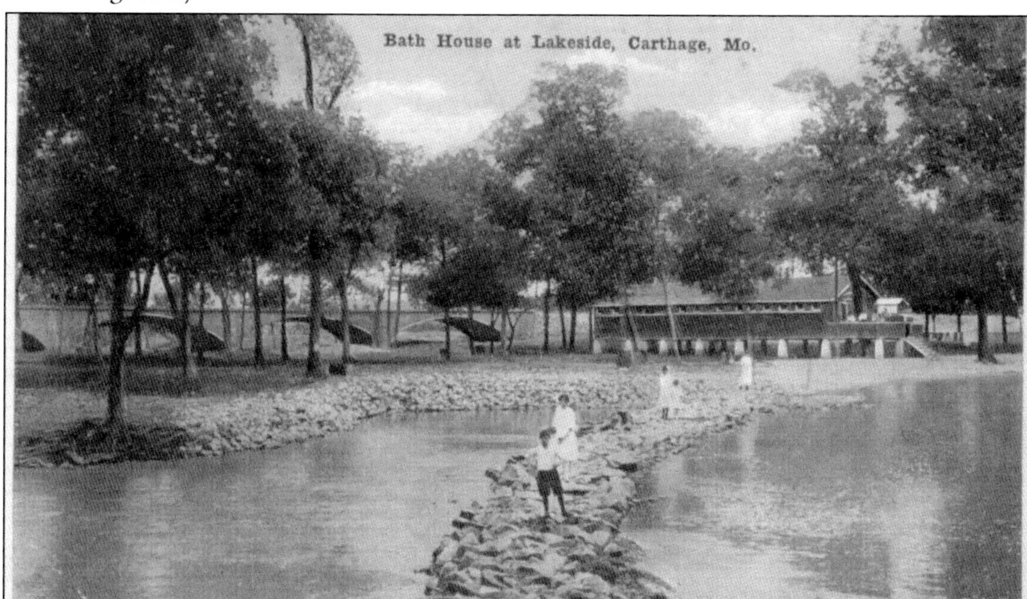

The bathing area included a bathhouse, beach, wading pool, and swimming hole. Swings, springboards, and toboggan slides delighted the children. Patrons could rent bathing attire. Lakeside's glory days began winding down after World War I. Since the park was built for trolley access, it was difficult to get there by automobile. The abandoned buildings eventually succumbed to decay and fire; the lake vanished with the removal of the dam. (Courtesy of Galen Augustus.)

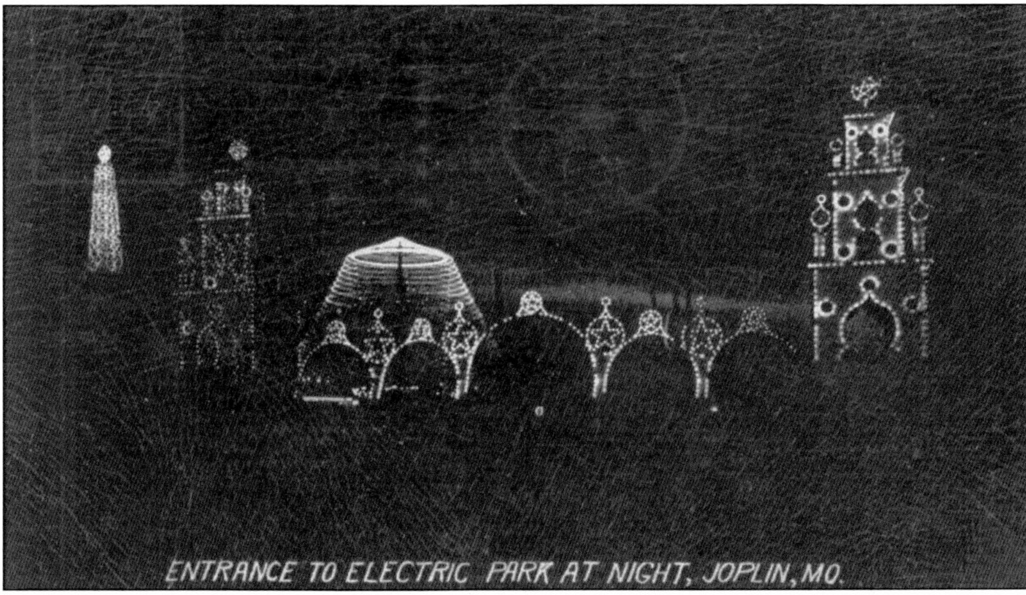

Opened in 1909, the Schifferdecker Electric Park, so named because of its 40,000 incandescent bulbs, was designed in the Moorish architectural style. The park featured rides, sideshows, musical performances, concessions, and souvenir stands. Other amenities included a dance hall, a skating rink, and a boating pond. The German Village beer garden paid tribute to the park's namesake Charles Schifferdecker, a German native who began his career in the brewing trade. (Courtesy of Galen Augustus.)

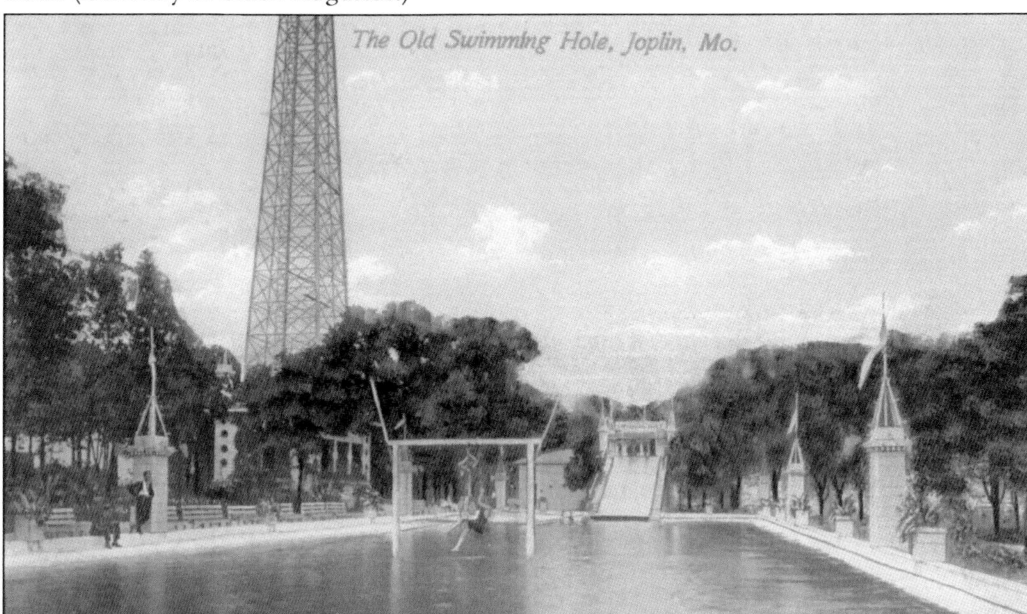

Schifferdecker Pool was Joplin's first public swimming pool. It featured a fancifully designed slide on one end and a beautiful colonnade on the other. Minarets decorated the top of the large slide as well as other structures around it. In the background loomed the 125-foot tower of lights. The pool was designed as a lagoon, with gently sloping sides leading into the water. (Courtesy of Rodney Blaukat.)

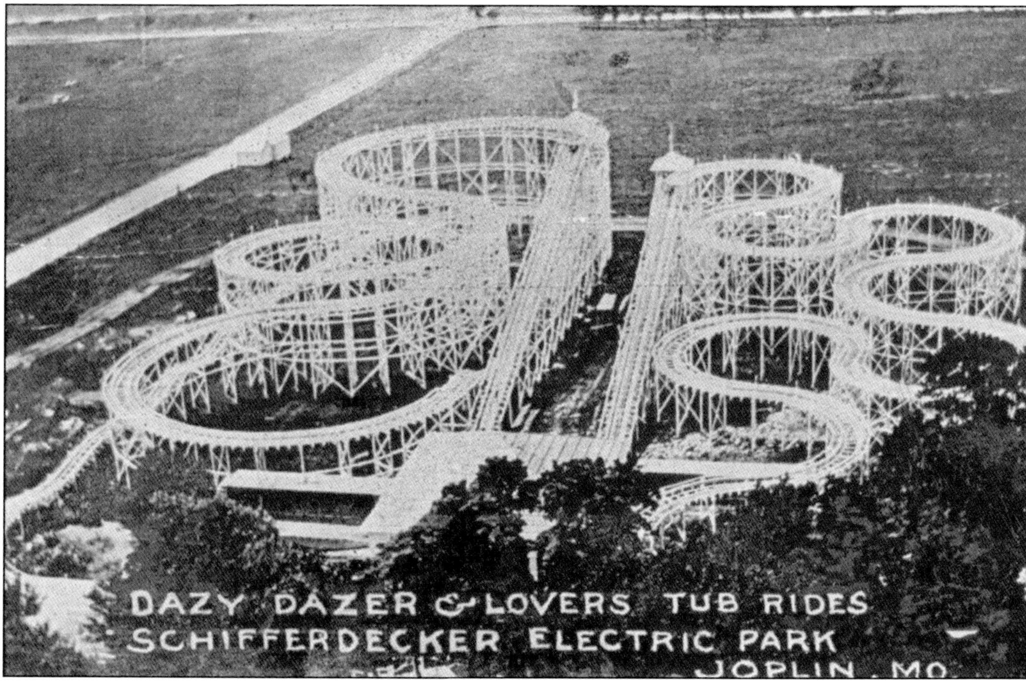

La Marcus Thompson built the world's first roller coaster in 1890; the wood contraption caught on all over the world. Schifferdecker Park offered the popular Dazy Dazer and Lover's Tub rides, both of which were constructed of wood and powered by electricity. Joplin's Figure-Eight roller coaster was demolished in March 1916, after it was deemed a menace to safety. Flowerbeds and tennis courts replaced the once-spectacular rides. (Courtesy of Rodney Blaukat.)

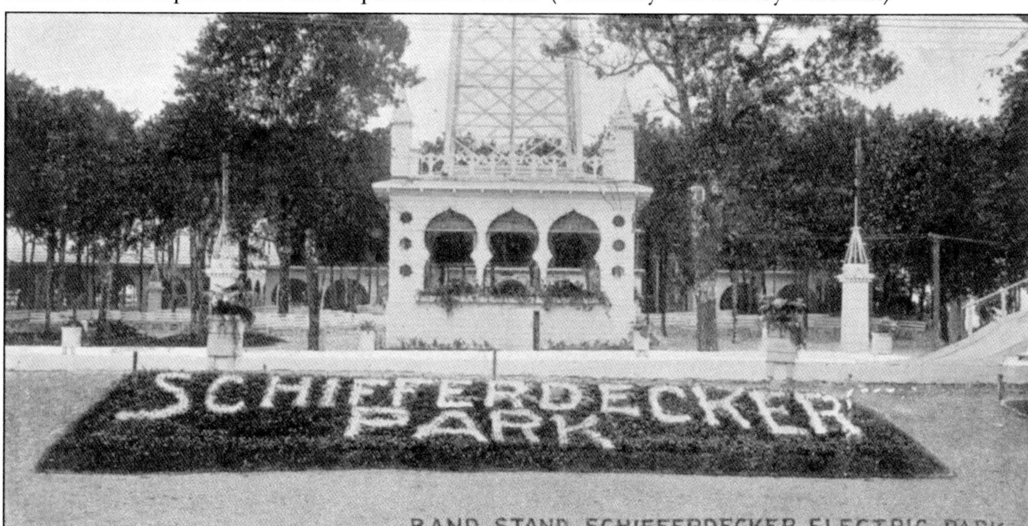

People flocked to Schifferdecker Park to stroll through the flower garden, have picnics, listen to concerts, and watch the animals. The zoo began on a small scale with five fox squirrels. Other critters added to the park included monkeys, black bears, beavers, an alligator, raccoons, bison, and exotic birds. Playful Betty Bear was a particular favorite. Her tombstone at the park reads "Betty Bear, 1920-1952. A long life given to entertaining visitors at Schifferdecker Park." (Courtesy of Rodney Blaukat.)

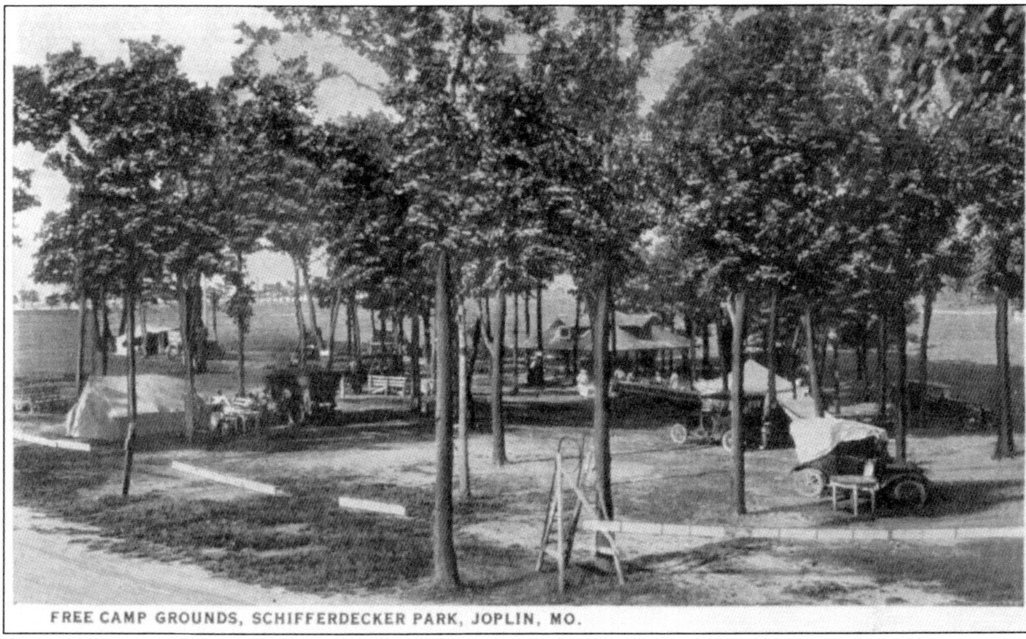

Campgrounds, such as this one at Schifferdecker Park, sprang up along the nation's roads in the 1920s and 1930s to accommodate travelers who needed a cheap place to stay. Tin-can tourists, a nickname for motor-campers, were very creative. They constructed homemade RVs out of old truck chassis, built shacks on two-wheeled trailers, or simply strapped their gear on any flat surface, such as the roof, running boards, or bumpers. (Courtesy of the Joplin Public Library.)

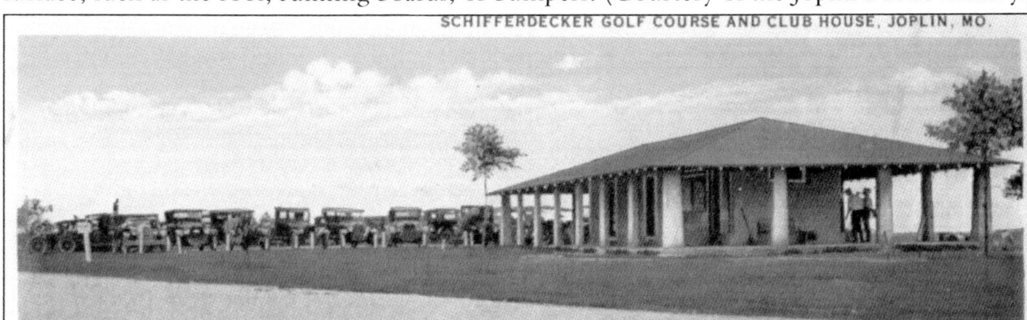

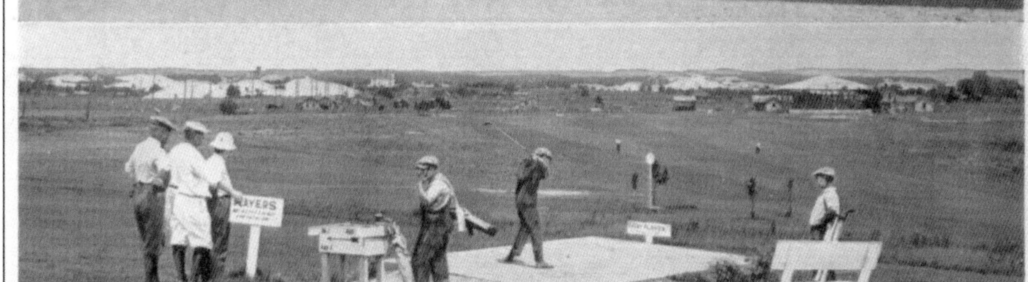

In 1922, city fathers established a municipal golf course at Schifferdecker Park. The top photograph shows the first clubhouse. Although golf tees were produced commercially in 1922, they had not made it to Joplin yet. The lower photograph shows the golfers preparing to tee off. Each golfer grabbed a handful of sand from the tee box, dipped it in water, and built a cone-shaped tee on which to place the ball. (Courtesy of Rodney Blaukat.)

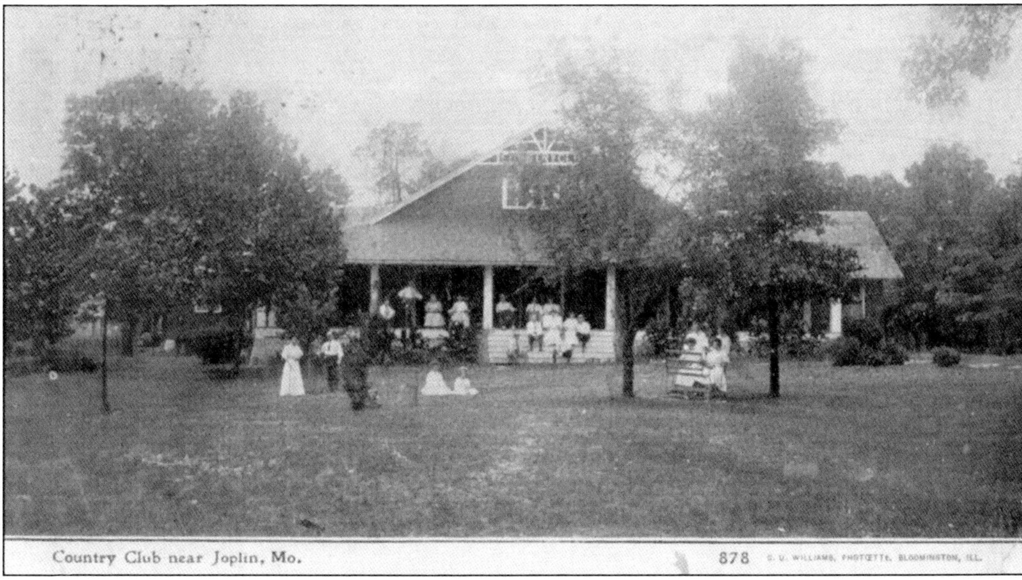

In 1905, a group of Joplin's elite organized a private social club and purchased 60 acres on the west bank of Spring River for construction of a country club. Sheltered by a grove of oak trees, the luxurious 22-room clubhouse provided a splendid setting for "gay, glamorous, and exclusive" society functions and an opportunity for the ladies to "dress to the nines," according to the *Joplin Globe.* (Courtesy of Galen Augustus.)

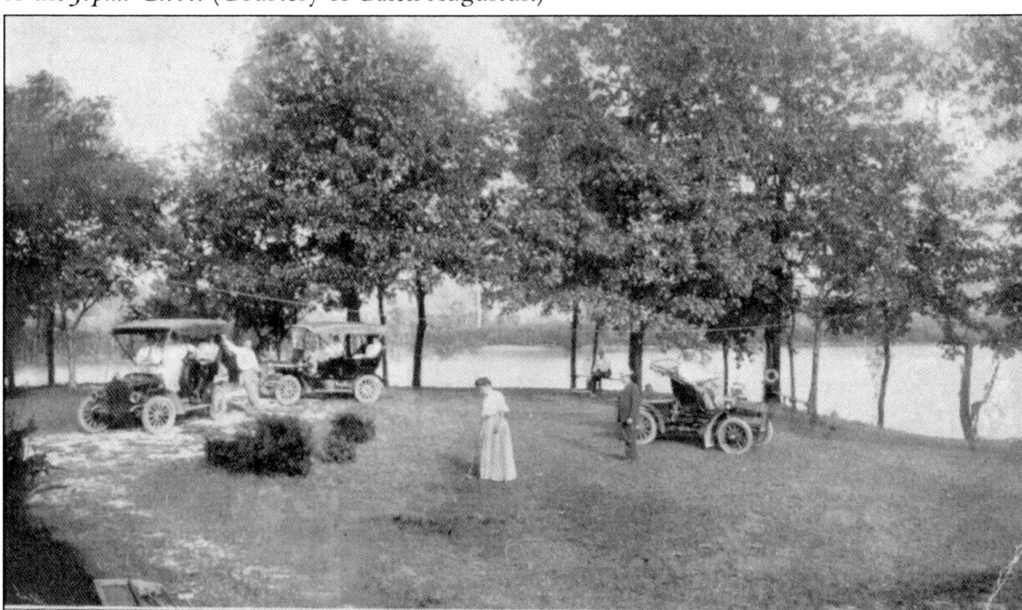

Boats, shady picnic grounds, tennis courts, and a swimming pool offered respite from the summer heat. Although members could take a trolley ride to the country club, they preferred to arrive in style in their flashy new automobiles. With membership dwindling during the Great Depression, the club disbanded and sold the property in 1932. Several years later, developers transformed the old resort into the popular Spring River Inn Restaurant. (Courtesy of Rodney Blaukat.)

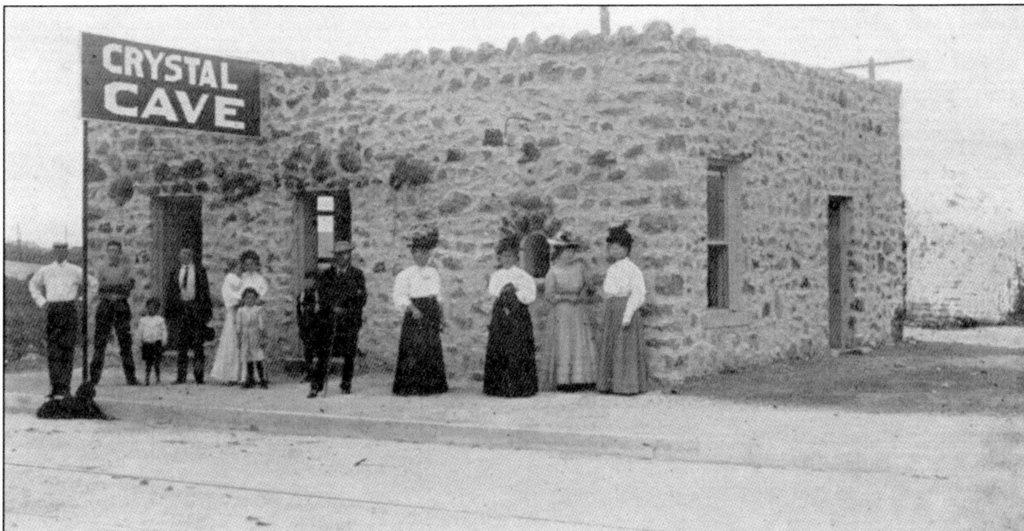

Entrance to Crystal Cave, Joplin, Mo. Entrance to the cave of Calcite Crystals.
At W. 4th St. & Gray Ave., " , " June 10th '09.

In 1893, James Roach made an astonishing discovery while excavating a mineshaft near West Fourth Street. He found a huge cave lined with giant calcite crystals 80 feet below ground. The sparkling chamber constituted one of the world's largest geodes. Roach Cave opened to the public as Crystal Cave on July 4, 1908. Tourists paid an admission fee to tour the attraction. (Courtesy of the Joplin Public Library.)

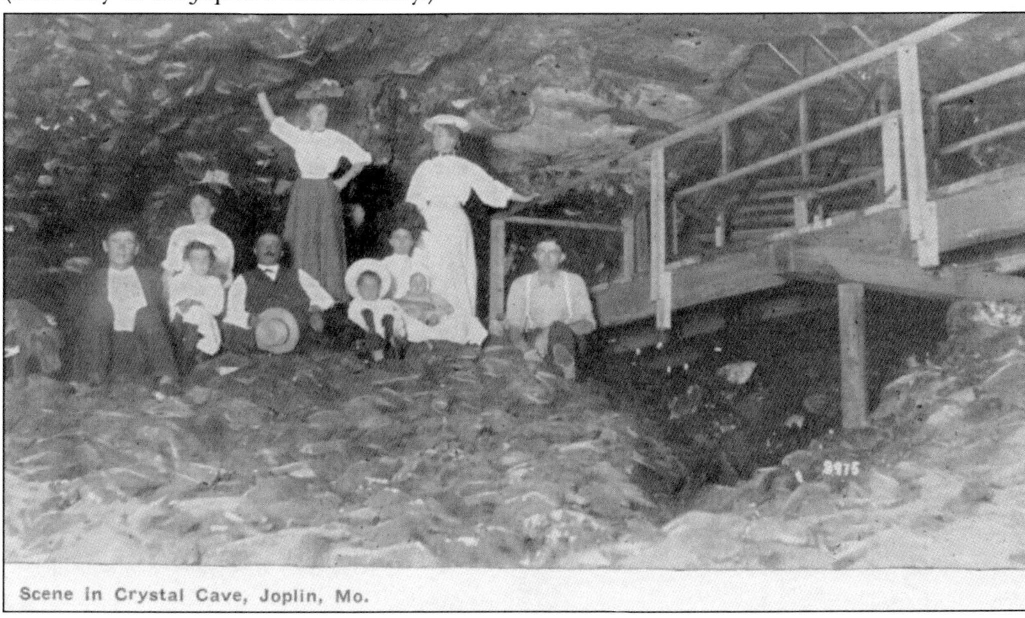

Scene in Crystal Cave, Joplin, Mo.

Furnished with walkways, stairways, and platforms with seats, the cave provided a great location for club meetings, parties, dances, and other entertainments. The cool cave made for a refreshing retreat from the blistering heat in the days before air-conditioning. Crystal Cave closed to the public in the 1930s. After mining-related pumping of groundwater was discontinued, the dazzling cave filled with water, never again to be enjoyed by sightseers. (Courtesy of the Joplin Public Library.)

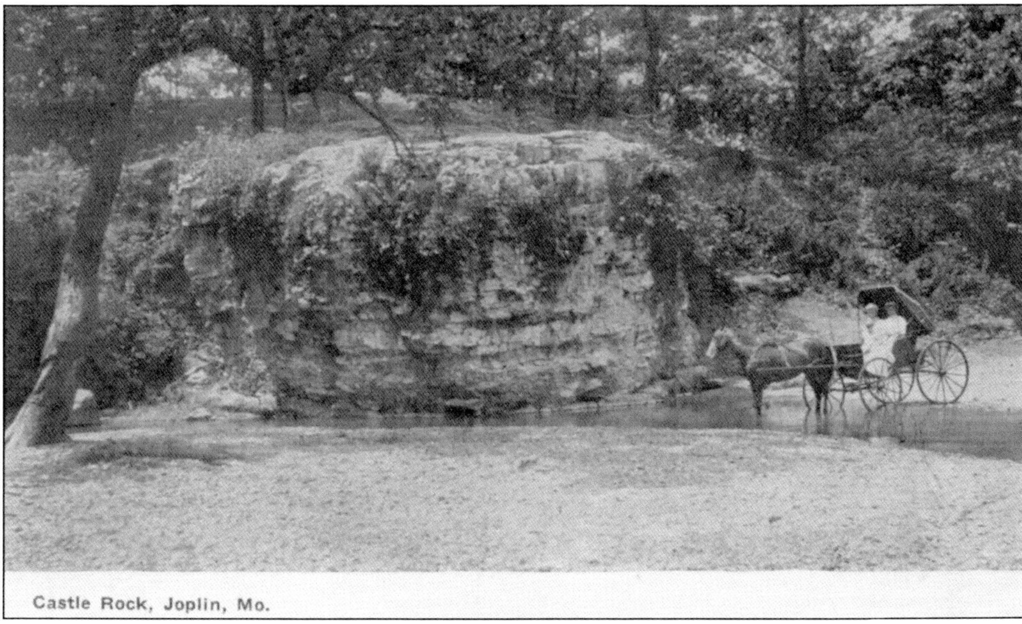

This serene locale, later known as Castle Rock, was well known to early residents, from Native Americans to the first white settlers. After Southwest Missouri Electric Railway ran a line from Carthage to Galena, it became an attraction at Midway Park, a trolley stop near Joplin. Castle Rock even fielded a baseball team that competed in the Trolley League. Countless daredevils have jumped from the cliff into the creek below. (Courtesy of the Joplin Public Library.)

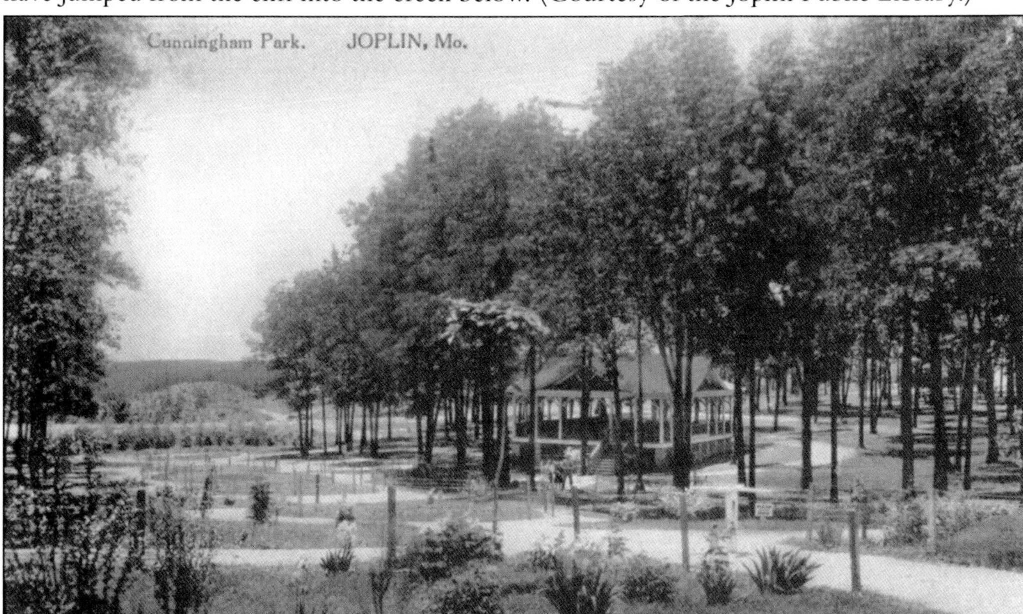

Thomas Cunningham contributed enormously to Joplin's development. He dabbled in everything from mining and farming to the wholesale and retail grocery business. He finally found his niche in banking. In 1898, Mayor Cunningham donated a seven-acre parcel of land between Twenty-Fourth and Twenty-Sixth Streets east of Maiden Lane to the city for use as a park. The city council voted to designate it Cunningham Park. (Courtesy of Rodney Blaukat.)

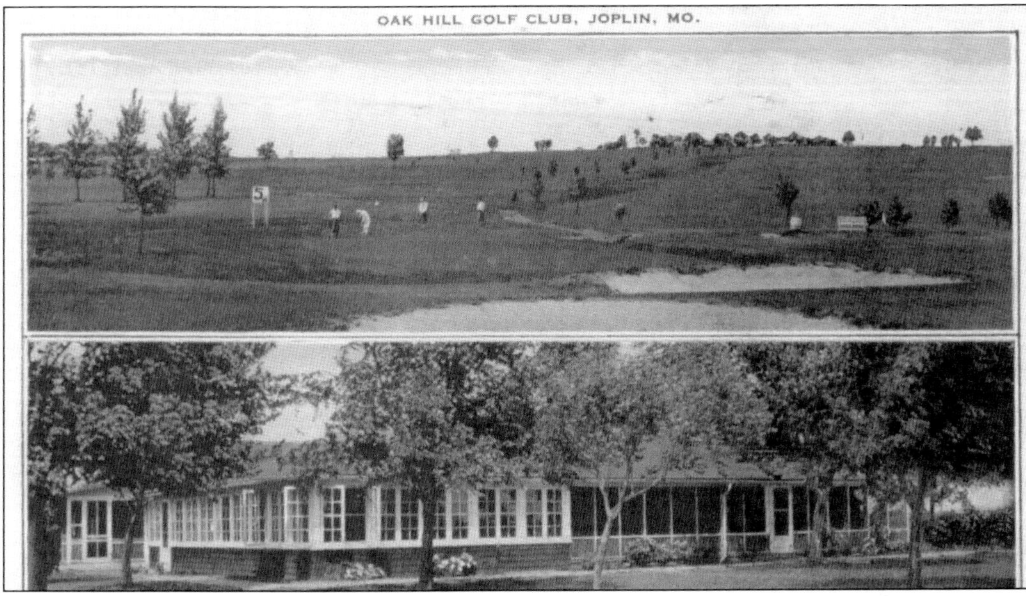

In 1911, Gus Mattes donated land for a nine-hole golf course. Englishman John Hood laid out the course and served as golf pro. The oldest golf tournament in the Joplin area commenced in 1922 at Oak Hill, now Twin Hills Country Club, with the first Tri-State Golf Championship. Three national golf legends, Ed Dudley, Ky Laffoon, and Horton Smith, began their careers as head pros at Oak Hill. (Courtesy of the Joplin Public Library.)

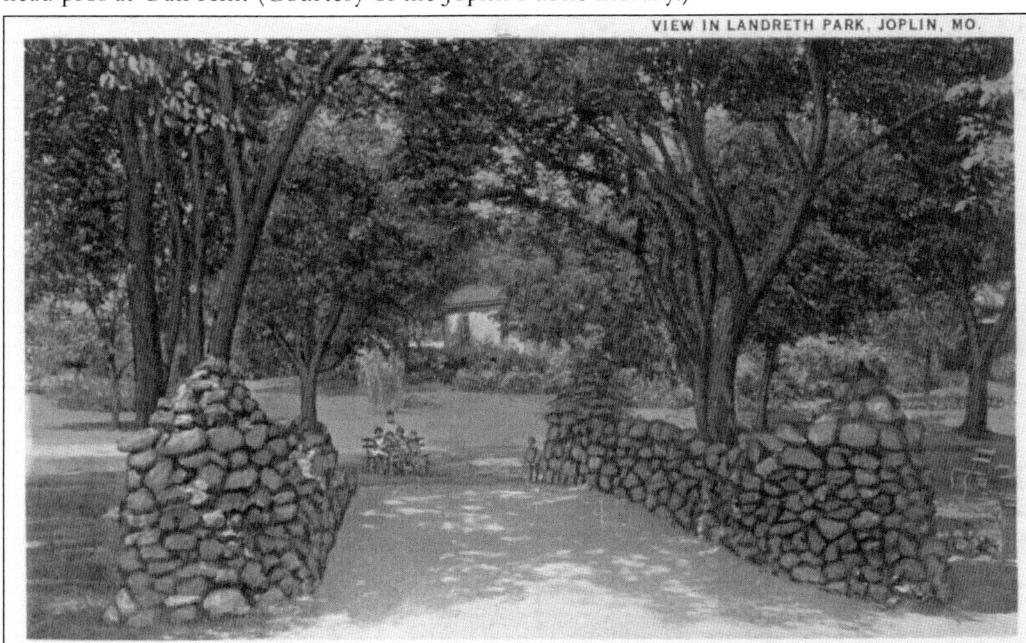

In 1928, Mr. and Mrs. William Landreth donated 100 acres of land north of the Broadway Viaduct and east of Union Depot along the railroad tracks and Joplin Creek. Unfortunately, the property abutted a red-light district that attracted gambling, prostitution, and squatters. In 1933, WPA workers cleared out the slums and created Landreth Park, which boasted a swimming pool, a playground, a tennis court, and flower gardens. (Courtesy of Rodney Blaukat.)

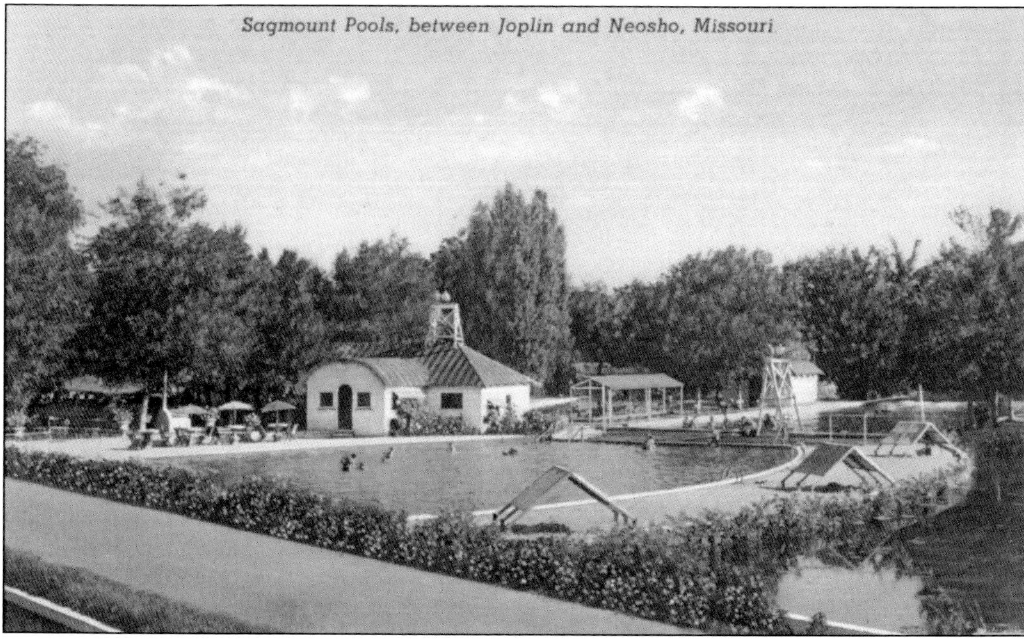

The community of Saginaw started as a mining camp at the end of the 19th century. Joplin businessman J. Frank Walker built a stone hunting lodge there in 1928. The scenic hillside and pure-water springs made it an idyllic vacation spot; old US Highway 71 provided easy access. In 1933, Walker developed his retreat as Sagmount resort; he built a 30-room hotel, cottages, and three spring-fed swimming pools. (Courtesy of the Joplin Public Library.)

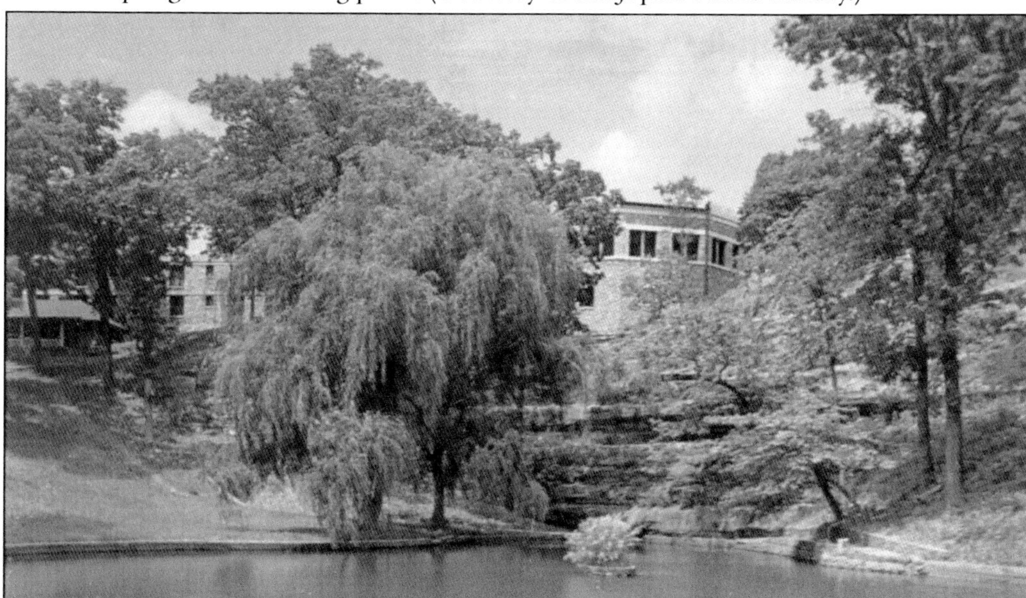

During World War II, Camp Crowder took over the grounds for use as additional housing for military personnel. Sagmount reopened as a resort after the war ended. It closed down in the 1950s, when evangelist Billy James Hargis began using the site as headquarters for his ministry. In 1960, the Missouri Baptist Bible Fellowship purchased the property for use as a retreat. (Courtesy of Rodney Blaukat.)

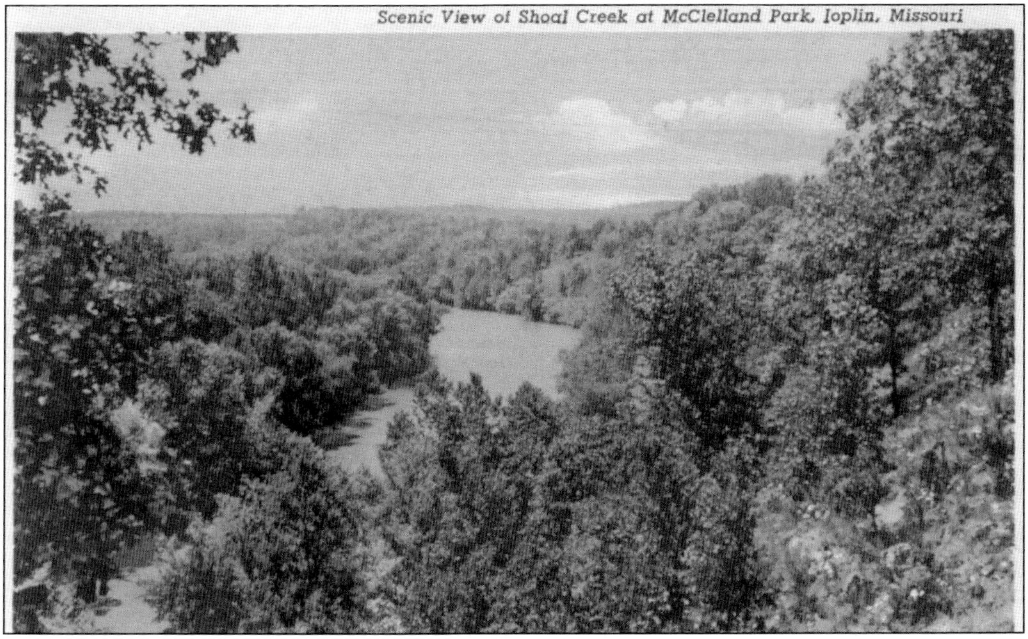

Shoal Creek spans portions of Newton, Lawrence, and Barry Counties. The 66-mile-long spring-fed channel joins Spring River five miles southwest of Joplin. In the 1830s, pioneers in Newton County settled beside its pure waters. In 1850, they established Shoal Creek Township. After lead mining commenced following the Civil War, several small smelters popped up along the creek. The major draw, however, continued to be the natural attractions. (Courtesy of the Joplin Public Library.)

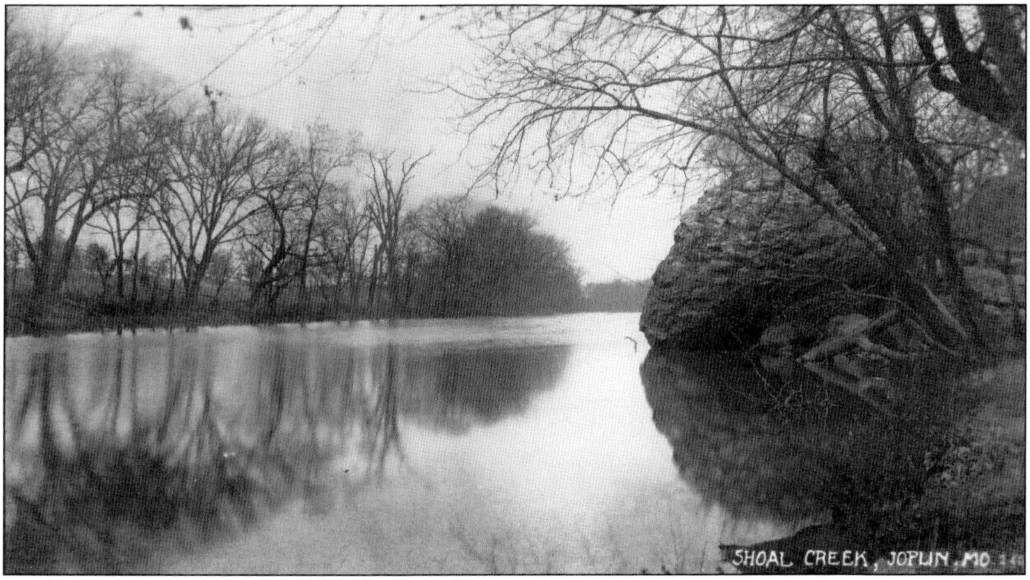

In his memoirs, LeRoy Calvin tells of swim parties at Shoal Creek in the 1890s. A group of Joplin swains and their steadies, with chaperones of course, would rent a horse-and-wagon rig and head south to Shoal Creek. The young folks stretched wide strips of canvas between trees to create dressing rooms where they changed into their swimsuits for a pleasurable frolic in the broad, placid waters of Shoal Creek. (Courtesy of Galen Augustus.)

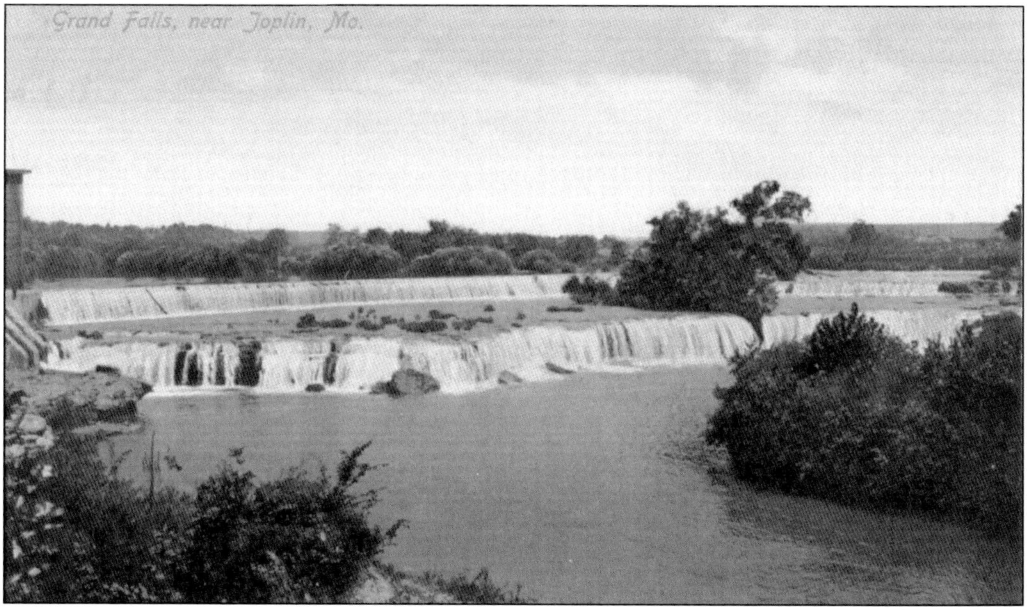

The largest natural falls in Missouri are located just south of Joplin on Shoal Creek. Long before white settlers came to southwest Missouri, Indians called it the place of the singing waters. In the 1890s, the turbulent spring-fed waters powered Joplin's first electrical power plant and furnished pure drinking water to Joplin citizens. Prone to flooding, the creek sometimes played havoc with the power plant and with nearby residents. (Courtesy of the Joplin Public Library.)

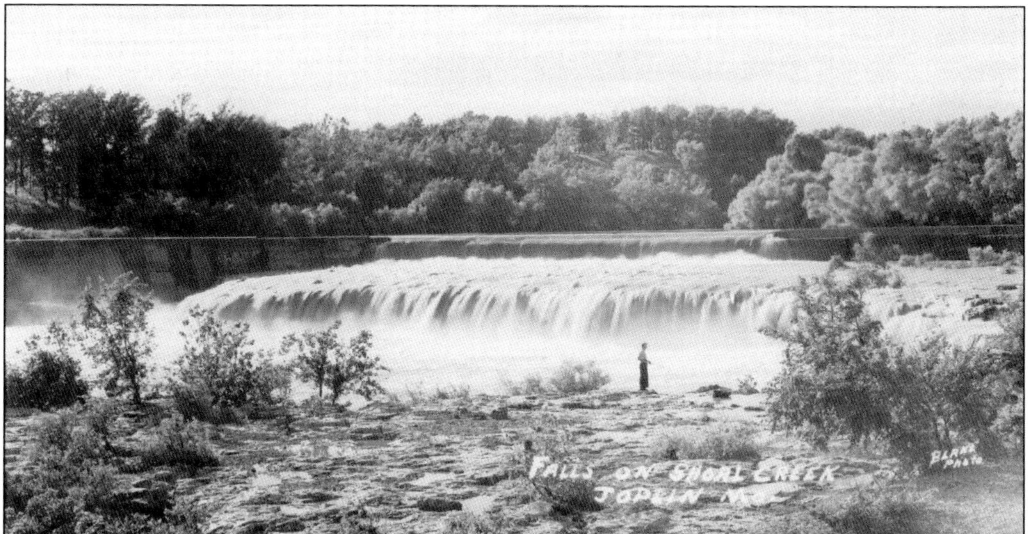

As Joplin grew, its people looked for ways to spend leisure time. In 1903, investors began developing Grand Falls Park as a pleasure resort complete with a vaudeville theater, a German village, and boathouses. Merrymakers ventured out in steam yachts and rowboats. A dance pavilion extended over the rushing water on the blue bosom of Shoal Creek. Missouri Pacific Railroad ran trains to the park on an hourly basis. (Courtesy of Galen Augustus.)

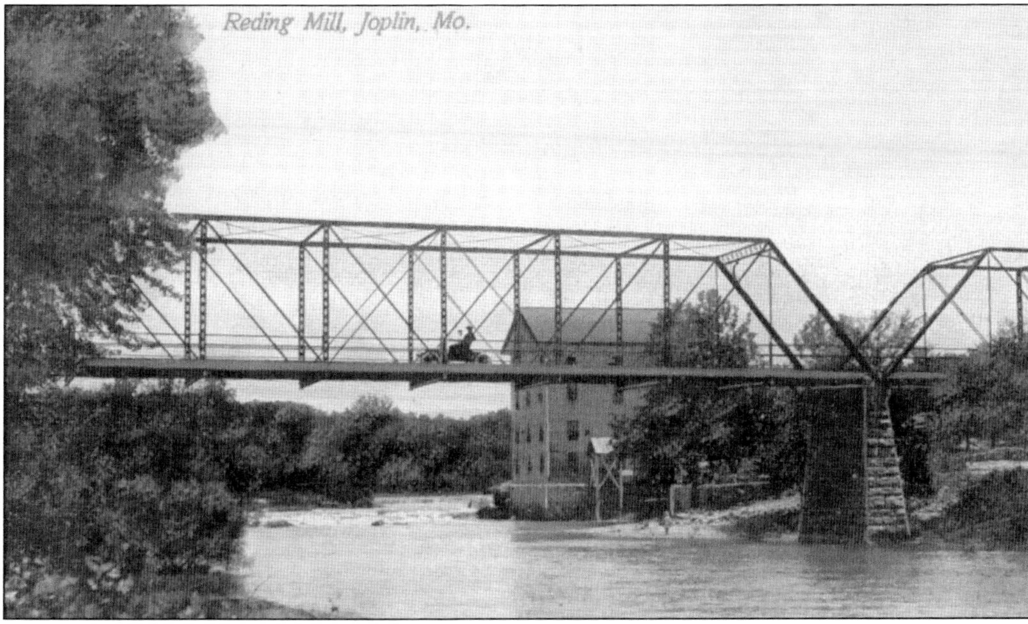

John Reding built his first gristmill on Shoal Creek in 1832 and founded a small village called Shoalsburg. In 1868, he erected the mill shown on this postcard. In 1932, the picturesque mill, one of the most photographed structures in southwest Missouri, burned to the ground. The one-lane steel bridge shown on the postcard was torn down in 1930, after a new steel-reinforced concrete span was completed. (Courtesy of Galen Augustus.)

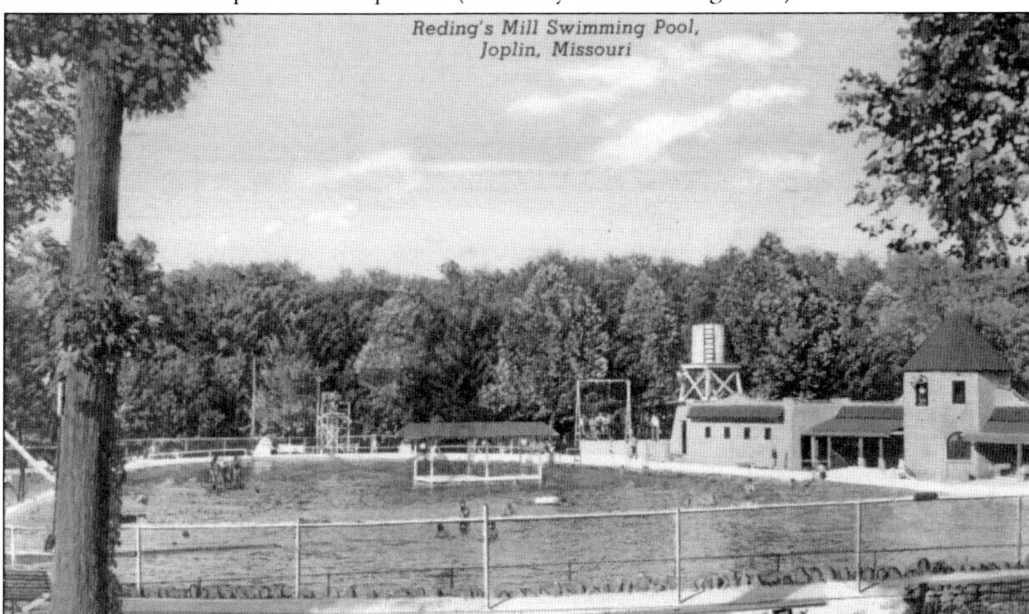

In 1926, Reding's Mill, Inc., began developing a posh resort south of Joplin. The oval swimming pool, the largest in the district, offered a variety of water sports, from swinging rings and a large toboggan slide to smaller slides. It boasted the region's coldest pool, filled with natural spring-fed water. West of the pool was the kiddie pool and an enchanting lagoon. A Spanish-style patio and pavilion added exotic ambience. (Courtesy of Rodney Blaukat.)

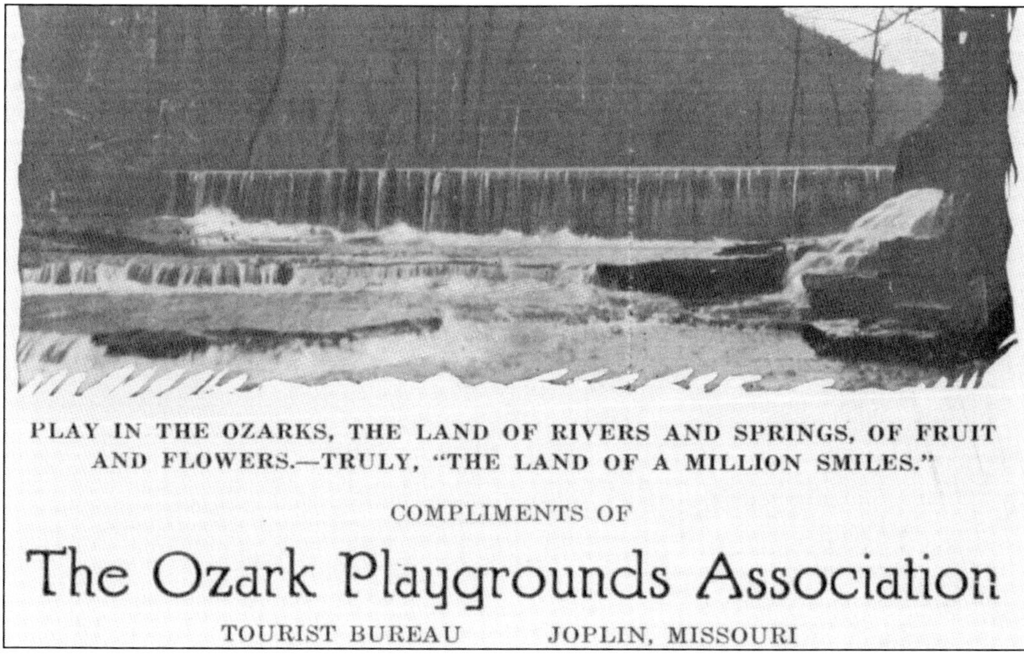

As tourists flocked to the great Southwest during the teens, Midwest promoters looked for ways to catch them as they passed through. They established the Ozark Playgrounds Association (OPA) to promote the gateway to the Ozarks. The association published maps, postcards, and brochures advertising area motels, tourist camps, restaurants, resorts, and attractions. It ran national newspaper ads and sponsored events, such as the Ozark Smile Girl contest, a beauty competition. (Courtesy of Galen Augustus.)

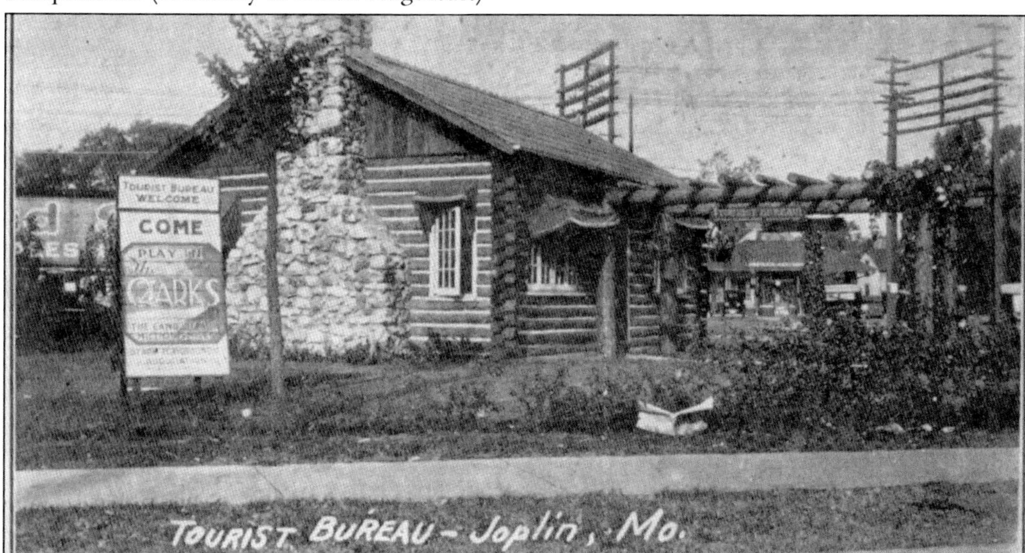

In 1920, the association constructed a characteristic Ozark log cabin at 602 Joplin Avenue. Joplin lyricist Homer Hardin turned OPA's slogan, "Land of a Million Smiles," into a catchy song extolling the beauty of the Ozarks. The tourist bureau moved in with the Joplin Chamber of Commerce in 1931. During its heyday, the powerful organization did much to boost tourism and the economy in the depressed 1920s and 1930s. (Courtesy of the Joplin Public Library.)

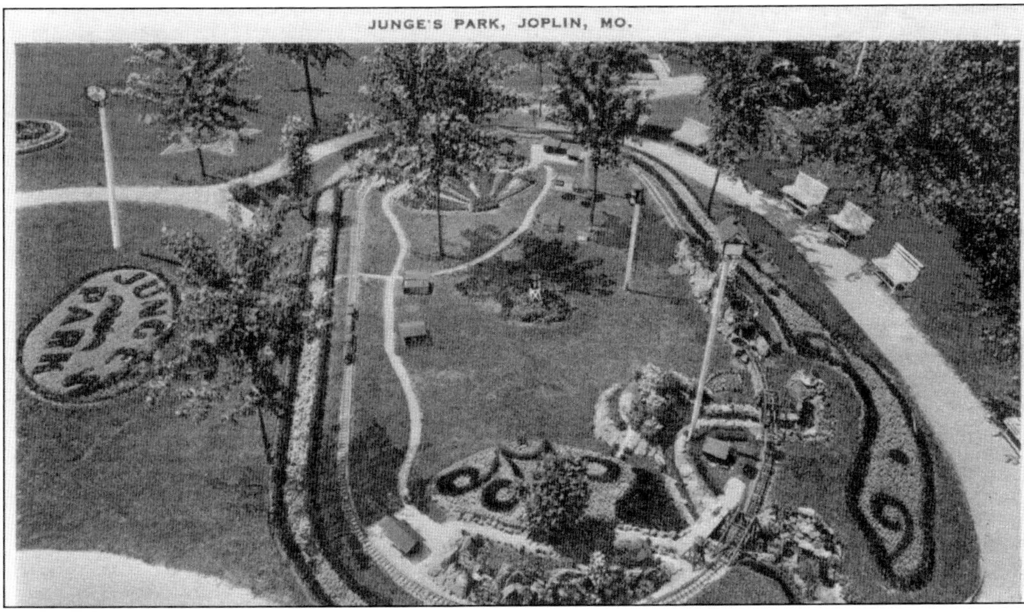

Junge Bakery genuinely cared about the people who helped the business prosper. In 1915, Albert Junge turned the lot next to the bakery at 1806–1814 Main Street into a beautiful park. It showcased a miniature train, a waterfall, a windmill, a miniature village, and elaborate floral designs. In 1929, Junge Park added a miniature automobile highway with a motorcycle cop, a mushroom bed, a fountain with goldfish, and animal figures. (Courtesy of the Joplin Public Library.)

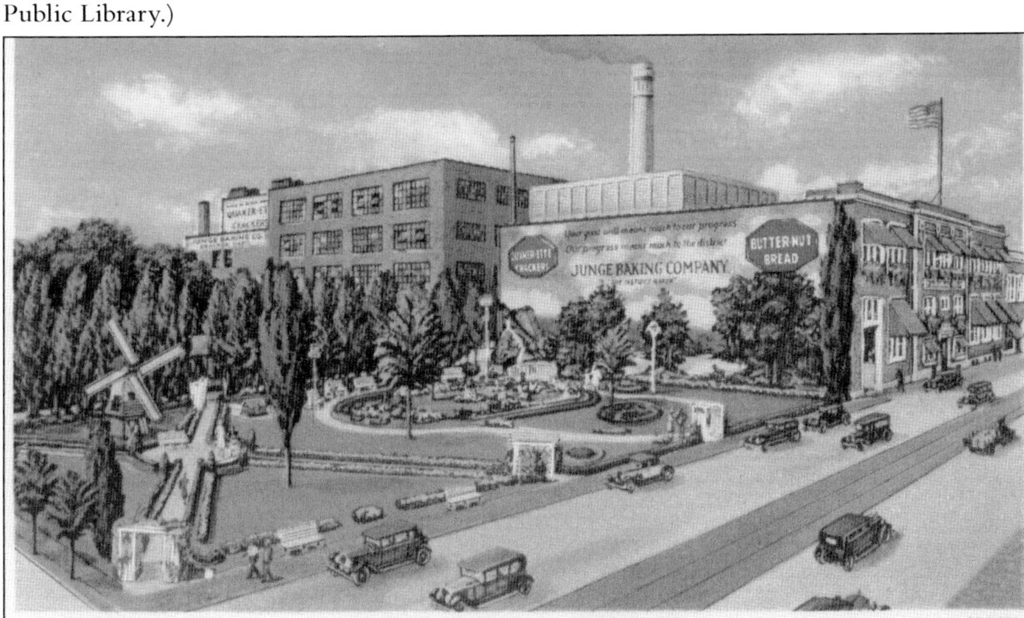

Each year, delighted spectators flocked to the park to see what delights the opening of the new season brought. Beginning in December 1936, Junge Park astounded visitors with a 22-by-65-foot, three-dimensional, animated greeting card. Some related to the holidays, such as Christmas and Easter, while others featured storybook themes. A patriotic sign, erected during the World War II years, listed the names of Joplin war casualties. (Courtesy of Rodney Blaukat.)

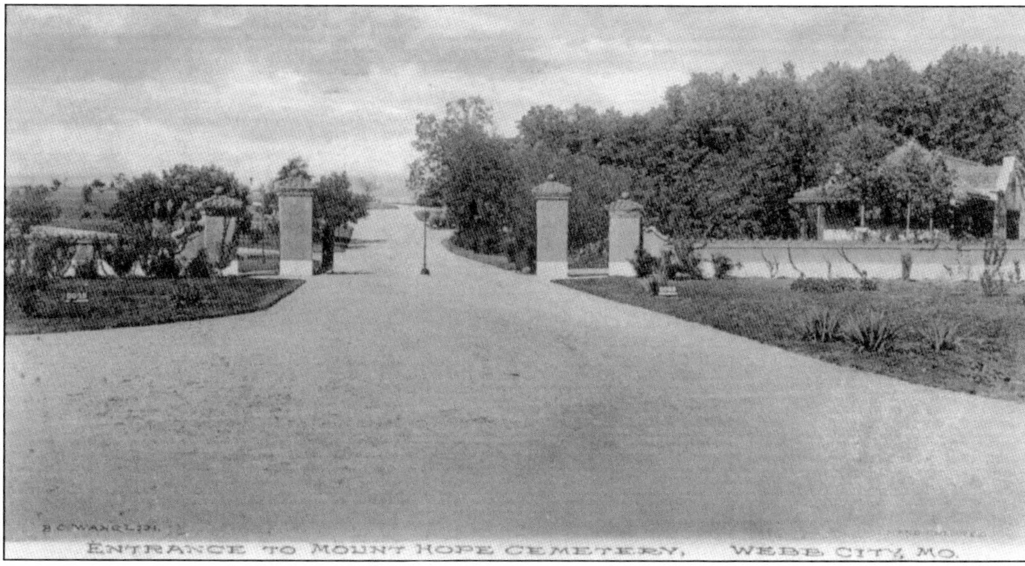

In 1905, the Mount Hope Cemetery Association organized to create a fine new cemetery centrally located between the two cities of Joplin and Webb City. The developers hired Sid Hare, one of the country's leading landscape architects, to design the layout of the cemetery with a "park-like appearance produced by clean undulating lawns, broken only by serpentine drives, trees and shrubs," as stated the Mount Hope Cemetery booklet. (Courtesy of Galen Augustus.)

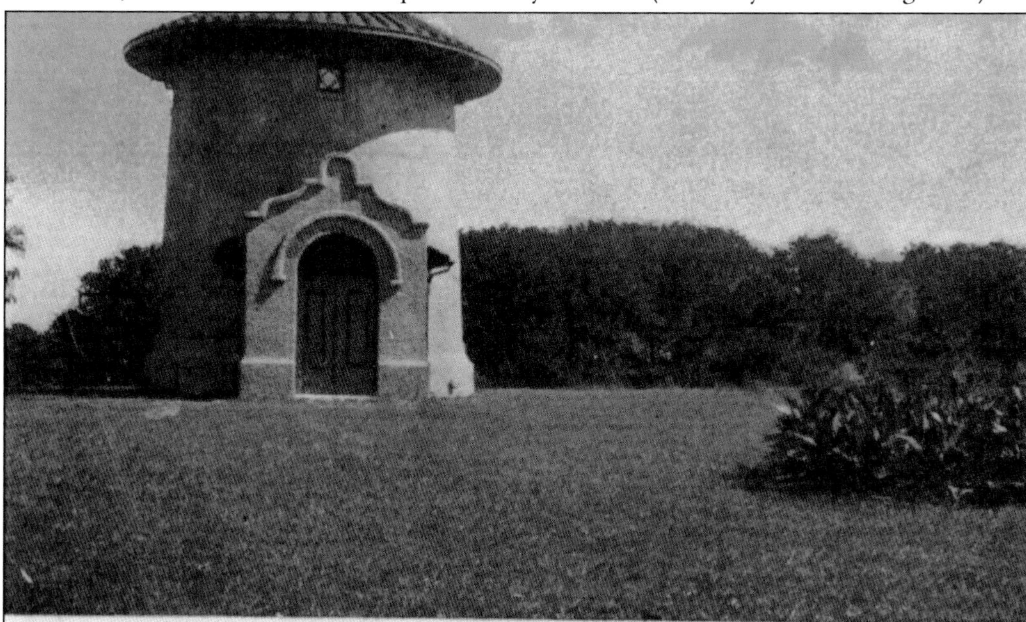

Hare's designs featured architectural entry gates at the corners and circular sections of lawn accented with naturalistic plantings. Not only were the grounds beautifully landscaped, but the buildings and mausoleums were architectural wonders as well. Mount Hope Cemetery featured several Spanish Mission–style structures, all with ivory stucco walls and red tile roofs. These included an office and a waiting room, a chapel, a two-story lodge, and a water tower. (Courtesy of Galen Augustus.)

Ten

Our Town

Many cities in Missouri—Carthage and Neosho, for example—were laid out neatly around a town square. Joplin's layout and development are unique for several reasons. First of all, there were the two towns of Joplin and Murphysburg that combined to form the original Joplin in 1873. As Joplin grew, it annexed many smaller settlements, such as Blendville (southwest), Chitwood (northwest), Villa Heights (east), Royal Heights (northeast), Oakland (northeast), Castle Rock (northeast), Stapleton (south), and Freeman Grove (south). This resulted in random, unplanned development. Since many of these communities already had a Main Street or a Broadway Avenue, street designations had to be changed to eliminate duplicate names and to accommodate the new thoroughfares. Also, the street grids in each little town did not always line up with the others. As a result, many of Joplin's streets take unexpected detours or dead end suddenly. One of the most unusual aspects of Joplin's layout is the length of its Main Street, some 52 blocks. In its infancy, the business district fronted on Main Street, with the residential district beginning one block over on Joplin Avenue to the west and Virginia Avenue to the east. This lack of planning immediately created problems, as the commercial district needed room to expand. As a result, many of the beautiful Victorian-era homes on Joplin, Wall, and Virginia Avenues were demolished and replaced with commercial structures in the early 20th century. This chapter presents a series of street scenes and aerial views, mostly of the downtown area, from 1900 to the mid-1960s.

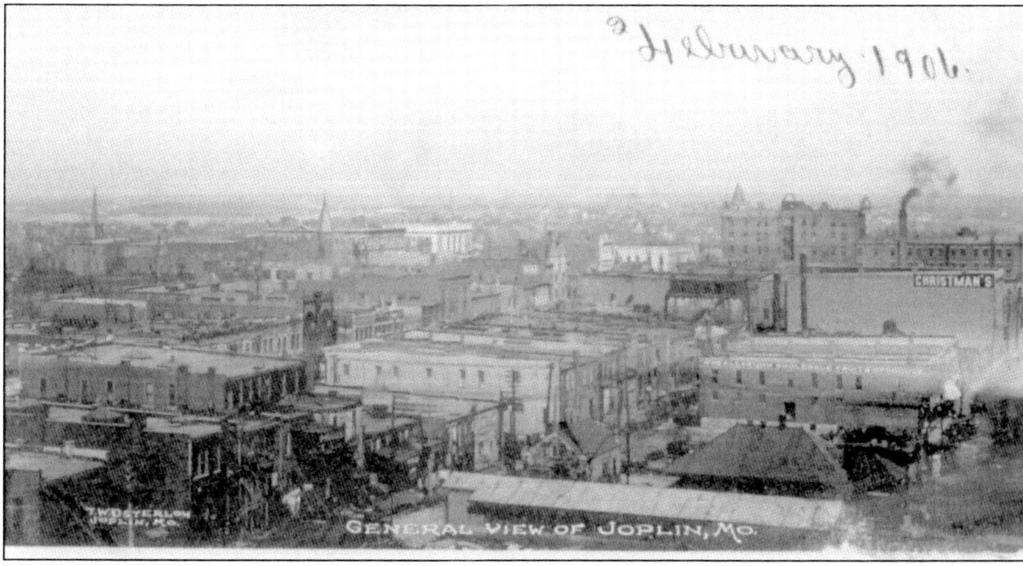

These c. 1906 postcards reveal a vibrant Joplin poised to take a giant leap forward. Both photographs, probably taken from the perspective of the courthouse at 701 Virginia Avenue, show a northwesterly view of the downtown district. The Keystone Hotel dominates the skyline, but the Connor Hotel would soon eclipse it. Visible in the distance are mine fields to the west and the residential area to the north. (Rodney Blaukat.)

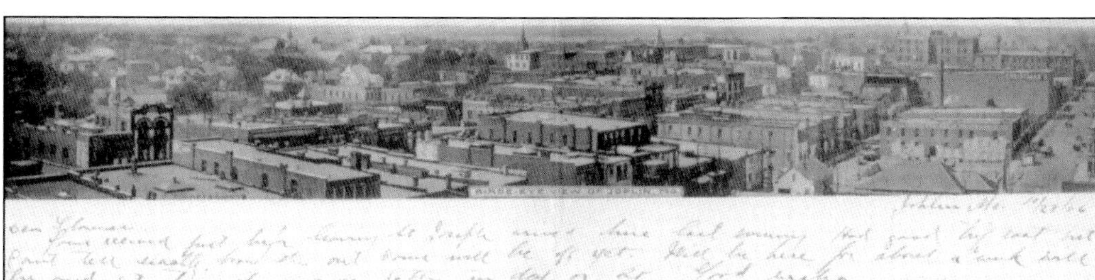

In the foreground are enterprises, such as O'Neall and Kuhn Wholesale Produce and Middle West Brewing Company. The proprietors of Christman's Dry Goods, just north of the brewery, must have been appalled by the water tanks, bottling works, ammonia compressors, and coal-fired steam engines residing next door to their fine retail establishment. Willow Branch creek provided the fresh water necessary for the brewery's daily production of 35 barrels of beer. (Courtesy of Galen Augustus.)

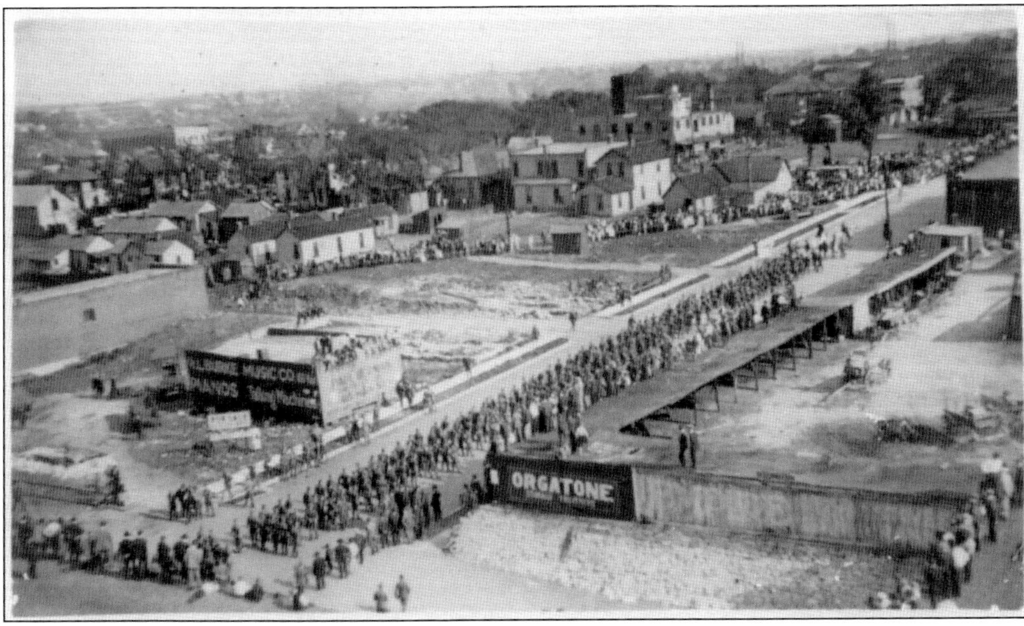

This 1918 postcard reveals the same area from a different perspective. Many of the buildings shown in the two previous photographs were torn down to make way for the Frisco Building, its railroad spurs, and its train sheds. This image documents Joplin's pride when its soldiers left to fight in World War I. The servicemen stood in formation as townspeople lined the streets and the building tops to bid them farewell. (Courtesy of Galen Augustus.)

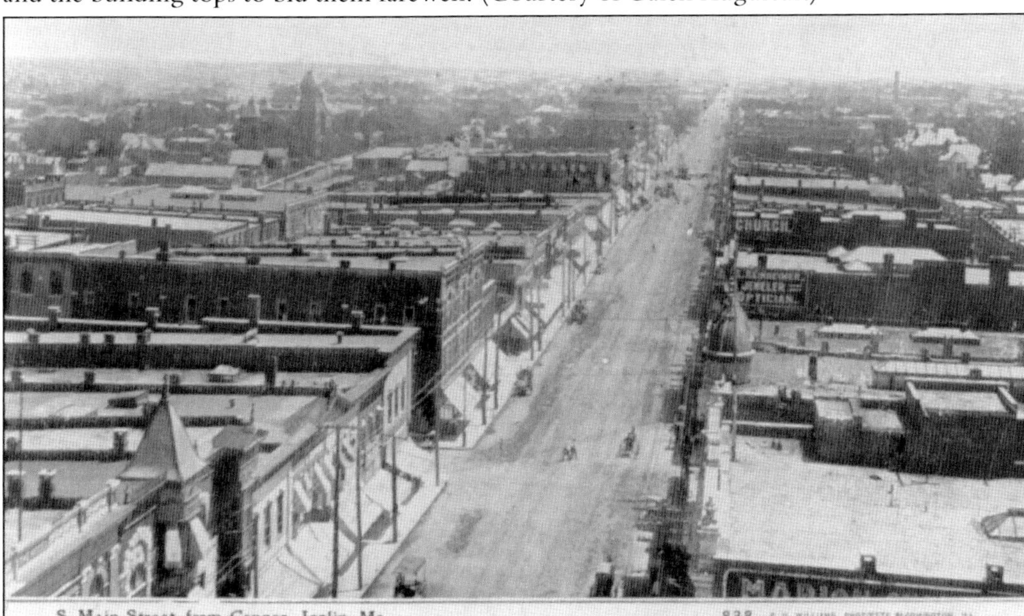

Bird's-eye views, which were extremely popular in the early 20th century, fostered pride in the community's growth. Here, the observer gazed southward on Main Street from a commanding vantage point, an upper-floor window of the Connor Hotel. This photograph must have been taken on a Sunday, when there was not much downtown activity. There are a few pedestrians and horse-drawn carriages along with a streetcar in the distance. (Courtesy of Galen Augustus.)

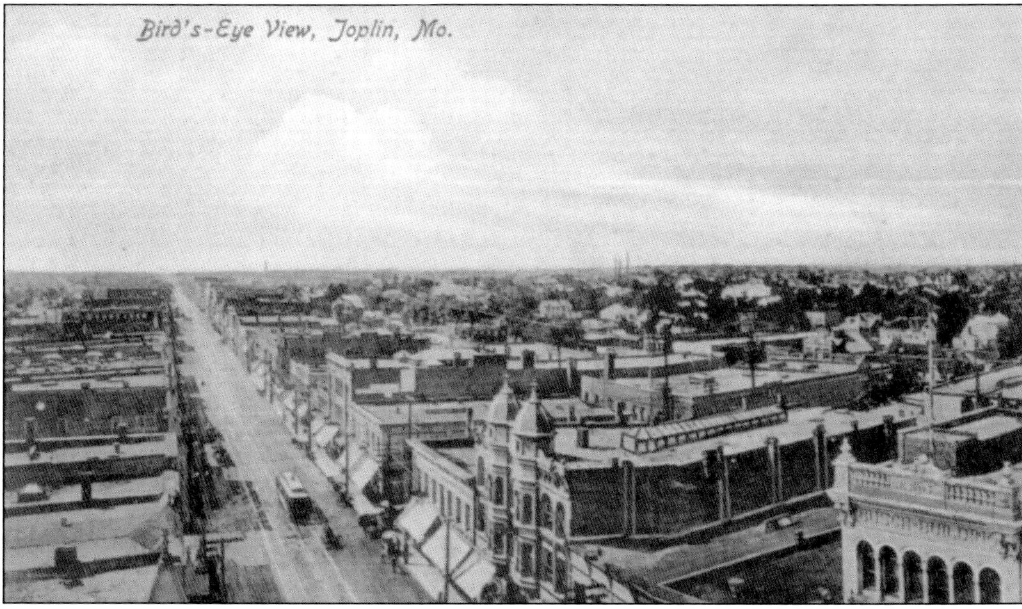

Looking south from an upper floor of the Keystone Hotel, one could see several prominent buildings. Visible on the right were the Busch Building at 410 Main Street and the Columbian Block at 420 Main with its elaborate stonework and twin cupolas. Stately homes lining Joplin and Wall Avenues would soon be torn down as the commercial district expanded toward the west. (Courtesy of Rodney Blaukat.)

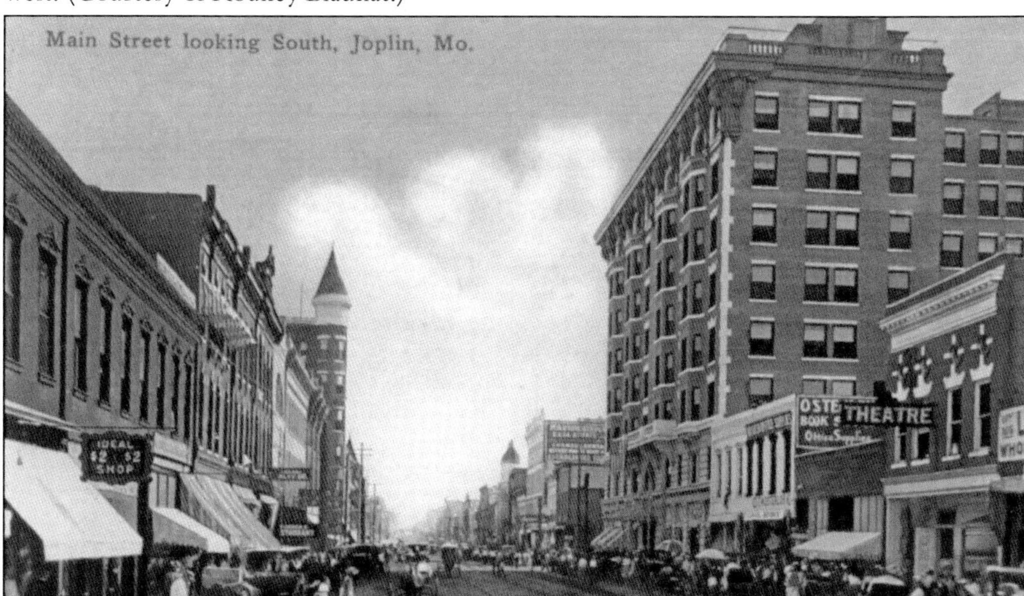

This c. 1909 photograph, taken facing south in the 300 block of Main Street, showcases the newly opened Connor Hotel. Across the street at 319 Main stands the legendary House of Lords. The three-story building housed a bar, restaurant, gambling tables, and female companionship. The lively establishment introduced customers to ragtime greats such as Scott Joplin. The House of Lords also played a role in launching Thomas Hart Benton's artistic career. (Courtesy of the Joplin Public Library.)

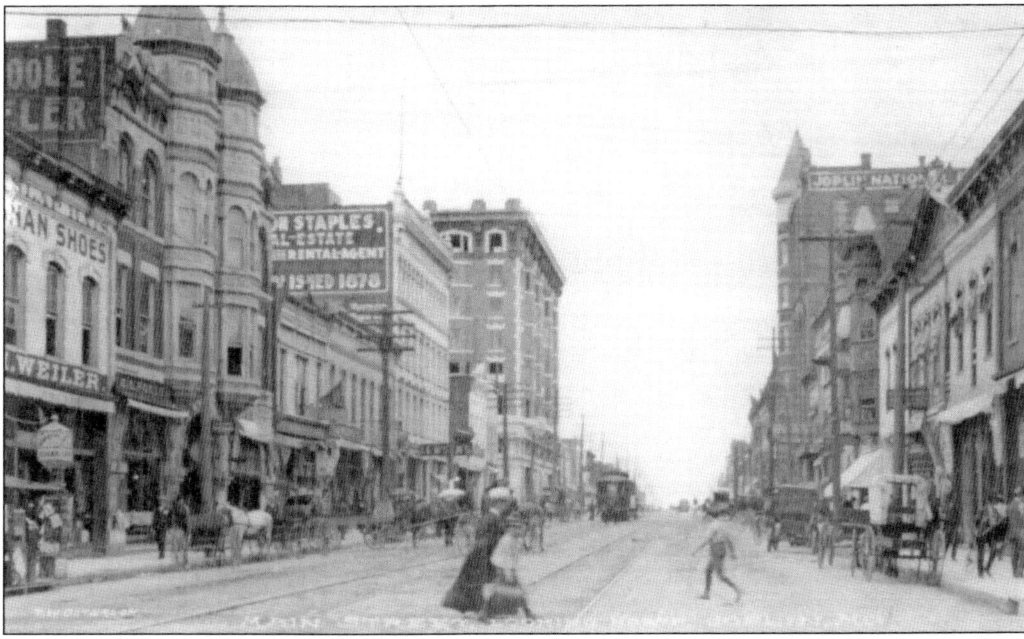

This 1908 image was taken facing north towards Fourth and Main Streets. Some of the buildings visible are the Perkins Block, the Columbian Building, and the Keystone and Connor Hotels. Retail establishments usually occupied ground floors of commercial buildings; upper floors provided office space and residential boarding. In addition to the numerous saloons on this block, there were also three banks and the prestigious Model Clothing store. (Courtesy of Galen Augustus.)

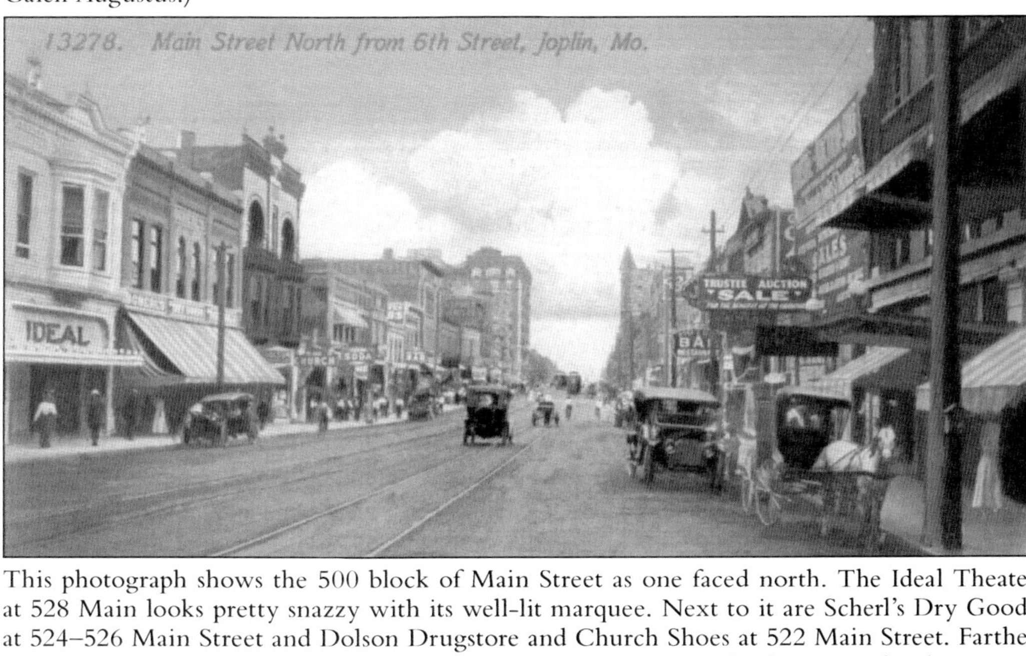

This photograph shows the 500 block of Main Street as one faced north. The Ideal Theater at 528 Main looks pretty snazzy with its well-lit marquee. Next to it are Scherl's Dry Goods at 524–526 Main Street and Dolson Drugstore and Church Shoes at 522 Main Street. Farther north are Poole Jewelers at 420 Main Street and the Connor Hotel. This scene also documents the different modes of transportation in use in the early 20th century. (Courtesy of the Joplin Public Library.)

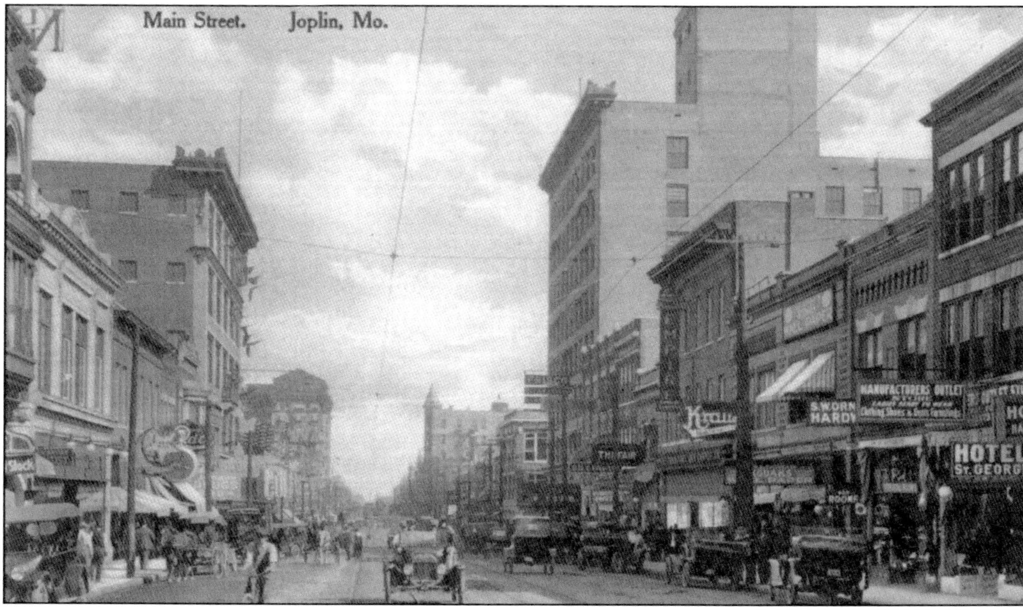

These two views of the 600 block of Main, taken as one looked north, show the changes that had occurred in 40 years. The first photograph was taken in the teens. What a sophisticated city Joplin had become! Two modern high-rises dominate the skyline—Newman's Department Store and the Frisco Building. Main Street teemed with activity by pedestrians, bicyclists, automobiles, and trolleys. (Courtesy of Galen Augustus.)

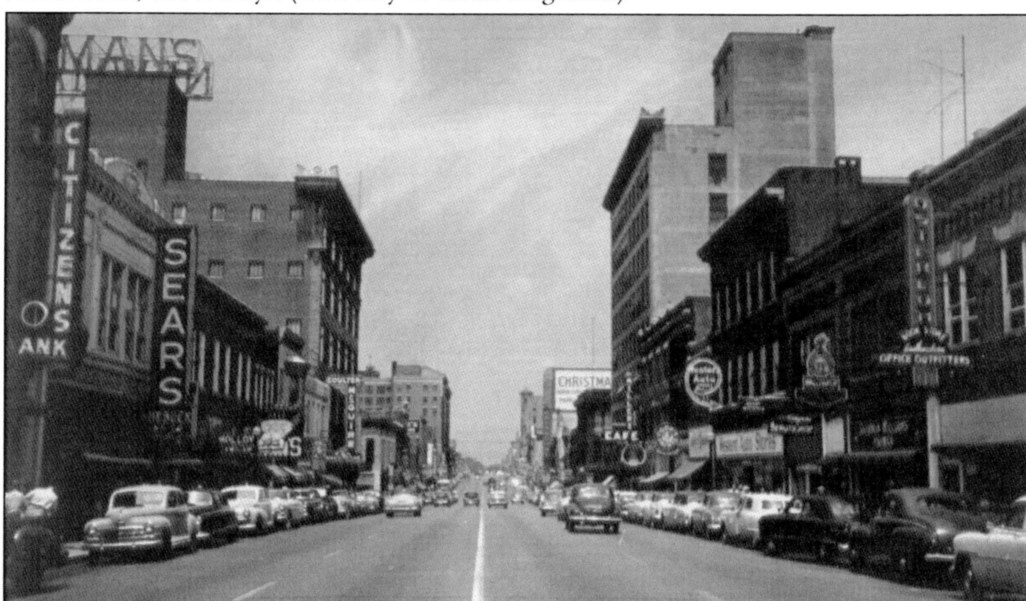

Life was good in downtown Joplin in the 1950s. The 600 block of Main was home to Citizens Bank, Sears & Roebuck, Molloy's Jewelry Store, Coulter-McGuire Men's Clothing, Newman's Department Store, Osterloh's Book Store, Sherwin Williams, Western Auto, Cook's Paint, Miller's Cafe, and the Frisco Building. However, this would be Main Street's last hurrah before urban renewal programs demolished 35 acres of buildings, including half of the ones shown here. (Courtesy of the Joplin Public Library.)

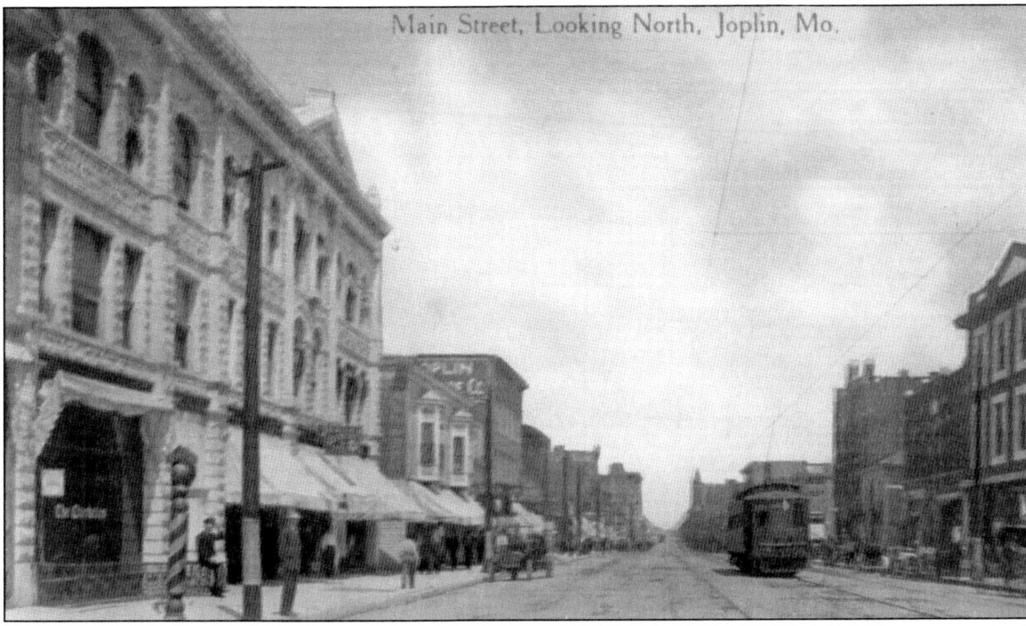

This photograph of the 700 block of Main Street was taken from the middle of the block facing north. On the left is the magnificent Clarketon Hotel at 718–722 Main, an imposing white limestone building designed in 1899 by architect August Michaelis. The hotel introduced an exciting novelty—electric lights! John King's book, wallpaper, and stationery store at 713 Main Street is the building on the right with the white-trimmed windows. (Courtesy of Rodney Blaukat.)

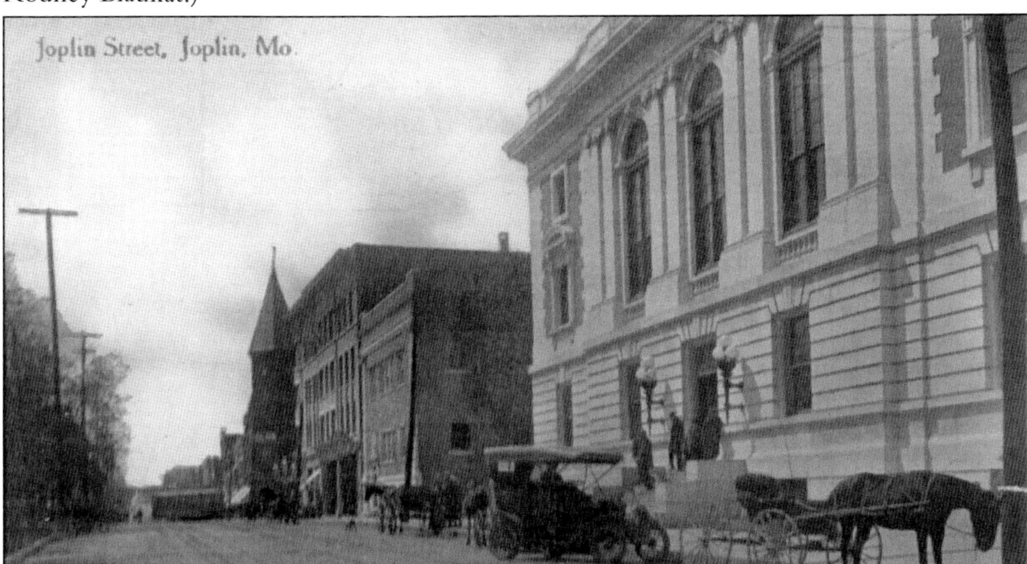

Looking south from the corner of Third Street and Joplin Avenue, one can see the federal building and post office on the right. Next to it is Home Telephone, which was completed in 1908, at 312–316 Joplin Avenue. Miners Bank opened in 1905, at the northwest corner of Fourth Street and Joplin Avenue. The pinnacled building visible across the street is the Club Theatre. (Courtesy of the Joplin Public Library.)

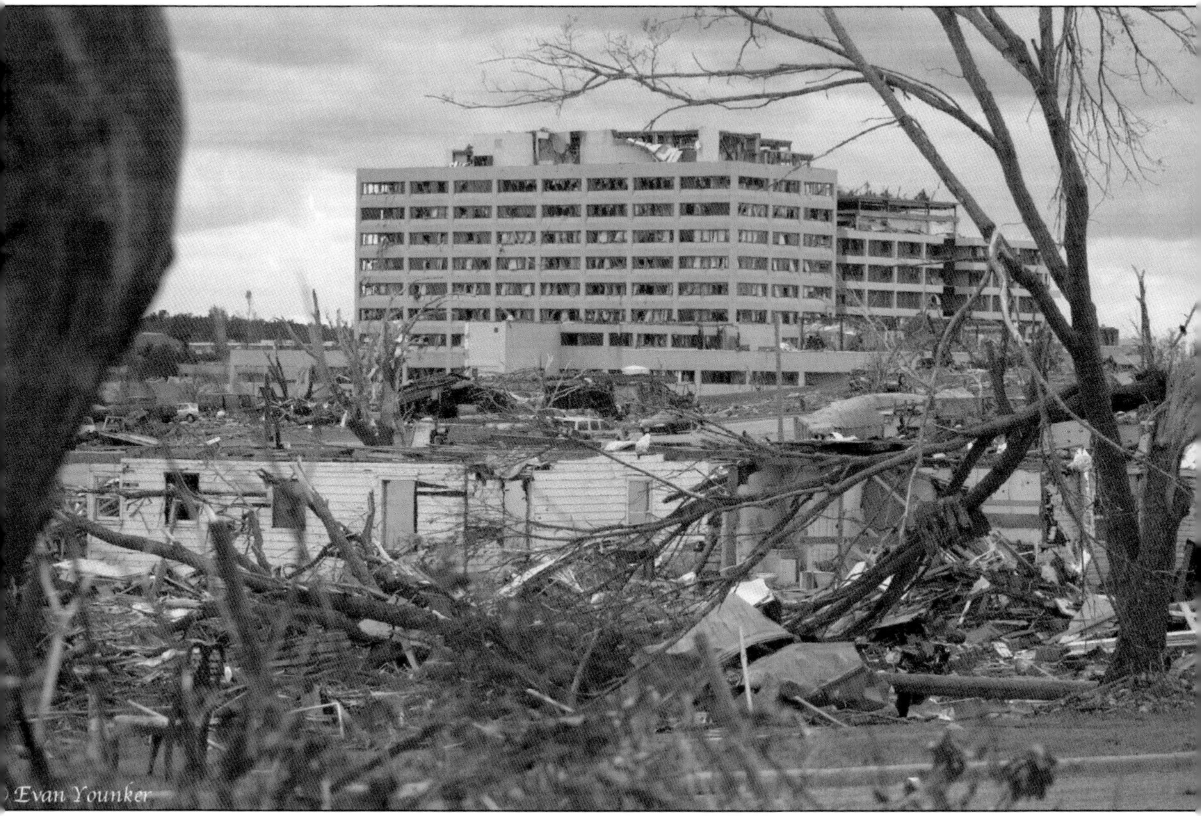

EPILOGUE: On a pleasant Sunday evening, May 22, 2011, an EF-5 tornado suddenly raged through densely populated south Joplin. It destroyed almost everything in its path for 13.8 miles in length and up to a mile in width.

The tornado smashed down in southwest Joplin, wrecking residential areas, Cunningham Park (page 108), schools, medical offices, and a major hospital, St. John's (page 31). It headed east, obliterating untold acres of late-19th- and early-20th-century houses. The storm's wrath intensified as it forged east, razing businesses along Main Street, more neighborhoods, and Joplin High School (page 98). It wiped out much of the lifeblood of Joplin's economy and the commercial strip on Range Line Road. It rampaged on, demolishing housing, banks, industrial buildings, and more schools and churches. It finally dissipated east of Joplin, after destroying or damaging an estimated 8,000 homes and 500 businesses. (Courtesy of Tricia Morse Courtney.)

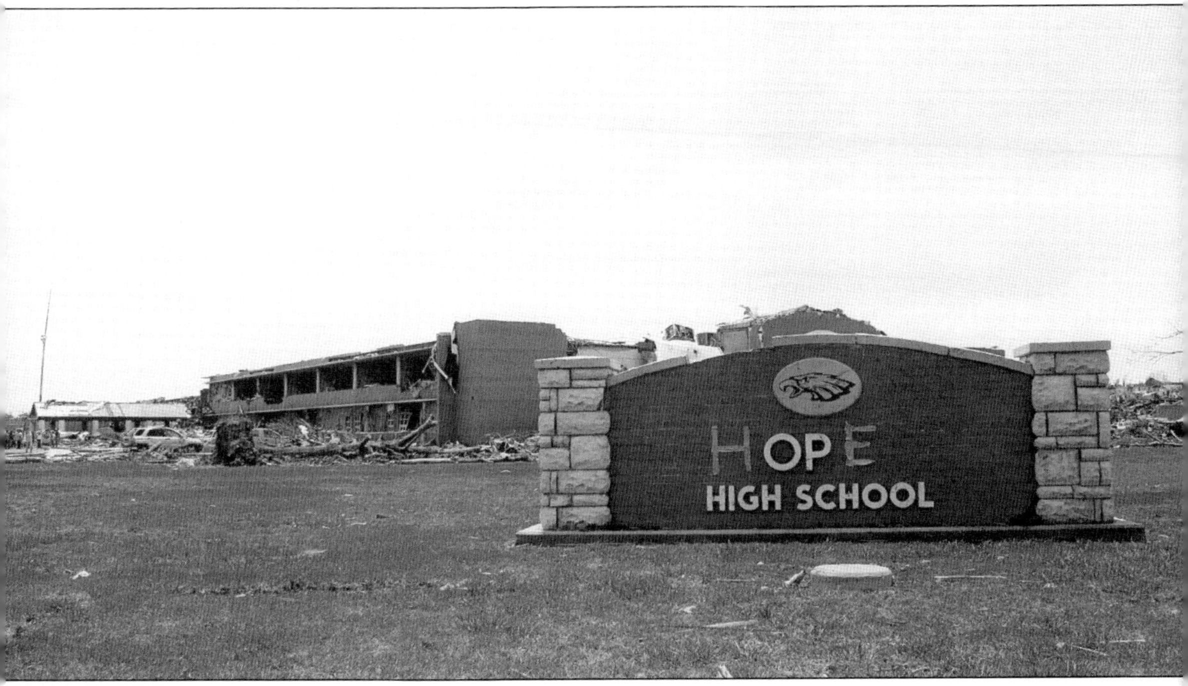

At the time of this writing, authorities have confirmed 159 fatalities, a number that continues to rise. More than 1,200 people sustained serious injuries. The Joplin tornado, the deadliest since modern record keeping began in 1950, ranks eighth among the deadliest tornadoes in US history.

We are in shock. We drive familiar streets yet cannot even recognize where we are. The cruel landscape of endless rubble and shredded trees reminds us of the human life, hopes, and dreams that have been destroyed as well. We have lost so much, and we are grieving on many levels. But our spirit is strong, as evidenced by the person who added the letters H and E in duct tape to the damaged Joplin High School sign. This book is my love letter to the city of Joplin, of which I am proud to be a citizen! (Courtesy of Sarah Thompson Craig.)

INDEX